DIAGNOSING JEFFERSON

*Evidence of a Condition that
Guided His Belief, Behavior,
and Personal Associations*

By Norm Ledgin

Comments by Temple Grandin

DIAGNOSING JEFFERSON

All marketing and publishing rights guaranteed to and reserved by

Future Horizons, Inc.

817-277-0727
817-277-2270 (fax)
E-mail: info@FHautism.com
www.FHautism.com

ISBN: 9781941765999

To my son, Fred, who has Asperger's Syndrome
and who caused me to wonder why he and
Thomas Jefferson were so alike.

CONTENTS

Relevant Chronology

1743	Born at Shadwell April 13 (April 2 by the old-style calendar)
1757	His father, Peter Jefferson, dies August 17
1760-62	Attends College of William and Mary, Williamsburg
1762-67	Studies law with George Wythe, Williamsburg
1769	Starts construction of Monticello
1770	Shadwell home burns, early records destroyed
1772	Weds Martha Wayles Skelton on January 1; daughter Martha (Patsy) born September 27
1774	Writes *A Summary View of the Rights of British America*
1776	Mother, Jane Randolph Jefferson, dies March 31 Writes Declaration of Independence for Continental Congress
1776-77	Drafts Statute for Religious Freedom for Virginia House
1778	Daughter Mary (later Maria and nicknamed Polly) born August 1
1779	Elected Governor of Virginia
1782	His wife, Martha Wayles Jefferson, dies September 6
1784	Leaves for France with daughter Martha, accompanied by James Hemings
1785-87	Arranges printings of his book, *Notes on the State of Virginia*
1786	Meets Maria Cosway in Paris Virginia Statute for Religious Freedom becomes law
1787	Daughter Mary, accompanied by Sally Hemings, arrives in Paris
1789	Returns to United States
1790	Named Secretary of State by George Washington Daughter Martha (Patsy) Jefferson marries Thomas Mann Randolph, Jr.
1794	Returns to Monticello after resigning as Secretary of State
1796	Starts remodeling of Monticello Elected Vice President
1797	Elected President of American Philosophical Society Daughter Maria (Polly) Jefferson marries John Wayles Eppes

Relevant Chronology (continued)

1800	Presidential election is tied between Jefferson and Aaron Burr
1801	Elected President by the House of Representatives, February 17
1803	Purchase of Louisiana Territory; Lewis and Clark Expedition begins
1804	Daughter Maria Jefferson Eppes dies April 17 Reelected President
1809	Ends his Presidency and retires to Monticello
1812	Renews his friendship with John Adams
1819	University of Virginia is chartered
1823	Monticello is completed
1826	Dies at Monticello on July 4

Prologue

Science has led us to a resurgence of interest in Thomas Jefferson, our third President, the author of the Declaration of Independence, and one of America's great intellectuals. The news about his likely fathering of Sally Hemings's son Eston in 1808 broke as I was completing a first draft for this book. Sally Hemings was his mixed-race slave and, as it appears from the evidence, a woman who shared affectionate companionship with Jefferson for thirty-eight years.

Confirmation of their liaison grew from a small dinner party among friends. Winifred Bennett of Arlington, Va., while visiting Eugene and Jane Foster in Charlottesville in 1996, had suggested that retired pathology professor Eugene should direct a DNA analysis involving descendants of Jefferson and Hemings. The result, she believed, might settle a two-centuries' controversy over the relationship once and for all.[1]

With the cooperation of descendants and with help from British and Dutch geneticists, Foster led a team that substantiated the often disputed Jefferson-Hemings love affair. The outcome of the study was announced in the scientific journal Nature, November 5, 1998.[2]

The media greeted that announcement as a significant news break. The story reverberated in newspaper opinion-page comments, magazine coverage, and television and radio talk-show treatment. Internet web sites emerged on the subject. Descendants of Sally Hemings restarted efforts to end racial differences and reunite with descendants of Jefferson.

At this writing I see new signs of interest in Jefferson—among people who are online with their personal computers, among those of my acquaintances who consider themselves amateur historians and are quick to raise the subject with me, and in recurring news accounts of attempted Jefferson-Hemings family reconciliation.

Past surges of interest in Thomas Jefferson revolved around such observances as the 250th anniversary of his birth in 1743. My family joined in what we called a pilgrimage in 1993 to Monticello and to Williamsburg, Va., where special display arrangements had been made. My reading about Jefferson dates back to an interest in his political theory that first held me when I was a student at Rutgers half a century ago.

The story about the DNA search and finding that appeared in the fall of 1998 could not have come at a better time for me. I had long accepted evidence offered by the late historical biographer Fawn M. Brodie in *Thomas Jefferson: An Intimate History* (1974) for Jefferson's having fathered all of Sally Hemingss children. The much-traveled Jefferson was present nine months before the birth of each of her eight babies (by my count). I had also accepted the logic for a long romantic relationship between "Tom and Sally" offered more recently by the law professor Annette Gordon-Reed in *Thomas Jefferson and Sally Hemings: An American Controversy* (1997).[3]

On another plane involving the personal life of Jefferson, I believed I had stumbled onto a discovery.

Moving through major biographies about him over a period of several years, I concluded by the summer of 1998 that the repeated mentioning of his various idiosyncrasies suggested a pattern of behavior begging for identification. I noticed Jefferson's biographers reached points in their narratives where they were forced to offer rationalizations for his oddities before moving on. I received such an impression not from just a few of the dozen or more mid-to-late twentieth century biographies of Jefferson but from all of them.

Thomas Jefferson thought of himself as a scientist more than ht did a farmer or lawyer or writer or architect or even a politician, although he was occupied in all those endeavors. That makes both interesting and rewarding the fact that todays science is helping us understand him better—the DNA search, computer science, and now the behavioral field into which I have leapt (with help from credential-carrying friends). After the DNA study verified the Jefferson-Hemings link I felt challenged to come up with a plausible explanation for that relationship in terms of my own study. Would my conclusions about his pattern of behavior accommodate a credible interpretation? Why did he choose Sally Hemings ahead of any other woman in 1788 as his companion for the remaining half of his life?

My search of additional sources and my effort to enter the mind of my subject convinced me that my observational diagnosis (conclusions based on reported behavior) embraced comfortably his having turned to Sally. As a matter of fact, I believed the confirmation of Jefferson's choice for female companionship reinforced my findings relative to his personal behavior.

No one, however, should misinterpret my meaning. There is no reason to believe Jefferson fell in love with a woman who was legally black because his quirkiness led him to do so. His personal need led him to it, and his special talent for logic eased his mind about it. Thomas Jefferson recognized he was a man apart from the mainstream in many respects, so why not cherish someone privately who was also outside that mainstream?

The liaison and its far-reaching implications for understanding Jefferson the man had nothing to do with power or subjugation and little if anything to do with lust. Regardless of how columnists in 1998 handled news about the affair, the evidence does not support their base conclusions. That evidence will be discussed in Chapter Three, which is devoted to Jefferson's logical choice of a consenting woman of African-American background for his very personal companionship.

Returning to my 1993 visit to Monticello, where two-dollar

bills bearing Jefferson's likeness are given as change for purchases, I wondered why he needed the dumbwaiters and other serving conveniences I saw there. He was surrounded by house slaves to do his bidding.

What I did not know then was the extent to which he was uncomfortable with slavery, that he referred to his slaves as servants, that he even paid some of them, that he seldom thought of them as being subject directly and quickly to his commands, and that he sought often to convenience them as well as himself.

What kind of person in his position of power would make such considerations? It would not be enough to say simply that Jefferson was kind and generous, which he was. In view of the aristocratic environment into which he was born and which he championed in politics and in trade matters, I believed there was a separate foundation for his becoming the leading dissenter in Virginia on slavery and the slave trade.

Such thoughts led me to realize that nearly everything about him was uncommon—his profound genius as well as his trust in people, his sentiments, obsessions, inventive tinkering, customary reserve, and his rituals and habits. With respect to the last, biographers have emphasized again and again his seeking the refuge of his writing desk. Writing was his principal response to every intellectual stimulus. In *American Sphinx: The Character of Thomas Jefferson* (1997), Joseph J. Ellis speculated that the computer would have been the "perfect Jeffersonian instrument."[4]

I have prepared an appendix for *Diagnosing Jefferson* to show the range of interests that an often-fixated Jefferson lent his pen. Another appendix lists internet websites featuring the public and private Jefferson. The websites also include several that describe Asperger's Syndrome, the condition I claim holds the key to understanding his behavior.

Perhaps my work will blaze a new trail for modern writers fascinated with the seeming contradictions in Jefferson's character. This fresh path may lead them to appreciate him more thoroughly and more fairly—if they would simply shift their focus from his character to his condition.

Notes:

1   Barbra Murray and Brian Duffy, "Jefferson's Secret Life," *U.S. News & World Report*, Vol. 125, No. 18, November 9, 1998, 60-61.

2   Eugene A. Foster, M.A. Jobling, P.G. Taylor, P. Donnelly, P. deKnijff, Rene Mieremet, T. Zerjal, C. Tyler Smith, "Jefferson fathered slaves last child," *Nature*, Vol. 396, November 5, 1998, 27-28.

3   Thomas, 1790-?; Harriet (1), 1795-97; Edy, 1796; Beverly, 1798-?; unnamed daughter, 1799; Harriet (2), 1801-?; Madison, 1805-78; Eston, 1808-?. Only sons Beverly, Madison, and Eston and the second Harriet are known to have grown to maturity, all four then having had children of their own. Sources: Fawn M. Brodie, *Thomas Jefferson: An Intimate History* (New York: W.W. Norton & Co., Inc., 1974) and Annette Gordon-Reed, *Thomas Jefferson and Sally Hemings: An American Controversy* (Charlottesville, Va.: University Press of Virginia, 1997).

4   Joseph J. Ellis, *American Sphinx: The Character of Thomas Jefferson* (New York: Alfred A. Knopf, 1997), 293.

CHAPTER ONE

A Truth Not Self-Evident

T homas Jefferson was eccentric in many ways. Until now his odd behavior has eluded explanation. Obviously his quirks were never considered worth examining. When those idiosyncrasies are assembled, however, a Jefferson emerges who is somewhat different from the man described by historians and biographers.

Although a politician and founder of a political party, Jefferson was neither a glad-hander, backslapper, nor buttonholer. He had no talent for public speaking. Up close he seemed uneasy with eye contact. To some his body language appeared odd and awkward. He sang under his breath constantly. Often he looked disheveled, and he drank too much.

If anyone brought him a grievance, he might not have shown the empathy one expected. If anyone became emotional in his presence, he was likely to have been discomforted noticeably. If anyone raised his or her voice, almost certainly Jefferson would have found a polite way to remove himself.

To date no biographer has elaborated on what might have been the basis for such enigmatic and unpredictable behavior. Now, however, there is a cohesive explanation available that accounts for all his oddities, including his careless and peculiar way of dressing, his stony-faced demeanor and awkward gestures in conversation, his inability to show affection to his daughters, his compulsion to jot down every financial transaction no matter how minor and, despite serious shortcomings in accounting, his lifelong obsession with the construction of Monticello.

This explanation accounts also for his relationships with women. After winning her hand ahead of other suitors largely because they shared music, Jefferson seemed happy in his marriage to the widow Martha Wayles Skelton. She died from her sixth childbirth after they had been together only ten years. A son born in her first marriage had died while she was being courted by the violin-playing and spontaneously-chanting Jefferson.

Jefferson's previous and then subsequent experiences with women, however, were idiosyncratic for his time. Among the early encounters was his offer of sexual companionship to a neighbor's wife, Betsey Walker. When it came to light, he admitted it and apologized. As a widower, he romanced an evidently agreeable married woman in Paris, Maria Cosway. Her devotion to Catholicism, however, made her an unlikely prospect for divorce. So there was no long-term point to that affair.

The relationship that made sense emotionally, and which apparently gave the widower Jefferson lasting contentment, was one he had no practical way of confessing to the outside world. That was his love for and thirty-eight-year affair with his slave Sally Hemings, half-sister to his late wife.

Martha Wayles Skelton Jefferson's father, John Wayles, had also fathered Sally by his mulatto slave, Elizabeth Hemings. When Martha died, Jefferson inherited Elizabeth as well as her children. Jefferson's alliance with young Sally was significant for its implications about his capacity for physical affection, which provided a sharp contrast with the arm's-length relationship he had with his daughters, Martha and Maria. Sally was closer to them in age than she was to Jefferson, and she was their blood-aunt.

The only explanation for the full range of Jefferson's idiosyncrasies is that he had numerous traits in common with Asperger's Syndrome, a form of high-functioning autism that occurs worldwide once in every 300 births. For reasons not yet known, it affects males at least four times as frequently as it does females.[1]

Autism is a brain-related developmental disorder that has probably been with us throughout human history but has only been given clinical attention and a name beginning in the mid-twentieth century. Leo Kanner, an Austrian-born child psychiatrist who headed the Johns Hopkins clinic in Baltimore, is credited with the discovery of autism as a type of disorder that had previously eluded clinical observation.[2]

In 1943 Kanner labeled as "early infantile autism" the cases in which he observed such differences as a child's failure to point to objects of normal interest and failure "to share interest and attraction with another person." By themselves such gaps could not result in clear diagnoses, but follow-up observation during pre-school years might confirm the diagnosis if children appeared not to understand what was being said to them or what was happening around them.[3]

By coincidence an Austrian pediatrician, Hans Asperger, was involved in a clinical study of "more able" youngsters. He appeared to be carrying Kanner's work to the next step, though neither knew the other, nor did either know what the other scientist was working on. That next step was the observation of a sub-group, actually autistics with relatively high intelligence.[4]

Hans Asperger (1906-1980) took a humanistic approach to his medical studies and clinical procedures, by best accounts. He believed children of above-normal intelligence who seemed to have inherited a personality disorder constituted a distinct class. He believed also that, although they were regarded as misfits owing to their strange behavior, they could be guided constructively. He was attracted particularly by their love of the arts and their special reasoning abilities. The paper he produced in 1943, published the following year, was his second doctoral thesis and was called, after translation by Uta Frith from the German, " 'Autistic Psychopathy' in Childhood."

Why was Asperger's landmark study of high-functioning autistic children ignored in the United States for so long—before its inclusion as a "first-ever translation into English" in Friths book, *Autism and Asperger Syndrome* (1991)? Asperger's work originated in wartime Vienna, which was at that time annexed to the Third Reich. I have heard suspicion voiced that a post-World War II bias against anything German probably slowed or inhibited circulation of that work. If that is so, a misunderstanding is to blame, for Frith has pointed to a heroic side of Hans Asperger: "Far from despising the misfits, he (Asperger) devoted himself to their cause—and this at a time when allegiance to misfits was nothing less than dangerous." As she explained, the Nazis were dedicated to "killing mentally handicapped and socially deviant people."[5]

Uta Frith, working in the Cognitive Development Unit, Medical Research Council, London, conceded that it will be some time before the patterns we now group under Asperger's Syndrome can be considered definitive to the satisfaction of the scientific community. Simply identifying "the core symptoms of autism" has consumed decades and has relied on "the happenstance of individual cases that come to the clinic." Reliable laboratory analysis of brain conformations and brain differences of autistics must await their deaths and depend also on their having willed their brains to science. Consequently, a definitive explanation will be available "only when we have full knowledge of the biological origins and their effects on brain development," according to Frith.[6]

In much the same way, and with plodding slowness, science has offered recently an analysis of abnormalities in the brain of Albert Einstein that appear to have accounted for features of his genius. For more than forty years the brain stood preserved on the shelf of the pathologist who performed Einstein's autopsy, Dr. Thomas Harvey. In 1996 Harvey furnished the "brain bank" of neuroscientist Dr.

Sandra Witelson at McMaster University, Hamilton, Ont., enough material for a team study. Witelson's group concluded that Einstein's brain was different in significant ways from normal brains and that those differences could possibly account for his genius in certain areas of thought.

Commenting in the cautious manner we have come to expect from medical science, Dr. Francine Benes, director of the Structural Neuroscience Laboratory at McLean Hospital, Belmont, Mass., said, "What you really need is to look at the brains of a number of mathematical geniuses to see if the same abnormalities are present." Obviously that kind of research is going to take time, first to select the subject geniuses, then to sign them up for future study, then to let them live out their lives.[7]

What the scientific community of autistic studies seems to be asking lay persons to do is, first, recognize that research is still in flux and, second, understand that any labeling now is like borrowing against something yet to be defined. And autism, whether high-functioning as in Asperger's Syndrome or low-functioning, is more likely to be defined in a laboratory than in a clinic.[8]

Meanwhile, society is burdened with limited perceptions whenever the word "autism" comes up. As the neurologist and writer Oliver Sacks has observed, the word represents for many "a child mute, rocking, screaming, inaccessible, cut off from human contact." Or the word calls to mind a "savant," a person with unexplained powers of calculation and memory, as in the movie *Rain Man*.[9]

Actually there are people between the strangely brilliant and the low-functioning who are also autistic. More individuals with characteristics of autism function as though they are normal than are numbered among the "inaccessible" Sacks described. The Asperger's incidence of one in 300 births is higher than that of the more severe type of autism receiving (and deserving) greater concern by the Autism Society of America. The ASA reports the more disabling type as occurring among fifteen out of every 10,000 people. That ratio translates to one in close to 700.[10]

Seemingly normal in so many ways, high-functioning autistics—people with the Asperger's disorder—will display odd and offbeat behavior. The enigmatic behavior of Jefferson reported in biographies attracted my attention because it resembled behavior I had observed in my family. Moreover, Jefferson seemed to possess more traits associated with high-functioning autism than the probabilities of coincidence would allow.

Over the past decade the most frequently recurring symptoms and traits of high-functioning autism have been assembled and reassembled by psychiatrists and other clinicians as diagnostic criteria. I have matched the applicable criteria with Jefferson and will explain those connections chapter by chapter. Yet in scientific terms the label of "Asperger's Syndrome" is not something to be pinned on him or others concretely. It is a condition still too newly uncovered for anyone to treat such a term definitively. The more evidence of traits, the better. In Jefferson's case there is good testimony by contemporary witnesses, but I wish there were more testimony available to lock in as full a diagnosis as would be acceptable to the stricter scientists. One can understand that problem best when one remembers, simply, that the man is dead and that medical scientists are leery of labeling without either biological evidence or substantial corroboration of observed behavioral features.

Yet from everything available about his manner, appearance, habits, interests, and reasoning, we can conclude Thomas Jefferson had an abundance of traits that appear on the high-functioning side of an autistic continuum. The continuum is a long line of factors and traits illustrating the range of the disorder from high-functioning to low-functioning. To be more particular, we can zoom in on the high-functioning portion of the line and focus on features assembled as primarily concurrent with Asperger's Syndrome. Then the line may be marked at a number of points to show which Asperger's traits Jefferson carried.

What kinds of traits, for example, may we identify with Jefferson? There are in the biographical literature frequently-mentioned signs of sensory problems involving sound and touch, several fixations of small and great importance, unrevealing facial expression, addiction to routines, and a few references to unsteady eye-gaze in conversation. They will be given fuller treatment in this and subsequent chapters.

Some so-called Asperger's traits are also to be found among low-functioning autistics. The eye-gaze and sensory problems are among them. They would then simply fall under the general heading "autistic traits." While Hans Asperger dealt only with the higher-functioning range, the effects of the problems on the individual seem the same. An autistic person either can or cannot bear the touch of scratchy clothing, for example, regardless of his or her functioning level of intelligence.

Turning again to Jefferson, his observed behavior in the historical biographies places him (as far as I am concerned, with support by authorities I will name later) firmly on the continuum of Asperger's traits. But not all those traits are shared by all people who belong on that continuum. Throughout this book we will be looking at the arrangement of traits that was peculiarly Jefferson's.

We will find that no other conclusion about Jefferson is available. We will find that all his behavior, strange or conventional, was at least compatible with what we know of Asperger's Syndrome. And it is equally important to appreciate that no other condition yet known to science provides an explanation for his bizarre behavior.

The most authoritative measurement available in the United States is the table of diagnostic criteria for the Asperger's disorder prepared by the American Psychiatric Association. It has been highlighted here with "bullets" to show which of the general areas can be associated with Thomas Jefferson.

DIAGNOSTIC CRITERIA FOR ASPERGER'S DISORDER
(Diagnostic and Statistical Manual of Mental Disorders, Fourth Edition, American Psychiatric Association, 1994)

A. Qualitative impairment in social interaction, as manifested by at least two of the following:

- (1) marked impairment in the use of multiple nonverbal behaviors such as eye-to-eye gaze, facial expression, body postures, and gestures to regulate social interaction
- (2) failure to develop peer relationships appropriate to developmental level
- (3) a lack of spontaneous seeking to share enjoyment, interests, or achievements with other people (e.g., by a lack of showing, bringing, or pointing out objects of interest to other people)
- (4) lack of social or emotional reciprocity

B. Restricted repetitive and stereotyped patterns of behavior, interests, and activities, as manifested by at least one of the following:

- (1) encompassing preoccupation with one or more stereotyped and restricted patterns of interest that is abnormal either in intensity or focus
- (2) apparently inflexible adherence to specific, nonfunctional routines or rituals
- (3) stereotyped and repetitive motor mannerisms (e.g., hand or finger slapping or twisting, or complex whole-body movements)
- (4) persistent preoccupation with parts of objects

C. The disturbance causes clinically significant impairment in social, occupational, or other important areas of functioning.

D. There is no clinically significant general delay in language (e.g., single words used by age 2 years, communicative phrases used by age 3 years).

E. There is no clinically significant delay in cognitive development or in the development of age-appropriate self-help skills, adaptive behavior (other than in social interaction), and curiosity about the environment in childhood.

F. Criteria are not met for another specific Pervasive Developmental Disorder or Schizophrenia.
    Reprinted with permission from the Diagnostic and Statistical Manual of Mental Disorders, Fourth Edition. Copyright 1994 American Psychiatric Association.

Five items are marked for Jefferson. To be diagnosed with the Asperger's disorder, only four such signs of developmental miscues are necessary. Assuming that believable links to all five of the marked criteria can be shown, and they will be, why not support straightforwardly a diagnosis of Asperger's Syndrome? Why hesitate and say instead that Jefferson and his idiosyncrasies belong on the Asperger's continuum? Again, Jefferson is no longer with us to observe. Contemporary observations that have come down to us seem fewer in certain areas than a quantity sufficient to persuade skeptics. So I must take the more conservative approach, and I invite readers to do that as well.

There is a reasonable explanation for most of his contemporary observers' not dwelling on Jefferson's oddities in his time. When a man has so many redeeming qualities as he had, people tend to overlook eccentricities. Particularly would this have been true on the part of Jefferson's closest associates. It is quite natural that they would have grown accustomed to such behavior and thus refrained from commenting. Probably they cautioned others waiting in anterooms who had never met Jefferson not to look surprised nor make much of what they saw that was unusual. Nonetheless, a few first-time visitors went away afterward and wrote in their journals that he was odd, and they described the ways in which that was so. Historians have found such notes and have passed them to us.

In the same way that people glanced aside when seeing President Franklin Delano Roosevelt's wheelchair and leg braces, many of President Thomas Jefferson's close contemporaries would have believed his greeting guests accompanied by an uncaged mockingbird or with his hair in disarray were items not worth belaboring. Presidents are customarily surrounded by polite society, and polite people tend to look for and deal with the substance and character of those they admire.

In the diagnostic criteria, notice also the exceptions near the end of the table. Had there been delays for Jefferson in such developmental areas as language or cognitive skills, the criteria would not apply. However, the relevancy of the American Psychiatric Association's having included those exceptions is in contention. Still, if there were such developmental delays, some believe, we might be dealing with an entirely different disorder, not the Asperger's condition.[11]

As it happens, there is little reason to believe that such delays characterized Jefferson's childhood. With reasonable assurance we can draw an inference from "family tradition" that would challenge the presence of such "late onset." Family tradition is information passed down by family members about one another. By such accounts young Thomas had read all his father's books by the age of five.[12]

Before anyone jumps to conclusions from the previous image of Jefferson and his pet bird, I must emphasize that nothing about the Asperger's disorder has anything to do with mental instability. Because Asperger's is a developmental brain or neurological condition that is listed in a medical manual of "mental disorders" (known widely as DSM-IV), we are using a source reference that some might find abhorrent. Inclusion of Asperger's in the manual and my linking him to it will probably assault people's long-standing reverence for Jefferson. I have the same problem, balancing what seems a harsh truth against my positive view of the man, his achievements, his reported good nature.

Regardless of what the resources are named that help me explain the evidence, however, I feel an obligation to come forward with my finding of the Asperger's connection. I challenge anyone to advance a better solution to the puzzle of his idiosyncratic behavior that has, for so long, eluded and haunted his biographers.

Having looked deliberately and contextually at Jefferson's eccentric side, I can agree with Joseph J. Ellis, Ford Foundation professor of history at Mount Holyoke College who wrote the popular 1997 work *American Sphinx*, that Jefferson was not "a mentally unstable person or a man with latent paranoid tendencies." The fact that Ellis would find it necessary to make such an observation at all (the context was Jefferson's early-1790s fear that a plot was afoot to reverse the Revolution) is an indicator of what compelled me to pursue my diagnostic process. While the secondary literature about Jefferson contains few such statements as that one by Professor Ellis, it is rife with asides about quirky and even bizarre behavior that I will highlight as elements of a pattern.[13]

Revisiting the topic of possible "late onset" and its doubtful applicability to Jefferson, we must concede that a 1770 fire in the Jefferson home at Shadwell blocked access to confirming documents of his childhood history—if such documents were ever available in the form of diaries or records destroyed by that fire. Later evidence points to a young man making normal or superior progress in his education if not his social development. With respect to his intellect he is shown in biographical histories and his writings as having advanced too fast for us to conclude the presence of childhood handicaps, but we simply do not know whether they can be ruled out as never having occurred.

As I mentioned earlier, the American Psychiatric Association may have blurred the diagnostic criteria by including exceptions D. and E., according to the Australian clinical psychologist and Asperger's Syndrome authority, Tony Attwood. But their inclusion forces us to weigh them because we lack the early childhood information that would contradict them.

We have sparse evidence about Jefferson's response to structured schooling, little more than his own ambiguous testimony that he was a "hard student." That could be taken to mean he was unusually conscientious about school or he had more difficulty responding to teachers than to self-instruction. Jefferson's noting he was still a "hard student" while nearing age seventy-six, however, inclines me toward judging him to have been a lifelong grind and insatiable bookworm.[14]

Regardless of how his childhood or student experiences may be measured or interpreted, we have a man whose apparent relationship to the diagnostic criteria for Asperger's Syndrome exceeds their minimum requirements. His traits, habits, and conditions matching all available diagnostic models for Asperger's reach, reliably, a total in number of roughly fifty.[15]

The evidence in a few areas such as eye-gaze problems and awkward body language is not nearly so strong as I would prefer to have, but there is enough testimony to prompt reasonable doubt of Jefferson's having had steady eye-gaze or having been graceful. I will persist in advancing my two-part conclusion: Jefferson's idiosyncratic behavior fell quite solidly on the continuum of Asperger's traits, and no other explanation applies to his collection of traits than high-functioning autism, which to many is synonymous with Asperger's Syndrome.[16]

What about that continuum? What is it, and how is it useful to our understanding of Thomas Jefferson? The Asperger's continuum is a string of atypical characteristics, largely behavioral, that are common among individuals judged to be disordered developmentally yet able to function as though normal. Many of the characteristics may appear to stand apart from tables of diagnostic criteria, but several are essentially offshoots or varying expressions of them. Such behavioral features are signs of a brain abnormality either inherited or the result of brain damage or disease. A person with the Asperger's disorder will have a collection of traits or characteristics appearing on the continuum. Another person tied to Asperger's will have a separate set of those features all his own. There is likely to be overlapping of shared characteristics between them.[17]

In their book *Asperger Syndrome: A Guide for Educators and Parents* (1998), Brenda Smith Myles and Richard L. Simpson, both with the University of Kansas Medical Center and writers in the Asperger's and special education fields, presented parents' profiles of four typical Asperger's Syndrome-diagnosed children—Brent, Michelle, Edward, and Andrew. Each child is different from the others, however, in the set of characteristics he or she carries that appear on the Asperger's continuum.

All four of the youngsters are highly intelligent. All interact poorly with peers and are loners. Andrew, the youngest, is described as having eye-contact problems. The other three have inexpressive faces or far-away looks. Brent and Andrew have touch sensitivities and low gross motor skills. Brent and Michelle fixate on objects or topics and have in common also an emotional detachment from family members, periods of depression, and engagement in acts of self-injury. While Brent is a boy of low energy, Michelle and Edward are hyperactive. There were birth complications for Michelle and her mother and pregnancy complications for Andrew's mother.[18]

I have prepared a list of traits such as those described above by borrowing from a number of tables used for diagnosis or used to describe common Asperger's-related behavior. It is a relatively long list of traits that the reader is welcome to consider an Asperger's continuum, but not necessarily "the official" Asperger's continuum, if there is such a thing. In the continuing study of the Asperger's condition no such list may yet be considered complete.

In what follows I have placed solid bullets alongside the traits that biographers furnished good evidence to have been present in Jefferson. I have placed checks beside the traits they gave me reason to suspect strongly also to have been present. Obviously the list is based on modern models or there would not be mention of such items as videos. The purpose is to help the reader understand the heterogeneity of the continuum and to profile Jefferson's relationship to it.

In view of our lacking anything that is both authoritative and all-inclusive for such a list, have I tailored it to incline its elements toward those behaviors the literature reveals about Jefferson? No, I have not done so knowingly and was, frankly, somewhat startled by the visual outcome.

A CONTINUUM OF ASPERGER'S TRAITS

- Behavior associated clearly with Jefferson by biographers or by Jefferson himself in writings
- ✓ Strongly suspected of Jefferson because of significant reference in biographies

Physical issues

✓ avoids eye contact in conversation
- wears an inexpressive face or far-away look
- appears stiff in stance or posture
- gestures awkwardly
✓ makes few meaningful nonverbal gestures
- sits awkwardly
  exhibits poor gross motor coordination
  rocks in seated position or flaps hands when nervous or distressed
✓ fails to swing arms normally when walking
- experiences sensitivity to certain types of clothing
- is hypersensitive to selected dissonant sounds and/or light and odors
- tolerates some loud noises (hyposensitivity)
- neglects grooming needs

- requires calming pressure at times
  seems excessively fearful of harmless objects
  lacks fear of actual danger
  appears to be insensitive to low pain levels
- suffers frequent headaches in youth and adulthood
  experiences eating or sleeping problems commonly
- tends to suffer bouts of diarrhea
- paces back and forth or in circles when distressed
- ✓ shows occasional signs of hyperactivity
- ✓ seems at times to have low energy level
- ✓ develops tics or odd mannerisms (throat-clearing, arm
  movements, etc.)
- speaks at times in strangely "swallowed" tone of voice
- ✓ stammers when nervous or has trouble starting conversation
  reacts exaggeratedly to sudden pain or physical sensation
  grimaces inappropriately
- ✓ reacts to some disappointments as though in seizure
  inflicts self-injury when distressed
  is compulsive about hand washing
- exhibits ambidexterity
- ✓ resists any touching that he or she did not initiate or invite

Social issues

- inclines toward being a loner and is regarded as shy
  interacts poorly with peers
- ✓ fails to recognize social cues
- seems unable to sense others' feelings
  is aggressive and ill-tempered in childhood
- ✓ lacks empathy when others disclose problems
  often rejects hugging or being touched affectionately
- cultivates those who are somewhat emotionally detached
  (engineers, scientists)
  indicates low self-esteem and depression frequently

lacks interest in group play
lacks understanding of play rules
when confused in conversation, changes the subject
- seems indifferent to peer pressures
intrudes or interrupts in social situations
- shares favorite topics by telling others more than they want to know
✓ displays a one-sidedness or lack of interest in others
shows impatience with others' mistakes
- engages at times in socially inappropriate behavior
- exhibits emotionally inappropriate behavior or seems aloof
in childhood appears deaf to cheery greetings
assumes his or her unshared thoughts and experiences are known to others
- tends to be vulnerably naive
shows impatience over waiting for others
✓ takes steps to avoid being teased
✓ in youth prefers company of adults who may tolerate odd behavior
- seeks company of persons with similar traits
- carries air of reserve that seems to attract others (charisma)
approaches others too closely
adheres rigidly to rules of right and wrong
- ignores middle ground for resolving conflict
needs excessive reassurance and praise
- is overly sensitive to criticism or imagined displeasure
- responds childishly in joy, anger, or grief
- lacks patience with social hierarchies
in childhood especially, asks stereotyped questions repeatedly
laughs or giggles inappropriately
becomes overly apologetic and may accept blame for others

Language and learning issues

- talks too little most of the time
- speaks or writes pedantically
- tends toward perfectionism and is impatient with own mistakes
- learns by seeing rather than hearing
- shows a talent for art or visual representations
  lacks understanding of abstract concepts
- ✓ fails to recognize or understand irony
  has trouble with words having multiple meanings
- ✓ customarily takes comments literally
  fails often to recognize subtleties
- believes some fiction to be real
- often views reality differently from others
- lacks artifice and fails to understand it
- ✓ tends to be deficient in what nonautistics call "common sense"
- exhibits remarkable memory
- exhibits somewhat rigid sense of logic
- adheres faithfully to routines, functional or not
  echoes what has just been said (echolalia)
  sometimes speaks too rapidly or in unregulated tone
- ignores need to adjust speech for others' understanding
  engages in repetitive speech patterns
- ✓ sometimes talks too much
- loves to tinker and improvise
  prefers to read directories, catalogs, data-based materials
- has a conspicuous talent for mathematics
- copies what he or she has enjoyed reading
  commonly has poor handwriting
  examines environment or objects by sniffing
- is detail-oriented in the extreme

Issues of restricted interests

- fixates on selected topics or data
- resists change in environment, preferring familiar place and routines

    has difficulty shifting to new tasks

✓ resists change in everyday activity

    makes poor use of unstructured time

    observes moving, spinning, patterned, or shiny objects closely

    forms attachments to objects

    watches some videos repeatedly

✓ aligns or arranges books, work materials, or toys

In *Thinking in Pictures—and Other Reports from My Life with Autism* (1995) the autistic lecturer/writer Temple Grandin referred to a few famous people she believed showed Asperger's traits. They included the originator of the theory of relativity, Albert Einstein; the painter, Vincent van Gogh; Charles Darwin, father of evolution; Gregor Mendel, geneticist, and Bill Gates, computer wizard and one of the richest people in the world. Einstein did not speak until he was three, was a loner as a child, and was relatively aloof all his life. He relied on visualization rather than verbalization, preferred soft clothing, and wore his hair in a wild and uncombed fashion. Van Gogh was aloof and a loner, ill-groomed, and had raspy voice problems. He spoke as though no one else was present. He showed poor empathy and engaged in childish behavior. His self-injury, cutting off an ear, is legendary.[19]

Skipping to Bill Gates, articles in *Time* have implied an Asperger's connection as far back as 1994. I went through a more recent *Time* piece about him with a highlighter and found twenty ways in which his interests, characteristics, and behavior matched Jefferson's. Gates's famous rocking when nervous was not one of them. Not everything in common between Jefferson and Gates appears on the foregoing continuum of Asperger's traits, but all their matching features are related to the list in some way:[20]

a love of tinkering with the technology of their time

faith in, and preparation for, the scientific technology of the future

prolific letter-writing (or e-mailing)

charitable interest in schools and libraries

powers of processing data mentally far beyond normal

possible savant skills

ambidexterity

shyness (or social awkwardness)

a preference for avoiding most social settings

conspicuous incuriosity about other people

low empathy

unhurriedness and perfectionism about the completion of their homes

reportedly poor eye-gaze in conversation

good story-telling abilities

unusual physical incapacity resulting from bereavement

unusually strong ties to old friends

emotional reserve

occasional release through solitary riding or racing (horses and cars)

childlike interests or behavior

charisma

The late Dumas Malone, who wrote the six-volume *Jefferson and His Time* from 1948 through 1981, furnished signs that a mystery might be begging for solution by diagnosis. In his first volume he referred to Jefferson as a "strong, strange man (who) did not wear his heart upon his sleeve."[21]

Before Malone died in 1986 he had taught at Yale, Columbia, and the University of Virginia, directed the Harvard University Press, and edited the *Dictionary of American Biography*. As Thomas

Jefferson Biographer-in-Residence at Virginia he won the Pulitzer Prize for the second volume, *Jefferson and the Rights of Man* (1951). But Professor Malone disappointed readers like me who search for the personal side of the people they admire. He disclosed smatterings of Jefferson's idiosyncrasies and then quickly set them aside. Malone's reasoning about their significance seemed laced with biases. About the Jefferson link to Sally Hemings, he was peevish and negative.

Another front-ranked twentieth-century biographer of Jefferson, Emeritus Professor of History at the University of Virginia Merrill D. Peterson, found his subject in *Thomas Jefferson and the New Nation* (1970) to be "an impenetrable man." Professor Peterson can also be faulted for expressing offensively some of the same biases about Sally Hemings as did Dumas Malone. As I have mentioned, Chapter Three will cover the Hemings affair and its Asperger's links with Jefferson's social handicaps.[22]

A few biographies treated the puzzles of Jefferson's oddly-patterned ways objectively and revealingly, including examination of unconventional expressions of his intellect. Joseph J. Ellis's *American Sphinx* stands out in that respect. Among other observations by Professor Ellis to be discussed in Chapter Four was Jefferson's knack for shielding himself against reality when fiction suited his romantic notions better. As will be shown, Jefferson's taking of such poetic license influenced the drafting of the Declaration of Independence.[23]

On a personal note, after I first observed that my son Fred's view of reality appeared different from most other people's view, my tracking of Fred's Asperger's condition started me also toward Jefferson's. I found other similarities between them inconclusive until I noticed Fred preferred to wear sweat pants instead of jeans. Curious about what I had remembered in my Jefferson readings, I retraced Dumas Malone's accounts of Jefferson's preference for soft clothing. Then I decided to probe the entire matter of similarities more conscientiously.

I asked a young man with Asperger's Syndrome to read roughly 100 pages of material I had prepared about parallels between Jefferson and the disorder. He is Jean-Paul Bovee, who has two masters degrees, one in medieval history from the University of Kansas and the other in library and informational science from the University of Missouri. He serves as manager of the Missouri Developmental Disabilities Resource Center at the Institute for Human Development, University of Missouri - Kansas City.

At meetings in Chicago and Kansas City I had heard Mr. Bovee speak with authority about Asperger's Syndrome. I knew that his knowledge in the field was broad—far beyond the limits of a disordered person's recounting solely his own experiences. When I asked him what he thought of my comparison of Thomas Jefferson's behavior to Asperger's behavior, he said, "It was as though you had written about me."

A close friend with whom I attended graduate courses in sociology and social psychology in the early 1960s also agreed to read my findings. Stanford Gerber received his social science doctorate from the University of Missouri - Kansas City in 1967, specializing in both psychology and anthropology. He then served as director of the Family Institute at the College of the Virgin Islands before beginning a twenty-two year stay at Clark University, Worcester, Mass., 1969-91.

At Clark he attained an associate professorship in several disciplines, including anthropology, before returning to Kansas City, where he teaches anthropology and ethnic studies at Donnelly College. Dr. Gerber's reaction was that I had made a believable match between Thomas Jefferson and the traits associated with Asperger's Syndrome.

Brenda Smith Myles, who lectures internationally on the subject of Asperger's, collaborated with Richard L. Simpson to write *Asperger Syndrome: A Guide for Educators and Parents*, mentioned previously. She received her Ph.D. from the University of Kansas and is associate professor in that university's Department of Special Education, whose faculty includes Dr. Simpson. She also co-directs the only master's degree program in Asperger's Syndrome in the United States.

Dr. Myles is president of the board and founding member of the Autism/Asperger Syndrome Resource Center, part of the university's Medical Center. Her writings include a new work, *Asperger Syndrome and Difficult Moments* (Autism Asperger Publishing Co., 1999). She edits *Intervention in School and Clinic*, the country's second-largest journal in special education. After she read an early draft, she called my work "important" and said I had "made a case" for Jefferson's ties with the traits of Asperger's.

Temple Grandin, author of the autobiographical *Thinking in Pictures*, was precise about the way I should state the connection between Jefferson and Asperger's. She pointed out that while the evidence was good, there was a short supply of it in a few areas. She cautioned me against trying to complete a firm diagnosis and urged me instead to show that his traits placed Jefferson on the Asperger's continuum.

Dr. Grandin believes strongly in referring to a continuum as a critical means for understanding the Asperger's condition and for appreciating its varieties from person to person. She did not make firm diagnoses of the famous people she referred to in her book, indicating instead that the traits they had were related to Asperger's, or high-functioning autism. "It's not a black-and-white disorder like diabetes," she emphasized.

Unhesitatingly, Dr. Grandin expresses pride in being autistic. She has a Ph.D. in animal science from the University of Illinois, is an associate professor at Colorado State University, and works internationally as a designer of livestock-handling facilities. She spends much time as a lecturer in high-functioning autism and Asperger's Syndrome, and a number of network television shows and magazine articles have featured her.

I turned out three drafts over a period of several months before Dr. Grandin was satisfied that I had gotten the point: that it was virtually impossible to make a firm diagnosis of a man no longer present, and unnecessary when I had sufficient grounds for placing Jefferson on the Asperger's continuum.

In order to help the reader understand more clearly Thomas Jefferson's links to Asperger's, I will give each of the five relevant criteria in the DSM-IV list the treatment of at least a full chapter. First, however, we should reacquaint ourselves with the author of our liberty—but on a more personal level.

Notes:

1   Tony Attwood, *Asperger's Syndrome: A Guide for Parents and Professionals* (London: Jessica Kingsley Publishers, 1998) (pb), 24, 151.

2   *Autism and Asperger Syndrome*, Uta Frith, editor (Cambridge, England: Cambridge University Press, 1991) (pb), 5. First used by psychiatrist Eugen Bleuler in 1908 in the context of schizophrenic withdrawal, the label "autism" fit the social detachment that Leo Kanner and Hans Asperger observed in the 1940s. *Ibid*, 6n. Also, Francesca Happe, *Autism: An Introduction to Psychological Theory* (Cambridge, Mass.: Harvard University Press, 1995), 11.

3   *Frith*, 2-3.

4   *Ibid*, 6.

5   *Ibid*, in which back cover notes by Dr. Oliver Sacks refer to Frith's work as the initial English translation; in support of Hans Asperger's heroic nature, see 7-10 and 90n.

6   *Ibid*, 6.

7   Michael D. Lemonick, "Was Einstein's Brain Built for Brilliance?", *Time*, June 28, 1999, 54. See also Sandra F. Witelson, Debra L. Kigar, Thomas Harvey, "The exceptional brain of Albert Einstein," *The Lancet*, Vol. 353, No. 9170, June 19, 1999, 2149-53.

8   *Happe*, 2.

9   Oliver Sacks, foreword for *Temple Grandin, Thinking in Pictures—and Other Reports from My Life with Autism* (New York: Doubleday, 1995), 11-12.

10 "Helping society solve the puzzle of autism...", leaflet of the Autism Society

of America Foundation distributed at the ASA National Conference on Autism, Kansas City, Mo., July 6-10, 1999.

11 In addressing a workshop in Denver sponsored December 9, 1998, by Future Horizons, Inc., of Arlington, Tex., Dr. Attwood suggested the DSM-IV section on late onset "really should be wiped out."

12 Jack McLaughlin, *Jefferson and Monticello: The Biography of a Builder* (New York: Henry Holt and Company, 1988) (pb), 37.

13 *Ellis*, 131.

14 *Thomas Jefferson: Writings*, Merrill D. Peterson, editor (New York: The Library of America, 1984), Jefferson to Dr. Vine Utley, March 21, 1819, 1416.

15 The Australian scale for diagnosing Asperger's Syndrome—one of several diagnostic tools and perhaps the most encompassing—lists about thirty abilities, skills, interests, and characteristics that may or may not be present in an Asperger's person in varying intensities. It is by no means all-inclusive, but it is one of the best guides available to the more common features. *Attwood*, 16-20.

16 Speaking in Denver December 9,1998, Dr. Attwood said he saw no difference between Asperger's Syndrome and high-functioning autism, except in the way "they are spelled." Others in this field have not been that certain.

17 *Frith*, 2.

18 Brenda Smith Myles and Richard L. Simpson, *Asperger Syndrome: A Guide for Educators and Parents* (Austin, Tex.: Pro-Ed, Inc., 1998) (pb), 115-32.

19 *Grandin*, 180-85.

20 "Diagnosing Bill Gates," *Time*, January 24, 1994, 25; Walter Isaacson, "In Search of Bill Gates," Time, January 13, 1997, 44-57.

21 Dumas Malone, *Jefferson and His Time* - six volumes (Boston: Little, Brown and Company, 1948-81), 1:161.

22 Merrill D. Peterson, *Thomas Jefferson and the New Nation* (New York: Oxford University Press, 1970), viii.

23 *Ellis*, 7/4 30-34.

CHAPTER TWO

Reluctant Celebrity

Thomas Jefferson was born into an environment that assured both the flourishing of his intellect and a generous measure of financial freedom during much of his life. His heritage also directed his interest toward agriculture, architecture, and the natural sciences, and it gave him an understanding of his obligations for public service.

Jefferson in his *Autobiography* (1821) described his father, Peter Jefferson, as a man of Welsh ancestry whose "education had been quite neglected." Nevertheless, wrote Thomas, his father's "being of a strong mind, sound judgment and eager after information" elevated the elder Jefferson into the company of men skilled in mathematics, surveying, and mapmaking.

Together with Joshua Fry, professor of mathematics at the College of "William and Mary, Peter Jefferson went into the field and charted the first map of Virginia. The activity gave Peter an advantage in selecting picturesque (if not always agriculturally workable) property in the piedmont that ascends west to the Blue Ridge Mountains. When he died in 1757 he left a large estate of lands and slaves to his widow and eight children. Thomas was fourteen at the time of his father s death and the elder of two sons.

In his memoir Jefferson offered little respectful recollection about his mother, Jane Randolph Jefferson, with whom he lived nearly twice as long as the time he enjoyed with his father. He noted in his *Autobiography* that the Randolph line traced back to England and Scotland, "to which let every one ascribe the faith & merit he chooses." Other than the fact that Jane Randolph married at nineteen (Peter was then thirty-two), that was all son Thomas believed significant enough to include about her in the life story he set out to write at seventy-seven.[1]

Several biographers have called attention to the shortage of comment or praise by Jefferson regarding his mother. That will be treated in terms of Asperger's traits in Chapter Eight. What differs from the short biography I am providing here and the stories of Jefferson's life that can be found elsewhere is that I will emphasize the personal side of the man, not necessarily the intellectual nor the political. Where Asperger's traits appeared to influence his intellect or his political involvement as well as his personal and social behavior, such connections will be shown.

More than likely the Randolph line carried the traits that my study of Jefferson has accumulated and revealed. Contemporaries of Jefferson furnished us descriptions of behavior by members of that family in that time, and those will be shared. Biographer Dumas Malone wrote of "instability in this branch of the Randolphs and, beginning with Peter, the Jeffersons served to offset it." Professor Malone added that the "remarkable clan" of Randolphs, which counted Jefferson, John Marshall, and Robert E. Lee in its line, "defies comparison with any other American family."[2]

Thomas had two older sisters, Jane, his favorite, who died unmarried at the age of twenty-five, and Mary. Thomas Jefferson was born April 2, 1743, at Shadwell, which adjoined the property he developed at Monticello. A calendar change in that period placed his birthday on April 13, which is the date accepted today. The same change affected the birth date of George Washington in 1732 by eleven days.

The sister born after Thomas was Elizabeth. Dumas Malone

described her as "subnormal," and a family friend wrote she was "feeble minded if not an idiot." She and her maid, Little Sail, drowned while boating when she was twenty-nine. Elizabeth's mental disability has received small attention from historians. Entries in Jefferson's *Memorandum Books* indicate, however, that she joined the family in travel and handled money for purchases or payments. She also had limited autonomy for moving about the large family estate in the company of others.

Elizabeth may have been autistic. The few available descriptions of her activity assign her to a functioning level below those of her siblings. Yet those descriptions fail to indicate a status so low-functioning as to have meant Elizabeth's total disablement. The family saw that she was cared for, treated medically as necessary, and never set apart nor given the period equivalent of institutionalization, according to Memorandum Book entries. Tony Attwood, international Asperger's authority, has written that some families have a history among their members of both classic autism and Asperger's.[3]

Jefferson's next sister, Martha, married his best friend, Dabney Carr. After her, Jane Randolph Jefferson bore a son, Peter Field, who died in infancy. Another son, unnamed, was either stillborn or died later on the day he was born. Daughters Lucy and Anna Scott were next and lived to maturity, followed by Jane's last child, Randolph, with whom Thomas "never found real congeniality," according to Dumas Malone.[4]

Peter Jefferson placed Thomas "at the English school" when he was five years old "and at the Latin" at nine, where he stayed five years. After his father's death he attended for two years a school operated by the Rev. James Maury, whom Jefferson described as "a correct classical scholar." While at Maury's, Jefferson established friendship with a boy three years younger than himself, Maury's son, also named James. Similar choices are noticeable among Asperger's teenagers, primarily to escape teasing by peers at their age level. I do not know whether teasing was a problem, but I think it was from the nature of descriptions I will cite in Chapter Ten. When nervous he stammered, and that alone could have prompted unwelcome notice or comment.[5]

At sixteen Jefferson entered the College of William and Mary, Williamsburg. There, apparently on his merits, he acquired or earned a privileged status as a member of what he called "a partie quarree." The foursome included law instructor George Wythe, who became a lifelong friend, William Small, science teacher and the only non-cleric on the College faculty, and Virginia Governor Francis Fauquier. The conversations at dinner in the Governor's Palace turned frequently to philosophy and gave Jefferson an intellectual and worldly-wise head start that he remembered gratefully. Such mentoring by older persons is a common need among high-functioning autistics, according to Temple Grandin. In her autobiographical *Thinking in Pictures* she wrote that mentors "explain the ways of the world."[6]

After attending William and Mary for two years, Jefferson remained in Williamsburg to study law with George Wythe. He entered practice in 1767. That year he began to keep legal notations and records of fees. The habit grew into a daily ritual of making Memorandum Book entries for the rest of his life. His recording of minutiae about expenditures evolved into an everyday exercise that served little if any purpose, for he lacked meaningful accounting abilities. I will cover such nonfunctional routines (and the comforts they brought him) in Chapter Six in terms of diagnostic criteria for the Asperger's disorder.

In the spring of 1768 Jefferson contracted work at Monticello to level a small portion of the mountaintop for a home. The project of constructing, tearing down, reconstructing, and then completing the dwelling was to command his attention with varying intensity for a period of fifty-four years. While that might be considered an Asperger's trait of "encompassing preoccupation"—a reference that appears in diagnostic criteria of the American Psychiatric Association—Monticello was hardly his sole fixation. An appendix showing the wide range of his writing interests reflects preoccupations of sometimes deep, sometimes recurring, or often short-lived focus. I will give the Monticello project a more complete description in Chapter Five.

The early part of 1769 carried him again to Williamsburg. Electors in Albemarle County had named the young attorney and promising member of the local gentry to be their representative in the House of Burgesses. As Jefferson noted in his *Autobiography*, "I made one effort in that body for the permission of the emancipation of slaves, which was rejected." At twenty-six his combined idealistic zeal and his seriously limited skills for vocal persuasion forced him into guaranteed defeat on the explosive issue of slavery. Earlier I identified both the unyielding perception of right and wrong and problems with public speaking as traits of people on the Asperger's continuum.[7]

Jefferson was burdened further in the pre-Revolutionary War period 1769-1774 by frustrations he shared with his countrymen over foreign rule. He advanced early in standing among leaders of Virginia's resistance to Britain. More importantly, perhaps, in that pre-war time he earned a reputation for summarizing those frustrations and inspiring that resistance on paper.

Patriots were organizing a "general Congress" among the colonies to meet in Philadelphia. Jefferson drafted instructions to Virginia delegates, but illness prevented him from delivering them to Williamsburg. He sent them ahead and was surprised later to learn they had been published and widely circulated on both sides of the Atlantic as *A Summary View of the Rights of British America*.

Although a landmark document of resistance to tyranny, *Summary View* revealed Jefferson's flawed perspective of reality. That was true particularly in his citing of Saxon history as bearing on colonists' rights. "In this doctrine," Jefferson wrote, "I had never been able to get any one to agree with me but Mr. Wythe." Biographer Joseph J. Ellis in *American Sphinx* treated Jefferson's historical distortion on that subject at length. Garry Wills in *Inventing America: Jefferson's Declaration of Independence* (1978) called attention to it. In Chapter Four I will discuss the flaw in Jefferson's historical perspective described by Professor Ellis and its significance as a sign of Asperger's impairment.[8]

Concurrent with Jefferson's deepening political involvement was his realization of prospects for a happy personal life. Such opportunity had eluded him through his twenties. As a college youth, he had been inordinately shy. Then he had behaved inappropriately by romancing the wife of his friend and neighbor, John Walker. Shyness as well as improper behavior are signs of social awkwardness and are compatible with Asperger's characteristics.[9]

After the 1770 Shadwell fire, when he was twenty-seven, Jefferson stopped living with his mother. The young lawyer, now shouldering responsibilities as a legislator and as self-appointed architect, established bachelor quarters in the only structure by then completed at Monticello, the small south pavilion. At twenty-eight Jefferson was attracted to a twenty-three-year-old widow, Martha Wayles Skelton. She was pretty, her figure "slight" but shapely, and her eyes were hazel and her hair auburn. They shared a love of music that gave Jefferson the advantage over other suitors, according to biographer Dumas Malone. Thomas and Martha were heard often joining in song, and he played the violin to her harpsichord accompaniment. The fact that he was tall, good-looking, strong of body, hazel-eyed, red-haired, and brilliant may have mattered, but biographers have stressed the musical tie. Thomas and Martha were married New Year's Day, 1772. They honeymooned in the south pavilion.[10]

Martha was the daughter of a law colleague, John Wayles, whom Jefferson admired as "full of pleasantry and good humor." Wayles must have been a robust man. He had put three wives in their graves and by all accounts was bedding his mulatto slave, Elizabeth Hemings, with apparent faithfulness and regularity. Wayles's death in 1773 resulted in an inheritance by Martha that, according to Jefferson, "doubled the ease of our circumstances." In another sense the inheritance of slaves and properties also enlarged Jefferson's responsibilities for care and management.[11]

Among personal responsibilities the new bridegroom had been prepared to accept was adoptive fatherhood for a son born to Martha in her marriage to Bathurst Skelton. But six months prior to the wedding, three-year-old John Skelton died. Fatherhood for Thomas Jefferson was not delayed seriously, however, for within ten months after their marriage he and Martha had a daughter, also named Martha, later nicknamed "Patsy." Of the six children they would have before Martha Wayles Jefferson died from childbirth complications in 1782, two reached majority. Their younger daughter, Mary, later Maria and nicknamed "Polly," died when she was twenty-five. Loss of those he loved was a recurring circumstance in that period for Thomas Jefferson. In 1773 his closest friend, Dabney Carr, died before he was thirty. Dumas Malone described Carr's ailment as "bilious fever," which may have been hepatitis. Jefferson kept a promise that he and his brother-in-law, Carr, had made each other: Whoever predeceased the other would be buried at Monticello, near an oak tree where the friends had shared books and conversations.

Martha and Thomas lost their second daughter, Jane Randolph, born 1774, when the child was seventeen months old. A son born in 1777, unnamed, survived a little more than two weeks. Mary came next in 1778, then Lucy Elizabeth in 1780, who lived only four and a half months. The birth of another Lucy Elizabeth in 1782 ended Martha's life soon afterward. The child succumbed to whooping cough at two and a half.[12]

Judging from his writings and his jottings in the notebooks he carried, Jefferson met personal loss in mixed ways. His mother's death in 1776 evoked nothing more than a factual Memorandum

Book entry. His wife's death in 1782, however, sent him into a paroxysm that will be described shortly from recollections of the person then closest to him, his daughter Patsy. She was not yet ten at the time her mother died.

Involvement politically in the American Revolution over this period might seem to have served as escape from the pain of personal losses, but Jefferson did not see it that way. He regretted that heritage and history had forced on him a succession of public responsibilities and preferred that he might have been allowed to stay at home, where he felt most comfortable even under the saddest of circumstances.

Lacking any appetite for the service that required him to be away, again judging from his writings, Jefferson appeared to carry the strong Asperger's trait of longing for sameness of place and routine. The characteristic of homesickness in high-functioning autistics was noticed in the 1940s by the pediatrician Hans Asperger and the child psychiatrist Leo Kanner. Although not universal among those with the disorder, homesickness crops up because of absence from daily routines that had brought comfort and security. That is not to say a longing for family members plays no part. Familiar engagement with relatives in routines and traditions, however, must be understood as primary in making "home" a magnet for people with traits of Asperger's Syndrome.[13]

War came in 1775, and many colonists felt compelled to apply talents where they might best answer the general need. With a constituency of gentry supporting this young Virginian of promise, Jefferson took his place in the Continental Congress in Philadelphia. There he was to produce a work that guaranteed his immortality.

Two of the three achievements for which Jefferson wanted to be remembered are associated with the year 1776, when he was thirty-three. They were the Declaration of Independence, penned for the Congress, which body disappointed the very sensitive man by excising significant portions of his draft, and his early steps toward crafting the Virginia Statute for Religious Freedom. Jefferson considered the religious-freedom bill important enough to set aside self-con-sciousness in public proceedings and pilot its circulation in the House of Burgesses. Regardless of the weight he gave it, however, the Statute for Religious Freedom was not to be approved for another ten years.[14]

The concept of separation of church and state was controversial then just as it is a matter of renewed debate today. But he was firm on it and commented that "it does me no injury for my neighbor to say that there are twenty gods, or no god. It neither picks my pocket nor breaks my leg." What was important was that every person be given the right to retain his freedom of intellect and choice in the matter and that the government should never sanction a particular body of religious doctrine.[15]

(The third achievement of which he was proudest was his fa-thering the University of Virginia very late in life. He ordered men-tion of that and his authorship of the Declaration of Independence and the Religious Freedom statute on his tombstone. Jefferson either trivialized presidential and other service by not mentioning any of it or he exhibited an unusual sense of humor.)

The connections between his *Summary View* and the Declaration of Independence have been topics of study by Jefferson scholars. While the premises of the natural right to liberty are the same between them, Congress eliminated from the Declaration an oblique reference to a link with early Saxon history. Congress also excised Jefferson's new and pointed mention of the evils of the slave trade. We are fortunate that Jefferson saved the original language of his Declaration draft in order that we might know where his heart and mind lay at the time. As I have indicated, I will revisit the Saxon theme as an Asperger's sign.

The need for reforms in Virginia to meet future challenges of independence captured Jefferson's attention in the years following the formal Declaration and its wide acceptance by colonists. Jefferson's model for public school education was a fundamental advancement for which he won approval of the Burgesses, as was his successful bill to shut down importation of slaves in Virginia. The educational system he crafted more than two centuries ago is largely the one used throughout the United States today. He was truly a one-person "legislative drafting bureau" in that time of colonial reformation. The attention he drew to himself for such efforts won him election by Virginians in 1779 as Governor.[16]

During his dynamic service in Virginia he developed his classic friendship with (and political dependence upon) James Madison. The choice of coming to know, admire, and trust Madison for his intellect and industry seemed fitting in terms of Asperger's Syndrome characteristics. For reasons of friendship and stability, wrote the Australian authority Tony Attwood in *Asperger's Syndrome: A Guide for Parents and Professionals* (1998), people with the disorder require "an opportunity to meet people with similar characteristics." James Madison had symptoms of epilepsy, a speech defect, and according to historian Fawn M. Brodie "a voice which like Jefferson's was almost inaudible from the platform." Epilepsy is a more severe sign of brain damage that is sometimes found among persons who are autistic.[17]

Although the states united by the Declaration were well into warfare with Britain, the periods of shooting were spread over vast lengths of time. The method of warfare carried out on the American side relied almost wholly on Gen. George Washington's non-confrontational policy. He hoped to wear down an enemy superior in training, experience, equipment, and numbers.

Critics faulted Jefferson as Governor for fleeing Monticello at the approach of British troops in 1781. Accusations of cowardice led to an investigation. But the weight of reason prevailed. As an official of some importance to the enemy, especially as he had committed a capital offense by authoring the Declaration, he could neither stand to be captured nor fend off soldiers with a sword and a few hunting and dueling weapons. He had already sent his family and slaves to positions of safety and was unable to organize effective means for local defense. I have never seen the question asked, but if General Washington could run as a practical course of action, why not

Governor Jefferson?

France, the dedicated enemy of Britain, had made a large commitment to the American effort, including a naval force. The help of France proved critical in Britain's defeat. Among those whom Jefferson befriended in that period was Washington's aide, the Marquis de Lafayette. A warm, lifelong rapport evolved between Lafayette and Jefferson, each man influencing the other in ways involving revolutionary politics on both sides of the Atlantic. Lafayette could not abide slavery, a practice unknown in his country, and he did not hesitate to let Jefferson know that.[18]

As the shooting war ended and diplomatic efforts were started abroad to legitimize separation between Britain and the United States by treaty, Jefferson penned his only book, *Notes on the State of Virginia* in 1781-82. (He never completed his *Autobiography*.) Later he took the *Notes* manuscript abroad for publication, where he hoped it would win interest in and friendship for the people of the United States.

In its time the book was an important work in natural science as well as in the sociopolitical features of a region that stood at the center of the new nation. Virginia provided much promise agriculturally. Furthermore, America's rich economic prospects relied to a great extent on harbors and trade along Chesapeake Bay.

Today, however, Jefferson's book is viewed differently. In light of unresolved racial tensions, modern readers of *Notes* tend to focus on his venturing into pseudo-anthropology to describe African-Americans. They see that as an overgeneralized and clumsy effort. By his failure to anticipate that freed blacks would become full citizens with the same powers of critical judgment held by humans of any other ethnic identity, Jefferson burdened his work with unfortunate liabilities to be discussed in Chapter Four. Furthermore, the book reflects his obsession with trivial details, such as measurements at the mouths of Virginia's rivers or dimensions of those rivers from point to point, or factual information about mineral resources, caves, springs, and countless other features of the landscape.

In that latter sense *Notes* stands also as an example of high-functioning autistic output, that of telling most people more than they want to know in specialized areas of interest. The practice is a prominent behavioral feature cited in three of the four sets of diagnostic criteria that Attwood carried in his book, *Asperger's Syndrome*, and a feature that Hans Asperger was beginning to track in the 1940s in his first-reported clinical study among children.[19]

During the calming period that followed British surrender, Martha Wayles Jefferson gave birth to her last child. She fell gravely ill as a result. After several months' decline, she died on September 6, 1782. Her passing provoked such a strange intensity of grief from Jefferson that his family and friends worried about his health and his mental well-being. He fainted, "fell into a state of insensibility," lay on the floor, stayed in his room for three weeks, allowing only his daughter Patsy at his side, paced "night and day," went out riding "incessantly" and to some extent recklessly, and he appeared generally to be in a "stupor of mind," by Patsy's later description. Commenting on Jefferson's grief, his friend Edmund Randolph found it to be "somewhat abnormal," according to historian William Howard Adams writing in *The Paris Years of Thomas Jefferson* (1997). Biographer Fawn M. Brodie wrote that his behavior "bordered on the pathological." The style of Jefferson's mourning as described by his daughter brings to mind what the autistic Temple Grandin called "emotions of a child," which she wrote in *Thinking in Pictures* are features of her own behavior.[20]

Family members found a few mementos of the relationship between Jefferson and his wife later, but Jefferson had burned their letters and thus destroyed significant information. The subject of their "unchequered happiness," as he described their marital joys nearly forty years later, was evidently considered by him too private to share. At the time of his bereavement, Congress renewed an earlier appointment for Jefferson to go to France. Jefferson wrote in his *Autobiography* that his "state of mind concurred in recommending the change of scene proposed."[21]

Jefferson's departure for London and Paris as minister plenipotentiary to France did not actually take place until the summer of 1784. Patsy and their slave James Hemings accompanied him. Though he had studied French as early as the age of nine by his own account, Jefferson was nevertheless uncomfortable with its sounds. He may have found them stranger than those he had studied in Latin and Greek. The new United States minister displayed an "awkwardness with spoken French," according to Joseph J. Ellis in *American Sphinx*, despite his ability to appreciate so many other features of the country where he was to spend five years. His discomfort with spoken French also contrasted with his known talent for writing in several languages, at times shifting to such material with obvious pedantry. Temple Grandin wrote in her autobiography that she "cannot pick words out of a conversation in a foreign language until I have seen them written first." In lectures she has said repeatedly that a feature of her autism is that she cannot learn well through the ear but relies on the eye and the visual images it helps her brain record. According to biographer Dumas Malone, Jefferson could not "learn through the ear" and had to write things down or "he was lost."[22]

Jefferson met and fell in love with the petite and pretty artist Maria Cosway in 1786. She was the wife of the rather foppish artist Richard Cosway, who appeared to waver in his firmness about their marital responsibilities to each other. The pursuit of Maria Cosway demonstrated that the widower Jefferson was not incapable of new romance or sexual interest. Biographers never said he had lost his capacity for loving another woman when his wife died. However, their treatment of his life after he broke up with Mrs. Cosway implied that he had finally soured on love.

That brings us to this question: Why would the normal interest shown for Mrs. Cosway (until their separation) turn suddenly into enduring celibacy for a healthy man of forty-three? As DNA testing results have shown, the implied rejection by Jefferson of women starting in late 1786 was a fiction by historians who ignored contrary evidence. They misled Americans toward an incredible conclusion regarding their icon, Thomas Jefferson: Despite his being on the rebound from an affair of the heart, he had lost all interest in women for the balance of his life. Most historians implied, and *some insisted*, he was incapable of companionable interest in a comely, light-skinned African-American teenager when she arrived with his daughter Mary Jefferson in Paris in 1787. She was a young woman likely resembling his late wife, someone he had known all of her life.

For so many biographers to have denied the Jefferson relation-ship with Sally that started in 1788 has in itself become a topic for debate. Logical explanations for denial must include racist mindsets by historical biographers, a belief that Jefferson in his mid-forties was too ethical to have taken a slave of fifteen to bed by holding the unfair advantage of his station over her, a suspicion that Sally's son Madison had made a false claim in 1873 that Jefferson was his father, or that, when tracking early biographers' doubts, a succession of copycat chroniclers simply added theirs.

The contradicting DNA finding has lessened confidence in the biographers who were most adamant in denying the relationship. Their logic was flawed, and their judgments of evidence for a mixed-race romance were harshly negative. We may never know for certain which writers among them also skewed interpretations affecting other areas of Jefferson's activity in order to sugarcoat his personal side.

A few writers—too few, in my opinion—understood Jefferson as a flesh-and-blood human in addition to his having been a great statesman. They were Fawn M. Brodie, despite one or two leaps of faith in her 1974 work, *Thomas Jefferson: An Intimate History*, which has already been cited; Winthrop D. Jordan in *White Over Black: American Attitudes Toward the Negro, 1550-1812* (1968), and Annette Gordon-Reed, who in her 1997 book, *Thomas Jefferson and Sally Hemings: An American Controversy*, levied specific censure against sev-eral historians.

Annette Gordon-Reed's targets included authors and works already mentioned here: Dumas Malone's six-volume *Jefferson and His Time*, a monumental effort that occupied him from 1948 until 1981; Merrill D. Peterson, *Thomas Jefferson and the New Nation* (1970)—and she added criticism of Peterson for *The Jefferson Image in the American Mind* (1960)—and Garry Wills in his 1978 study, *Inventing America: Jefferson's Declaration of Independence.*

A lawyer talented in matters of logic, Ms. Gordon-Reed also censured John Chester Miller, *The Wolf by the Ears: Thomas Jefferson and Slavery* (1991); Andrew Burstein, *The Inner Jefferson: Portrait of a Grieving Optimist* (1995); Alf J. Mapp, Jr., *Thomas Jefferson: A Strange Case of Mistaken Identity* (1987), who repeated his doubts of the liaison with Hemings in *Thomas Jefferson: Passionate Pilgrim* (1991); Willard Sterne Randall, *Thomas Jefferson: A Life* (1993), and Virginius Dabney, a descendant of Dabney and Martha Jefferson Carr and author of *The Jefferson Scandals: A Rebuttal* (1981).

Joseph J. Ellis's *American Sphinx* was just coming into print in 1996 when Professor Gordon-Reed was completing her study. Because Ellis had not denied the affair, she excluded him from criticism. In fact, while serving as a helpful reader of Ms. Gordon-Reed's manuscript, Professor Ellis walked a center line on that topic in his own book. He did suggest prophetically, however, that unless the Thomas Jefferson Memorial Foundation allowed exhumation of remains for "DNA testing on Jefferson and some of his alleged progeny," the matter would remain a mystery.[23]

Two years after *Sphinx* was published, however, and the year after Ms. Gordon-Reed's book appeared, a DNA test was run without anyone's having to dig up Jefferson's body. It was accomplished by tracing Y-chromosomal DNA haplotypes from male-line descendants of Thomas's paternal uncle, Field Jefferson. Significantly, Professor Ellis expressed disappointment over the outcome. He wrote in a letter to *The New Yorker* that Jefferson "is more a sphinx than ever before" and that "he was living a lie." In my own interpretation of the Jefferson-

Hemings relationship in the next chapter I will track the affair to diagnostic criteria for Asperger's Syndrome—and to other Asperger's traits not enumerated specifically in those criteria.[24]

Fawn M. Brodie included a helpful analysis of biographers by Sigmund Freud in her *Intimate History* of Jefferson. We can read it now in the context of our knowing Jefferson's behavior contradicted several biographers' preferred image of him, whether as a cardboard character or as a candidate for plastic sainthood.

> Biographers frequently select the hero as the object of study because for personal reasons of their own emotional life, they have a special affection for him from the very outset. They then devote themselves to a work of idealization, which strives to enroll the great man among their infantile models, and to relive through him, as it were, their infantile conceptions of the father. For the sake of this wish they wipe out the individual features in his physiognomy, they rub out the traces of his life's struggle with inner and outer resistances, and do not tolerate in him anything savoring of human weakness or imperfection; they then give us a cold, strange, ideal form instead of a man to whom we could feel distantly related. It is to be regretted that they do this, for they thereby sacrifice the truth to an illusion, and for the sake of their infantile phantasies they let slip the opportunity to penetrate into the most attractive secrets of human nature.[25]

Jefferson witnessed a number of the events that marked the early period of the French Revolution. He was in touch with leaders including Lafayette, and he can be said to have meddled somewhat in their proceedings. The place where Jefferson breaks off his *Autobiography* for want of further patience with it is the moment of his return to the United States in 1789, at the height of France's internal conflict. He had devoted approximately a third of his life's story to describing the ebbs and flows of French revolutionary politics that preceded his leaving France. He had shown halfway through the autobiographical work his weariness with the writing effort. ("I am already tired of talking about myself.") During his long stay in France he corresponded with James Madison about the development of the Constitution and later the Bill of Rights. While history has credited Madison correctly with piloting those efforts, the influence of the absent Jefferson was clear from the letters between them.[26]

President Washington named Jefferson in 1790 to his cabinet as Secretary of State. In that capacity Jefferson began his sharp feud with Alexander Hamilton over their vision for America along opposing lines of central authority (Hamilton) and states' rights (Jefferson). Modern political analysts might see the two poles as Hamilton's disposition toward promoting passive acceptance among the governed and Jefferson's effort to promote active self-advocacy among the self-governed. George Washington pleaded with them to settle their differences, but fresh issues divided them frequently. Their policy disagreements were so consuming of Jefferson's tolerance that he resigned at the end of 1793.

Jefferson's return to Monticello in 1794 lifted his hopes that he had finally retired from public service, but the period that followed also brought gloom over agricultural failures. His family was growing by the addition of nieces, nephews, and grandchildren who headquartered at Monticello, so Jefferson in 1796 undertook a remodeling of the home, which eventually more than doubled its space.

Political parties in that time were seen more as necessary evils than they are today, despite current widespread disenchantment. Unable to shake off the responsibilities of leadership and by an arrangement of electoral outcomes we would find puzzling today, Jefferson the Republican became Vice President in the 1796 election under President John Adams the Federalist. In that new capacity he dissented frequently because he was convinced Adams's followers were dedicated to dismantling freedoms won in the Revolution and secured in ratification of the Bill of Rights. Jefferson opposed bitterly and even clandestinely the Alien and Sedition Acts which sent editors to jail for criticizing Adams in print.

Having been a "reluctant candidate" in 1796, Jefferson seemed more interested in the opportunity that a Presidential candidacy in 1800 gave him for setting things right.

The New York Republican Aaron Burr was also in the field. Burr's electoral total tied Jefferson's over the defeated Adams. That stalemate forced a decision upon the House of Representatives. The House chose Jefferson and placed Burr in the Vice Presidency. Even Hamilton preferred Jefferson over Burr, who not only proved something of a rascal in later adventures but who killed Hamilton in an 1804 duel.[27]

Jefferson's first term was marked by national economic prosperity. A highlight also was the opportunity Napoleon's war-spending spree furnished for the United States' purchase of Louisiana Territory, which transaction would place new cash at the French conqueror's disposal. The first term also showcased Jefferson's style of executive leadership, which contrasted with Washington's and Adams's. Jefferson preferred to make himself relatively inconspicuous. He did so partly to avoid pompous ceremony that he thought his predecessors had overdone, and he did so partly because he preferred to spend as much time as possible in solitary writing, another reflection of Asperger's I will cover in an appropriate context. Jefferson's bad fortune continued with respect to the loss of loved ones, however, for his daughter Mary (Polly) died in 1804 as her mother had, from childbirth complications.

Jefferson's bid for a second term grew from his wish to reinforce the status of the liberal Republican philosophy. The vision of the Democratic-Republicans, as his political faction was coming to be known, was his preferred model for the young nation. He fostered the establishment of a political dynasty of his philosophical heirs in the President's House, later the White House. It lasted through a number of successors, James Madison, James Monroe, and to an extent John Quincy Adams, who as a boy had known and admired Jefferson. To add Andrew Jackson and Martin Van Buren might distort the image of a legacy somewhat, but they gave evidence of

Jefferson's influence. There would be risk in attempting to associate with his successors precisely the same vision that Jefferson carried in his mind, with the possible exception of James Madison.

Jefferson pictured trade route capabilities for an expanded United States. The nation would reach the Pacific Ocean, regardless of prior claims to that land by Indians, or Native Americans. We cannot know whether that vision represented imaging common to many people with Asperger's Syndrome or whether Jefferson's far-sightedness stemmed from his having been son of a self-taught map-maker. Nor can we rule out mental imaging as a precursor for his resetting of the nation's boundaries. We do know that he engaged in such imaging, such "thinking in pictures." In his famous dialogue written for Maria Cosway titled "My Head and My Heart" (1786), Jefferson referred to his ability to think pictorially. He wrote of visualizing "architectural 'diagrams and crotchets' (jointed wood used as building supports)" as a means for relaxing in order to fall asleep.[28]

Jefferson's second term was quite different from the balmy first term. A stormy accompaniment to it was the war between Britain and France. He attempted to keep the United States out of it. Jefferson and Congress established an embargo against trade to avoid dangers from war on the high seas. But the embargo carried out in roughly the final year of his term proved disastrous to the economy. In advancing such a move he had failed to promote and win the public support that was needed to sustain it. The embargo expired at the end of his term in 1809. He and Secretary of State Madison had been postponing the inevitable, for a fresh war with Britain came anyway in 1812, during President Madison's administration.

In the years of his retirement to Monticello starting in 1809, Jefferson enjoyed the company of his large family. (His daughter Patsy had twelve children, all but one of whom lived to maturity.) Periodically, however, when visitors overwhelmed him he fled to other estates he held in the region, such as Poplar Forest. His daily regimen included long periods of letter-writing, up to ten hours' worth. He enjoyed riding about his properties to monitor the status of farming efforts. The habit of writing for long periods was symptomatic of his Asperger's tendency toward being a loner and of yet another trait—resistance to changing a comforting everyday activity. Without expressing suspicion about its origin, Joseph J. Ellis observed that inclination toward self-isolation by Jefferson in American Sphinx, just as other biographers have written of his preference for study or writing in seclusion.[29]

Three situations are worthy of note here about Jefferson's final years. For one, his involvement in organizing the University of Virginia was of such a depth and intensity as to include architectural plans, mapping of the curriculum, hand-picking the faculty, prescribing student living arrangements, and personally cataloguing its 6,860-volume library four hours a day over a period of several months. The last type of activity has been said by Temple Grandin to be closely associated with "savant-like memorization skills." There were disappointments in the university project, some of them of his own making. But the institution has lasted as a tribute to his genius and, I have no doubt, as a monument to obsessive behavior linked strongly to traits of Asperger's Syndrome.[30]

The second situation, a sadder circumstance in that same period, was Jefferson's realization that his debts had outrun his income and that the family would not be able to retain Monticello for very long. Self-deluding Asperger's characteristics—believing that, somehow, everything relating to money management would end well, together with his keeping of irreconcilable financial records—had evidently induced the situation. His co-signing of a large loan for a friend also proved disastrous, because the friend defaulted. For Jefferson that was another consequence of his vulnerable naivete.

To offset the decline of his finances Jefferson proposed that Virginia authorize a lottery to assure the family sufficient funds to pay debts and keep the home. The lottery was designed to dispose of portions of Jefferson's property at "fair value," with proceeds to go toward satisfying creditors. Jefferson argued that his public service had entitled him to special consideration. He had willingly given low priority attention to his personal financial well-being in the process of serving Virginia and the nation. Officials in Richmond criticized the lottery at first. Then, as they realized what was at stake, they granted authorization. Lottery ticket sales, however, were so disappointing as to doom the project.[31]

The third item of interest from this late period was a letter-writing reconciliation with John Adams. We have a small sign of Asperger's in that area, because Jefferson at first sought rational if not perfect closure through Abigail Adams after intense political disagreement had separated him from John Adams for so long. Jefferson "perseverated" in the matter, an almost esoteric concept used frequently by Asperger's analysts. It means belaboring a topic endlessly, sometimes with benefit, more often without. The correspondence with Abigail had started in 1804 after she sent a condolence letter for the death of Polly. Jefferson's responses had strayed into what some might judge a nagging perseveration—until John Adams shut it down curtly. When Adams and Jefferson renewed direct correspondence in 1812 by the intervention of a mutual friend, Dr. Benjamin Rush, the letters became a treasure and a rich record of the outpourings of contrasting geniuses. They were united in passion for their creation, the United States. On July 4, 1826, as the nation marked the fiftieth anniversary of the Declaration, death claimed both Founding Fathers.[32]

Notes:

1   *Writings*, 3-4.

2   *Malone*, 1:12-13.

3   *Ibid.*, 1:38; *Jefferson's Memorandum Books: Accounts, with Legal Records and Miscellany*, 1767-1826, James A. Bear, Jr., and Lucia C. Stanton, editors - two volumes (Princeton, N.J.: Princeton University Press, 1997), 1:212, 287, 370n; *Attwood*, 141.

4   *Malone*, 1:38.

5   *Writings*, 4; *Malone*, 1:42, 83.

6   *Writings*, 4; *Grandin*, 101.

7   *Writings*, 5.

8   *Ibid*, 6-10.

9   *Malone*, 1:153-55; *Attwood*, 195.

10 *Malone*, 1:158.

11 *Writings*, 5; *Gordon-Reed*, Genealogical Tables, xxiii.

12 *Malone*, 1:160-61,434.

13 *Asperger/Frith*, 73n.

14 "I was myself the mover & draughtsman," *Writings*, 36

15 *Malone*, 1:274-80.

16 *Ibid*, 1:280-81; *Writings*, 34; *Peterson*, 112, quoting Julian Boyd, Jefferson papers editor and historian.

17 *Attwood*, 52; Robert A. Rutland, *James Madison: The Founding Father* (New York: Macmillan Publishing Company, 1987), 8; *Brodie*, 178; *Happe*, 28.

18 *Brodie*, Reminiscences of Israel Jefferson, 481-82.

19 *Attwood*, 195-201; *Asperger/Frith*, 45-46, 53-54.

20 *Malone*, 1:396; *Peterson*, 246; William Howard Adams, *The Paris Years of Thomas Jefferson* (New Haven: Yale University Press, 1997), 34; *Brodie*, 169; *Grandin*, 87.

21 *Writings*, 46.

22 *Ellis*, 84; *Grandin*, 55; *Malone*, 1:126.

23 *Gordon-Reed*, 107, 82-83, 169-170, 107, 111-12, 4, xviii; *Ellis*, 304-5.

24 *Foster et al.*, 27; *The New Yorker*, January 11,1999,5.

25 *Brodie*, 30, from Sigmund Freud, *Leonardo da Vinci: A Study in Psychosexuality* (Modern Library edition, 1947), 109.

26 *Writings*, 43, 71-74; see also *The Republic of Letters: The Correspondence Between Jefferson and Madison*, 1776-1826, James Morton Smith, editor—three volumes (New York: WW. Norton & Company, 1995), 1:435-637.

27 Noble E. Cunningham, *In Pursuit of Reason: The Life of Thomas Jefferson* (New York: Ballantine Books, 1987) (pb), 221.

28 *Grandin*, 25; Andrew Burstein, *The Inner Jefferson: Portrait of a Grieving Optimist* (Charlottesville, Va.: University Press of Virginia, 1995) (pb), 18-19.

29 *Ellis*, 38; *Malone*, 1:56, 58; *Peterson*, 9.

30 *Grandin*, 107; *Peterson*, 537-38; *Ellis*, 282, 286-87.

31 *Malone*, 6:473-82.

32 *The Adams-Jefferson Letters*, Lester J. Cappon, editor (Chapel Hill, N.C.: The University of North Carolina Press, 1959) (pb), 268-82.

CHAPTER THREE

A Logical Choice

One of the five diagnostic criteria for Asperger's Syndrome applying to Thomas Jefferson reads, "The disturbance causes clinically significant impairment in social, occupational, or other important areas of functioning." To arrive at an understanding of factors that led Jefferson to Sally Hemings in 1788, we must look at his problems in the social and other areas that demonstrated his impairment. We must also move past the negative connotation of the word "impairment" and understand that people who fall in love often do so at low points of disappointment, trouble, or confusion in their lives.

Because I share the view that his affair with Sally was a positive factor in Jefferson's life (or else he would not have been a party to letting it run so long), I feel obliged to show the relationship was a rational choice for him. Less is known about the influences upon Sally Hemings at the start of the affair, but it probably was a rational choice for her as well.

The key to unlocking the mystery of this secret romance lies in the question of why the widower Jefferson never remarried. In his fifties, before he became President and then after he attained that office, he need not have worried that finding a wife would affect his daughters directly. They were grown by then and charting their own futures.

Nor is there need for concern that a middle-aged Thomas

Jefferson lacked the interest or vigor of a bridegroom. The sole Sally Hemings birth that DNA tracking has attributed to his paternity occurred when he was sixty-five. Now, struck by logic since the DNA announcement, historians appear to be coming around to the view that sixty-five would hardly have been the age for starting an affair, that there was indeed a relationship between Thomas Jefferson and Sally Hemings, and that its Paris beginning when Jefferson was forty-five was far more likely (which is what his son Madison Hemings tried to tell us more than a century ago).[1]

To find the key we must go back several years before they began their affair—to a time when Jefferson had only a peripheral awareness of young Sally and when neither of them had the slightest inkling they would someday be loving companions for thirty-eight years. A single act on September 6, 1782, placed them on that path.

As Martha Wayles Jefferson lay dying at Monticello that morning, nine-year-old Sally was in the room along with her mother, Elizabeth, or Betty Hemings, and Sally's older sisters, Bett, known as "Betty Brown," twenty-three; Nance, twenty-one, and Critta, thirteen. Apparently the only other house slave present was Ursula, an older woman who was considered Patsy's and Polly's "Mammy."

That a dying Martha should call upon her late father's mulatto mistress, Betty Hemings, and upon her own mixed-blood half-sisters for comfort is significant to our assessment of the dynamics of the scene that unfolded. As told "often" to the wife of Edmund Bacon, who was the Monticello overseer beginning 1806, the Hemings women and girls "stood around the bed" as Martha gave her husband Thomas "directions about a good many things that she wanted done." After a moment of emotional difficulty, the dying woman said, by Bacon's second-hand account, "she could not die happy if she thought her four children were ever to have a stepmother brought in over them." Actually only three of Martha's children were alive at the time. Historians have blamed the reported error on the confused mind of a dying person.[2]

Martha Wayles Jefferson had lost her own mother shortly after she was born. When Martha was three years old her father, John Wayles, remarried. John lost his second wife and remarried again when Martha was eleven. The major female constant in the Wayles household through all of that was Betty Hemings, who was thirteen years older than Martha and who later became John Wayless mistress.[3]

A question also arises whether Martha Wayles Jefferson's expressed fears about stepmothering over her daughters might have been indirect praise for the care she received from Betty Hemings in her own childhood. People who are dying have an enlarged sense of drama about whatever they say that may be remembered well. It is the very last thing they leave us.

By itself the strong presence of the Hemings women during Martha's dying at Monticello appeared to confirm an interracial bond in that time that most Jefferson biographers have ignored. Had such a bond been acknowledged realistically by historians it would have skewed their accounts, not only of the Martha Wayles Jefferson death scene but of subsequent family history, in ways most of them have scrupulously avoided. The presence in that time of mixed-race family members on such occasions was either uncommon in plantation Virginia or more common than reported.

Jefferson's widowed sister, Martha Carr, and his daughters Patsy and Polly were also near or present by other accounts. But it was the proximity of the Hemingses to Martha's deathbed in those moments that added weight to observations that Betty's family enjoyed a remarkable role in the lives of the Jeffersons.[4]

Jefferson's response to his wife's final plea was that he would "never marry again." Reason goes against anyone's believing he would have chosen such a moment to negotiate over a technicality and propose at least delay in remarrying until the girls were grown. He was in no frame of mind to catch subtleties of the situation in which he found himself. Although not present at the time, overseer Bacon, who served Jefferson fourteen years until 1822, added this observation: "He was then quite a young man and very handsome, and I suppose he could have married well; but he always kept that promise."[5]

In a later and calmer moment, using his wits and superior intelligence to draw a proper inference (biographer Merrill D. Peterson estimated Jefferson's intelligence quotient at 150), Jefferson could have looked back, assessed new circumstances, and decided upon an adjustment. He might have rationalized that he had kept his word according to Martha's general intentions and, next, altered his position in light of reason. However, according to Francesca Happe, research scientist in the Cognitive Development Unit of the Medical Research Council, London, a person with an Asperger's disorder must understand another's intentions fully to draw a proper inference from the exchange. We have no reliable quotation from the dying Martha to know exactly how the plea was put to Thomas. We have only a general basis of stepmothering avoidance for the request, then Jefferson's indirecty-quoted but evidently *un*ambiguous response.

Without great clarity, which is hardly ever available in a room where someone is dying, the surviving person with strong traces of Asperger's will simply take literally the clearly-remembered words uttered between the principals.[6]

Jefferson's inability to cope with any contingencies associated with Martha's deathbed wish was compounded by the universal and pragmatic question, When does a father stop being a father? His first obligation under the plea and the promise was to his daughters. There was no discussion of an end point, no future release from his pledge. The Asperger's clinician Tony Attwood has pointed out that a strong tendency among persons with traits arising from Asperger's Syndrome is to take instructions and commitments literally. Furthermore, there is a reinforcing factor in Asperger's that was represented in this instance—the ethic of the pledge. Once given, a promise has been made for all time, a rule of life. Asperger's people play strictly by the rules. Factoring in the powerful sense of "place" and his primary obligation to those around him, we have a man who on September 6, 1782, was locked by *literalness*, *rules*, and a *commitment* witnessed by relatives present at his wife's dying. Such an array of Asperger's influences upon Jefferson added up to impairment—more precisely to an inability to act independently in both his social and emotional interests in eighteenth-century terms. The combined factors set the stage also for his selecting Sally as his mate when they were in Paris, a choice that evidently gave both of them enduring happiness.[7]

An event closer to Sally's arrival abroad fostered further the atmosphere for their relationship. In the summer of 1786 Jefferson fell in love with the artist Maria Cosway. They saw each other daily, enjoyed the sights of Paris and its surroundings, and probably enjoyed each other sexually. Jack McLaughlin, the Humanities Division head at Clemson University who wrote *Jefferson and Monticello: The Biography of a Builder* (1988), noted that Jefferson was too much of a scientist not to have known about contraception then coming into use. His purchase of a syringe that was probably applied to such a purpose appeared in Jefferson's records during the time he was spending with Mrs. Cosway.[8]

Maria Cosway's marriage and her subscription to Catholicism ruled out any hope for a formal or long-term commitment between them. In a display of vanity rare for Jefferson he tried to impress Mrs. Cosway with his agility while they were on a leisurely late-summer stroll September 18. He attempted to vault a fence or a low wall, and the effort resulted in an accident that left him with a dislocated right wrist. He came down hard and received an injury that disfigured his right hand for life, for the physicians who attended him failed to reset the bones correctly. He never gave the violin serious attention again. The affair cooled quickly, regardless how historians judge the romantic dialogue which Jefferson subsequently wrote left-handed and sent Maria Cosway. It was entitled "My Head and My Heart"—amounting to a twelve-page tribute to her that biographer Dumas

Malone called a "feat of ambidexterity." Significantly, the "Head" prevailed, thus providing the sensitive intellectual Jefferson the closure he evidently required over an affair doomed from the start and fraying badly after the accident.[9]

Nevertheless, Jefferson brooded over the broken affair. Not only did he put off a number of commitments to let his wrist and his heart mend, he soon took a long-desired trip in the hope such a change of scene would speed recovery. For three months he traveled to the south of France, to northern Italy, and across southwestern provinces to Brittany. Although the trip filled his mind and his notebooks, it did little for his injured wrist and hand. Meanwhile, Jefferson had been arranging for his daughter Mary, or Polly, to join him in Paris. His youngest daughter, Lucy Elizabeth, had died in Virginia of whooping cough at the age of two and a half shortly after his arrival in Paris in 1784. That was what prompted him to send for Polly, who had recovered from the same illness. Transoceanic arrangements required such long intervals of time that it was not until the summer of 1787, when Polly was almost nine, that she arrived by way of London.

John Adams and his wife Abigail were living in London at the time, for he was serving as America's first minister to Britain. Upon Polly's arrival with fourteen-year-old Sally Hemings, Mrs. Adams wrote Jefferson and showed ambivalence over Sally's worth as Polly's maid or traveling companion. "The Girl who is with her is quite a child," Abigail wrote, adding that the ship captain believed he should take Sally back on his return trip. Sally, she added, "seems fond of the child (Polly) and appears good naturd." What Abigail Adams probably did not know, because all who lived at Monticello seemed to guard family privacy as closely as was reasonable, was that the relationship between Sally and Polly was also one of aunt and niece, not simply slave and mistress, or maid to Jefferson's daughter. I find it difficult to believe that Polly, young as she was, had no awareness of their blood tie. But she would also have known at her age that others might find such a truth too sensitive for her to confide.[10]

Upon the arrival of Polly Jefferson and Sally Hemings in Paris on July 15, 1787, Thomas Jefferson and his older daughter Patsy gazed upon two members of their Virginia household whom they had not seen for three years and who had not seen them. Dumas Malone commented of Polly, "She had totally forgotten her sister, but her father thought she showed signs of faintly remembering him." Shortly after Polly's arrival Jefferson boarded her in the Abbaye Royale de Panthemont, the supposedly non-proselytizing convent that Patsy, soon to be fifteen, had been attending for some time. What Jefferson expected Sally Hemings to do next under such circumstances was another matter, and no chronicler has given the problem adequate consideration.[11]

At this point elementary logic dictates a dialogue that would certainly have taken place between Sally and her older brother, James, who was then cook at the Hotel de Langeac quarters of Jefferson and his retinue and who had been in Paris three years. Unless Sally Hemings already knew, James would have taken her aside to tell her they had been emancipated, technically, simply by being in France, a place which gave no recognition to slavery. There can be no doubt of it. People who were slaves did talk about such things. We know that Sally viewed such a circumstance as her technical freedom with some seriousness two years later. But a revelation as enormous in its implications as that one would have leapt to her conscious mind frequently as she was taking on assignments in the Jefferson suite and observing the events beginning to boil into revolution in Paris. Again we are encountering in the story of this household a situation that Jefferson's Asperger's traits would soon bear upon strongly.

Sally Hemings had no reason to disbelieve her twenty-two-year-old brother about the fact of their freedom. She had also known Jefferson all her life, evidently looking upon him as a father-figure. Her own father, John Wayles, had died the year she was born. If she had wanted verification of so important a possibility as her sudden freedom (in law if not in fact), Jefferson the lawyer-diplomat was the logical person to whom she would turn to confirm it. Again, I have no doubt they, too, discussed the matter on a few occasions, long before she and James used it with Jefferson as a bargaining point we will learn about. Records neither reveal nor suggest what Jefferson's early thoughts may have been as he considered the matter.

Unlike the customary relationship between master and slaves then current in American environments, theirs was one of employer and "servants." That is the reference Jefferson preferred to make to slaves, and he paid James and Sally for their work. As Sally's Paris stay lengthened, increased payments for her appeared in the *Memorandum Books*—for clothes, lessons, wages, and amenities. Rather than enter the argument about why such payments escalated, I prefer to move ahead and link the relationship to Jefferson's Asperger's condition. Those who denied their affair argued that the payments were intended to make Sally more presentable while accompanying Patsy when Jefferson's older daughter was not attending the convent. Those like historian Fawn M. Brodie believed the increased payments represented forms of Jefferson's increasing attention to Sally. For me, the argument whether the affair took place is at an end, and it would appear the Brodie school has won that argument.

Because I believe Jefferson's Asperger's condition directed his decisions about Sally and governed a number of other choices, I am obliged to offer for consideration the following realities of that time in Paris that required reconciliation:

❑   Jefferson was lonely, still smarting from his wrist injury, rebounding from a brief romance, experiencing occasional sieges of migraine or tension headaches, and in that time of his life seeking female company.

❑   A reportedly stunning and maturing young woman in her mid-teens, Sally Hemings, likely resembling his late wife to whom she was a half-sister, was present with him and the only female present in their relatively confining Paris quarters.

❑ Though Sally was his inherited slave and his servant in Paris, her presence in France made her free, which also rendered her (at a level of civil status) essentially Jefferson's equal.

❑ Sally was about the same age as his daughter Patsy, actually several months younger. She was also a friend from home, witness at one of his darkest moments, the death of his wife.

❑ Thomas Jefferson could never look forward to female companionship through remarriage. He was sworn not to, and Sally knew that for she had been present to hear his pledge.

❑ Coincidental circumstances left Thomas and Sally alone much of the time. Jefferson's not-very-busy secretary, William Short, was in pursuit of the Duchess de la Rochefoucault and absent from Langeac much of the time. The household maitre d'hotel, Adrien Petit, was often shopping and, when not busily occupied, free to return to the nearby Champagne district, his home. James Hemings was attending an academy for chefs so that he might cook in the French style when he returned to Monticello. The girls, of course were boarded at the convent for their schooling.[12]

❑ If Thomas Jefferson and Sally Hemings were moving toward an affair that they might have thought about continuing at home, they would later be violating Virginia law, for she was one-quarter black. But for nearly the entire period 1788-89 they were not in Virginia.

Once again, the element of literal interpretation is on the table, particularly with the last of those facts. If Sally was a free woman, and neither French law nor natural law was being violated, Jefferson would be without guilt of wrongdoing. Was the thirty-year difference in their ages a factor that could invite shame? Probably not in those days. It would certainly not have been a prominent problem when mixed among so many stage-setting circumstances as those above.

Jefferson was in a position to take literally the fact of Sally's freedom in that place and in that time and, further, that there would be no transgression of law by allowing nature to take its course. The Asperger's considerations of literal interpretation and strict adherence to rules thus served the start of the affair, but only the start. As we shall see, yet another and more complicated Asperger's dependency maintained the affair after they returned to the United States.

How may Jefferson have dealt with the fact that, slave or not, Sally was his servant? Could that condition have raised an ethical question for him? As a matter of fact Jefferson was very impatient with social hierarchies. He demonstrated his intolerance of that feature of society's system a number of times when he was President. It is probable he had always found class to be a foolish barrier to human interaction. Using his favorite means for interacting, he corresponded with and appeared to respect any and all persons, no matter how lofty or how humble. Another Asperger's trait came into play when he ignored Sally Hemings's servant status, and that was his inner disdain for class distinctions.

Reason dictates there had to be a practical consideration for someone's eventually placing Sally in charge of Jefferson's wardrobe. After they returned to Monticello the job became hers for the rest of Jefferson's life. I have called attention to problems about the way Jefferson dressed. He tended to dress oddly and neglect his grooming. The ways in which he was perceived regarding that will be elaborated in Chapter Nine. But to look tacky in Paris was unseemly for an American diplomat. It seems quite logical that William Short, Jefferson's secretary, would have called upon Sally Hemings for help. She came as close to being Jefferson's sister-in-law as anyone might have found conveniendy. Short would have been the person likely to have urged Sally, who was talented in sewing and probably attentive to her own dress, to try to do something about Jefferson's clothing. If such a plausibility can ever be found to have had a basis in fact, yet another Asperger's trait may have helped ignite the Jefferson-Hemings liaison.

As someone so obviously affected physically by autism (postures and gestures yet to be described, manner of walking, manner of sitting, sensory problems), Jefferson often required calming pressure on certain parts of his body, most notably his chest. The way he dressed provided clues to that need, for he wore a vest that others noticed was conspicuously small and tight, and that one over *another* vest. He might have received similar satisfaction from simply hugging his children, but he was undemonstrative toward them. Such an arm's-length stiffness toward them indicated emotional deficiency that was also compatible with Asperger's. Besides, his daughters were away at school most of the time, exactly where he wanted them to be.

For a lonely man known to be inept about showing affection toward his young daughters, yet who craved physical relationships with women, the embrace of a "good naturd" woman promised satisfaction and calming pressure. And the fact of her being a young, attractive, "down-home" woman, a relative by marriage with whom he was alone much of the time, would have enhanced the pleasure of such an embrace.

Taking Sally's perspective, she had observed this man all her life. She knew his power was great, that his appeal had won her half-sister, that his physical condition was youthful and strong, that his talents appeared limitless, that his tastes were intriguingly rich, that his interests were arty, wide-ranging, and fascinating, and that he had recently closed the book on a disappointing love affair that had left him injured physically. He was lonely, vulnerable, and seemed to a watchful eye enchantingly disoriented.

Unfortunately, we cannot end the story of love's first bloom for Thomas Jefferson and Sally Hemings with the touching prospect of their first embrace. Nor can we simply fast-forward the affair to the significant and poignant observation that it lasted longer than many marriages, because Tom and Sally would soon be going home. Daughter Patsy's expressed desire to be a nun hurried arrangements for quitting France. Jefferson and Sally would return to a hostile environment where legal prohibitions against their liaison were clear, where they would resume roles of master and slave, where very few people would understand such an affair tolerantly. Jefferson faced the dilemma of balancing at home a private benefit that was taboo against his public image of propriety as a respecter of law and custom.

Here I must pause to explain something about high-functioning autistics. To put it simply, they live mentally and perhaps emotionally on two planes. They live in our world of nonautistics, but they carry with them a separate and otherworldly "reality"—*their* reality. The rest of us see it as idealism, but autistics seem to convert it into something palpable. A glance back at the traits on the Asperger's continuum (see Chapter One) would help a nonautistic lay reader conclude that people with autism operate in several respects on two planes, ours and theirs, often more successfully when they can remain on theirs. In order to understand Jefferson's inner adjustment over the affair when he returned to the United States in 1789, we must also understand how strategic is that second available plane, how vital to autistics is the quality of their self-isolation over social discomforts, and how essential that withdrawal becomes to escape pressures the rest of us bring to bear on them.

In the matter of the separate planes and pressures, it is as though they are "in" this world but "of" another. But is such a dichotomy a fair standard for our referring to all autistics as socially "impaired"? What manner of social structure have we created that rates harmless unorthodoxy so negatively? We nonautistics govern our own lives and values from far outside the realm of autism and give little thought to their world when we set standards and norms. Simply because they do not meet our standards, do Asperger's people believe themselves hobbled in the way we believe they are? Perhaps we should think of them as passive nonconformists. They do understand very well, by the way, that they are deviating from nonautistics' norms. But they resent the tightness of negative references we use to describe those deviations. They have little power to do anything except ignore the biases of normals the best they can.

Because we nonautistics make the rules, the test measurements, and the judgments, autistics may be thought to require guidance about what norms to follow. As a matter of fact not all of them have that need, for many autistics appear to carry an innate sense of right and wrong that is uncanny for its spontaneous expression and consistency and for its practical validity. Because they know what our standards are, that the application of ours to them leads often to misunderstanding, and that we are famously hypocritical about adhering to our own standards, people who are high-functioning autistics have often felt like aliens. They have the gift of reason but are made to feel uncomfortable about whether they truly have the freedom and right to exercise it.

What would Jefferson's judgment of his own behavior have been over the seeming incongruity between staying within the rules of France but venturing outside the rules of Virginia? In an Asperger's sense his judgment would have been, and I contend it was, that the subject had moved rather quickly beyond the range of anyone else's concern. It was so private after having matured into a loving relationship by the time they sailed home, so dear to him and to Sally that, for Jefferson, it was almost a secret he could keep from himself. When the "scandal" about their relationship appeared in newspapers in 1802, President Jefferson simply declined to comment.

Consider this: When Joseph J. Ellis plumbed Jefferson's character for *American Sphinx*, he wrote that Jefferson in 1798 responded to daughter Polly's concern over an alcoholic relative by suggesting "prudent obliviousness," in Ellis's words. By such mental discipline one could bolster an "imaginary ideal" and perhaps let that ideal pass for the reality of the situation, Ellis wrote. Jefferson's point to Polly was that it was better not to discuss it. Professor Ellis saw in such a Jeffersonian code an effect in which "one not only kept secrets from outsiders; one kept secrets from oneself."[13]

Jefferson had a keen talent for dealing with reality differently from the way others managed it, especially if he was to avoid the discomforts of conflict. The biographer Ellis is probably the first among interpretative historians to discover that two levels of reality served Jefferson. Ellis wrote that Jefferson was capable of creating inside himself "separate lines of communication" that would sort conflicting signals. My Asperger's interpretation simply adds this: On the one hand there was reality as you and I know it, and on the other hand there was a Jeffersonian reality that the rest of us tend to see as idealism. Jefferson could shut out the first as though it did not exist and maintain the second as though he were Elwood P. Dowd escorting, as his friend, a giant white rabbit named Harvey. The two levels are common to persons with high-functioning autism, and they deal with those separate realities daily in ways not yet clear to nonautistics.[14]

An area in which Jefferson's otherwise deft handling of the affair with Sally Hemings failed him was in his assumption it would be only their secret. Where he succeeded, however, was in separating the reality of its harsh perception by others from the reality of its belonging to the private world of his mind and heart—and in his holding to that privacy at all costs. Sally was the only person he allowed into that private world of deeply-felt emotion for the final thirty-eight years of his life. Martha Wayles Jefferson most certainly had been there, or Jefferson would not have been so quick to destroy all evidence of their intimate secrets when she died. Had Maria Cosway ever been admitted? Available character descriptions of the fickle Maria cast strong doubts on that possibility.

By the ethics of a nonautistic society we would call Jefferson's adroit handling of the affair the use of a double standard. But by the more complicated and Asperger's-influenced ethics of Jefferson, society was in no position to force its judgment upon him regarding the relationship. Society had charted unacceptable courses for his behavior that presented only terrifying choices: Either he must rationalize differently and expediently the promise he had made his dying wife in order to find socially-approved companionship, or he must survive somehow without the company of a woman.

Within the framework of that first course were requirements of reentering, in middle-age and sans violin, the game of courtship, of accepting what may have begun to look like nonsensical ceremony, of taking legal steps in behalf of a new spouse's secure place, of trusting her to run a household that was unlike other households in many respects, and of tutoring her to meet the special social demands of Virginias aristocracy. Naturally, society in that time and perhaps in ours would judge someone who sidestepped such games of opportunity for companionship to be socially impaired.

Within the framework of the alternate course that society's rules left him were the aches of personal loneliness and of celibacy—for a forty-five-year-old man of great sexual appetite. The surprise to me is that so many of Jefferson's biographers, unable to accept the reality of a relationship with the consenting Sally Hemings because she was a woman of African-American descent, crafted instead a fictional choice by Jefferson that made him appear superhuman.

Another Asperger s-related factor enabling Jefferson to transfer the affair to Virginia arose from his knowing he had deficits (by others' observations) as a social being. How could he not know? He had been retreating habitually from discomforting social engagements, seeking his writing desk or a book, realizing others stayed to chat and enjoy one another's company because they were different with respect to the activities that gave them pleasure. Jefferson could not have avoided knowing he was a person apart from others socially.

As I have pointed out also, people with problems of autism seek the company of others with similar problems. Yet those others' problems need not always be autism-related, only similar. In that regard we must consider whether Sally Hemings was a person fully-integrated socially, and of course she was not. Her status as a house slave constituted a form of social impairment separate from but as real as

Jefferson's. By some manner of reasoning—definitely Jefferson's manner of reasoning—they were a pair well suited to each other.

Those who would judge Jefferson harshly over the affair might instead consider gratitude. His enjoyment of the almost-secret life he thought necessary to his well-being probably freed him for such complicated achievements as the Louisiana Purchase, the completion of Monticello, and the establishment of the University of Virginia.

Sally and James Hemings did not overlook the new autonomy that their presence in France had brought them. Before surrendering their temporary freedom by returning to Virginia, they negotiated bargains with Jefferson. If James would teach another person at Monticello his skills as a French chef, he could look forward to freedom soon after. In Sallys case, according to Madison Hemings, the situation was more complicated. Sally had become pregnant. She asked Jefferson to promise that all children they would have together would be freed. It is important to notice the implication that Sally Hemings was, for emotional reasons known only to her, ready to have more children with Thomas Jefferson.

As it turned out she lost the baby she conceived in Paris shortly after their ocean voyage home, although another version, unverified, has it that the child, Thomas, survived and was adopted out. I cannot believe Jefferson would have allowed such a separation between mother and son. He did not permit slave families to be divided when bought or sold, and that contributes to doubt about his allowing the adoption of young Thomas. Jefferson later kept all promises to James and Sally Hemings that he made when they were about to leave French soil in 1789. Several Hemingses went free in Jefferson's lifetime, but not Sally. After they returned from France, she took charge of his suite along the south side of Monticello, including his library, his cabinet/study, and his bedchamber with its famous alcove bed. On the basis of evidence still unwinding, Sally Hemings was unconcerned about her personal freedom while Jefferson was alive, clearly because she did not wish to separate herself from him.[15]

When Madison Hemings told his story to a reporter from the *Pike County* (Ohio) *Republican* in 1873, he was sixty-eight years old. Critics including distinguished biographers have accused him of seeking gain from that. Their skepticism raises such questions as why Madison Hemings would have waited until he was an old man to tell such a story, and why his critics overlooked the fact it took Thomas Jefferson's heirs more than half a century after his death in 1826 to liquidate his debts, so there was nothing for Hemings to gain.[16]

Law Professor Annette Gordon-Reed in her analysis of the Jefferson-Hemings controversy wrote that the historical biographer Dumas Malone "set the tone" for an out-of-hand rejection of evidence for the affair. Other historians and biographers chorused that rejection clear into the 1990s. Comments in Volume Four of *Jefferson and His Time* (1970) suggest that the matter for Dumas Malone became one of attitude over reason. He dismissed any thought of Jefferson's being capable of such a "vulgar liaison." Malone wrote that he agreed, essentially, with earlier analyses by biographer Merrill D. Peterson. The same year Malone's fourth volume appeared Professor Peterson produced *Thomas Jefferson and the New Nation*. He maintained the Tom and Sally story was fraudulent "unless Jefferson was capable of slipping badly out of character." What I find offensive about the views of Malone and Peterson on the subject is that they allowed the only significant variable, race, to muddy their logic on this point while maintaining clarity on so many other matters of Jefferson's life.[17]

When the topic of miscegenation, or race-mixing, comes up in current debate about Thomas Jefferson, writers often turn to a letter Jefferson wrote to Edward Coles in 1814 as ostensible proof that Jefferson was against mixing. Coles earlier had helped Dr. Benjamin Rush broker the restarting of correspondence between John Adams and Thomas Jefferson. Later Coles became politically prominent in antislavery affairs, and the people of frontier Illinois elected him Governor in 1822. Writers including biographers have lifted this sentence about blacks out of context from the Jefferson letter to Coles: "Their amalgamation with the other color produces a degradation to which no lover of his country, no lover of excellence in the human character, can innocently consent."

When the letter is read in its entirety, the reader realizes Jefferson was encouraging Edward Coles to work toward eventual emancipation of slaves and to move ahead in that effort without him. It was a cause in which Jefferson admitted he had failed and was now too old to lead or lend meaningful participation. Taken in that broader context the offending sentence turns out to have been a lament about social consequences for those who were racially mixed, consequences he had observed personally at Monticello. It was not a condemnation of race-mixing.

Remember, Jefferson was inclined to take literally what he heard or read and to mean literally what he said or wrote (when he was not using metaphors). That is a characteristic of many people with the Asperger's disorder. For that reason we should look at the key word, "degradation," and in what other forms Jefferson used it. An early passage from the same letter will help:

> The love of justice and the love of country plead equally the cause of these people, and it is a moral reproach to us that they should have pleaded it so long in vain, and should have produced not a single effort, nay I fear not much serious willingness to relieve them & ourselves from our present condition of moral & political reprobation. From those of the former generation who were in the fulness of age when I came into public life, which was while our controversy with England was on paper only, I soon saw that nothing was to be hoped. Nursed and educated in the daily habit of seeing the degraded condition, both bodily and mental, of those unfortunate beings, not reflecting that that degradation was very much the work of themselves & their fathers, few minds have yet doubted but that they were as legitimate subjects of property as their horses and cattle.[18]

On the matter of the word "degradation" or forms of "degrade," Jefferson preferred to use it in the transitive sense, to show what one set of people had done to another set of people. He appeared to shun the intransitive meaning, by which one would assume the problems of the latter people were of their own making through self-neglect or by their somehow inviting corruption. As a matter of fact the portion quoted above puts the blame for "degradation" squarely on *slaveowners and their heirs.* In such a context the sentence about "amalgamation" constitutes Jefferson's condemnation of bigots' depriving the race-mixed of their dignity by means of destructive taunting.

Jefferson lived with a family that was the product of race-mixing, the Hemingses. He noticed or heard about frequent acts of petty indignities against those of mixed blood, in all probability. The practice of such taunting of mixed-race children and adults has been a common problem in the American culture and will probably continue for some time. Were his words, then, an attack on the abusers for assaulting his idealized (and naive Asperger's-related) vision of the country's charitable spirit? Was he condemning such taunters for having lowered the level of their own "human character" by behaving in that way? Did the final passage of the sentence imply shame for any who would be a party to such behavior by tolerating it? Only an affirmative answer to such questions is in conformity with the widely-shared view of Thomas Jefferson's character and his attitude in that time of his life.

Biographer Fawn M. Brodie confronted the same sentence from the letter to Edward Coles. Realizing that some scholars had read it out of context and were misunderstanding it, she came nearly to the same conclusion as mine (minus the semantic analysis) in her 1974 work, *Thomas Jefferson: An Intimate History.* Her point of view provoked criticism, however, by John Chester Miller in *The Wolf by the Ears: Thomas Jefferson and Slavery* (1991). As Professor Emeritus of History at Stanford University, Miller believed Jefferson feared race-mixing "would prove fatal to the republic."[19]

In writing African-American mathematician-inventor-astronomer Benjamin Banneker twenty-five years earlier, Jefferson had chosen a pattern for associating the word "degraded" with the lot of blacks. But it was free of meaning they had brought such a condition upon themselves, or that acts on their part had caused their degradation. He referred in the Banneker letter to "the degraded condition of their (blacks') existence both in Africa & America." By that use he indicated in 1791 a preference for the word's meaning "humiliated by others" rather than "corrupted by their own dereliction." People associated with Asperger's Syndrome are clear about their use of logic and about their sense of right and wrong, allowing no middle ground or subtleties to slow their direct and often literal approaches. Therefore, Jefferson would never have written nor implied to a black man that the latter's very existence in either environment, Africa or America, was a *prima facie* evil.[20]

Another combination of logic with an understanding of Thomas Jefferson's character is available to us over the disputed passage in the letter to Edward Coles. Before I present that argument, I must be candid and admit that Jefferson did not always hold charitable views about black people. In Chapter Four we will treat Jefferson's pre-Paris notions about race, which were abominable, which reflected prevailing folk prejudices, and which he expressly regretted later.

For reasons associated with his Asperger's condition, Jefferson had long been standoffish with his daughters. Madison Hemings complained Jefferson was "not in the habit of showing partiality or fatherly affection to us children," meaning those by Sally. Because we do not understand everything there is to know about Asperger's Syndrome, I find it both exceptional and surprising that such inhibitions do not always hold true in relations with grandchildren. That seemed to have been the case for Jefferson, who let Monticello be overrun with them and was happy to do so. Offspring of Patsy and Polly, the latter daughter having died in 1804, those grandchildren were contemporaries of Madison Hemings, who was born in 1805. Such circumstances as seeing Jefferson at play with his grandchildren added to Madison's melancholy over lack of affection from his father. He had long held as well a self-image that he was technically a slave for the first part of his life.

The issue here, however, is whether Jefferson would have intruded upon the self-esteem of his one-eighth-black offspring, Sally's and his children, so insultingly as to declare them (in his 1814 letter to Coles) corrupted from birth. My verdict on the basis of his Asperger's sense of right and wrong is that Jefferson would not have done so, for he had been a party to giving those children life through acts of loving intimacy with Sally Hemings.

My overall conclusion is that Jefferson gave Edward Coles no judgment whatsoever about race-mixing. Instead he condemned the atmosphere of degradation with which bigots were known to surround it.

Notes:

1 Brent Staples, "Fighting for Space at the Jefferson Family Table," *The New York Times*, August 2, 1999, A18.

2 *Jefferson at Monticello: Recollections of a Monticello Slave and of a Monticello Overseer*, James A. Bear, Jr., editor (Charlottesville, Va.: University Press of Virginia, 1967) (pb), 99-100.

3 *Malone*, 1:432-33.

4 *Brodie*, 168; *Monticello: A Guidebook* (Charlottesville, Va.: Thomas Jefferson Memorial Foundation, 1997), 104.

5 *Monticello: Recollections*, 100.

6 *Peterson*, 13; *Happe/Frith*, 236-38.

7 *Attwood*, 76-78.

8 *McLaughlin*, 196; *Memorandum Books*, 1:636.

9 *Malone*, 2:73, 75.

10 *Adams-Jefferson*, 179.

11 *Malone*, 2:136.

12 *Ibid*, 2:149; *Memorandum Books*, 1:585n; *Brodie*, 235; Peterson, 535; *Malone*, 2:6, 136.

13 *Ellis*, 136.

14 *Ibid*, 89.

15 *Brodie* (Madison Hemings), 472-73; Staples/*NYTimes, op. cit.*

16 *Malone*, 6:511.

17 *Gordon-Reed*, 107; *Malone*, 4:214, 494-98; *Peterson*, 707.

18 *Writings*, 1343-46.

19 *Brodie*, 432-33; John Chester Miller, *The Wolf by the Ears: Thomas Jefferson and Slavery* (Charlottesville, Va.: The University Press of Virginia, 1991) (pb), 207.

20 *Writings*, 982-83.

CHAPTER FOUR

Separate Realities

The criterion for diagnosing the Asperger's condition of Thomas Jefferson that we must give further treatment before moving on to others is the seeming catchall that reads, "The disturbance causes clinically significant impairment in social, occupational, or other areas of functioning." In this chapter we will observe how impairment—which resulted largely from his literal interpretation of legend and fiction and from his inclination to follow a moral precept against slavery—brought him serious discomforts. His uneasiness was plain when the Continental Congress adopted an edited Declaration of Independence. The issue of slavery haunted him throughout his life.

Jefferson ignored certain realities because he had romantic notions about the way the world ought to be. It was next to impossible to shake him from the rosier features of his deeply-held convictions, from his faith in humankind's ultimate perfectibility. For such reasons John Adams, ever the realist, maintained jokingly that "Jefferson was always a boy to me."

Adams's co-worker in the Continental Congress, in which service they formed the defining bond of their relationship, was the tall, red-haired Virginian, Jefferson, who still carried the blush of youth on his cheeks while in his early thirties. For a man so talented with his pen Jefferson seemed utterly naive and, of course, "could not speak in public" during that greatest of debates by representatives of the thirteen American Colonies over separation from Britain.[1]

Biographer Joseph J. Ellis analyzed a basic irony of the Declaration of Independence that Jefferson was asked to draft. Indictment of Britain for exercising power abusively had flown from Jefferson's pen before, in his 1774 work for Virginia representatives entitled *A Summary View of the Rights of British America*. Jefferson's paper for the Continental Congress, which he presented in 1775 after the start of war, carried the vivid title, *Declaration of the Causes and Necessity for Taking Up Arms*. The same assumptions on which Jefferson based those two earlier works became an underlying feature of his 1776 Declaration of Independence.

In essence Professor Ellis explained in *American Sphinx* that the situation called for a popularly-credible we-versus-they theme when representatives asked Jefferson to be the wordsmith of grievance and remedy. To justify the Colonies' separation from Parliament and the British monarchy they had to see themselves clearly as victims. The rest of the world required persuasion, it was thought, of Americans' injured innocence as a circumstance of history.

In order to assemble such a moral case for the triumph of good over evil, Jefferson responded to his Asperger's inclination to treat fiction as fact, and he dipped far into old legends about English-speaking people. He came up with "Saxon myth"—that feudal monarchs had overcome a pristine, prospering society and held the Saxons hostage for centuries by the power of the sword. The same brand of might was being held lately, he maintained, over British expatriates who had found the initiative to make their way to these shores, for whatever opportunity the New World offered. Where did Jefferson find such a story? There never was such a society historically. There was only a myth that British Whigs had exploited similarly in their own political struggles. Nor did emigration to these shores by Britons or any other people deserve such simplistic characterizations. But such stories "fitted perfectly with the way his mind worked," according to Ellis. Jefferson's similarly-based background themes had been published prior to the Declaration in *Summary View*. Though such themes were mostly excised from the 1776 document, their heroic tone lingered.[2]

As historian Merrill D. Peterson noted about Jefferson's clinging to his historical fiction, "Early committed to the Saxon myth, Jefferson never abandoned it." The clinician Tony Attwood has observed that once "on a particular track," as Jefferson was with Saxon myth, the Asperger's child or adult seems unable to change his mind, "even if the track is clearly wrong."[3]

The myths that partly underlay eventual separation from Britain were not the only examples of Jefferson's preferring legend to reality and ignoring contrary evidence. His long-standing interest in fiction about classic heroics gave support to his persistent view of early cultures as pure and unspoiled.

Shortly after his wife died in 1782 Jefferson's interests turned increasingly to poetry. Already devoted to Ossian, purportedly a Celtic poet of the third century, he sought the original work in Gaelic. But seven years earlier, in 1775, the widely-quoted English lexicographer and writer Samuel Johnson had exposed the Ossian works as fraudulent. They were the creation of a contemporary translator, James Macpherson. He had invented the heroically romantic poetry, and he had invented Ossian himself. Despite the evidence, Jefferson saw every bit of the Ossian works as genuine, quoting from them frequently and maintaining enthusiasm for the adventures of Ossian heroes a quarter century past Johnson's trashing them.[4]

By continuing to believe in such poetic tales, Jefferson brought them to life. Dr. Attwood wrote that some Asperger's children find it difficult to tell the difference between fiction and reality. When reading books of fiction or watching television and movies, "They accept the events as reality," and their retreating into an "inner fantasy world" may persist through adolescence.[5]

Jefferson appeared never to have outgrown the few fantasy worlds he enjoyed, those that fit his sense of right and order. And his failure to mature in that respect is one reason he was regarded as childlike. Furthermore, his relative immaturity along such lines was what made him an either-or person, one who judged on the basis of perceived right or wrong without contingencies.

There was little use of letting the mind chase into middle ground, where it could become lost among subtleties and in gray areas. Such pursuits could only clog his "all-or-nothing-at-all mentality," by Ellis's view. As tools of communicating and understanding, words were to be taken literally, and he took seeming fact as literal truth. He was unsuited for playing games of debate that required cunning and artifice.[6]

One might question why he was asked to participate in the world of realpolitik. The assignment to Paris that he finally accepted could be viewed as an appointment pressed on him in sympathy over the loss of his wife. It kept him a participant if not a major player in the developing post-Revolutionary government. At that he was somewhat lost in his European role. The principal success he achieved in his work abroad was a tough financial deal with Dutch bankers that he admitted was beyond his full understanding.[7]

An eyewitnesses to violent excesses of the French Revolution, Jefferson seemed too willing to excuse them. His zeal for struggles by which people sought political liberty clouded his reason. He compared the French experience with the American revolutionary success and added that it had global significance, a view which caused John Adams to think Jefferson had lost his mind.[8]

An interesting twist could apply to the condition of a person's social impairment that is called for in the criteria of the *Diagnostic and Statistical Manual*. What if impairment does not occur for society, as a general result of acts by a person with the Asperger's disturbance? What if social *gain* is the consequence instead? Whether or not myth survived in the final Declaration of Independence, myth inspired Jefferson nonetheless, and Jefferson's words inspired the founding of a nation.

Although Jefferson was sensitive to such tampering with his work as the removal of Saxon analogies and of tales of emigration by innocents, he showed resentment much longer over the excising of original Declaration draft references to slavery and the slave trade. It was regarding that subject that he was to become least understood.

A scientist in natural history of some renown in his day, Jefferson was also—by present standards and perhaps by measurements of scientific inquiry in his own time—a deplorable anthropologist. He seemed fettered by prevailing fears and biases. A fear was current that the numerical power of blacks in Virginia could be turned into a force for rebellion against slaveowners' abuses. Biases woven into the fabric of a gentrified upbringing contributed to an intellectual nearsightedness and a subjective musing in the unfortunate passages on race he wrote in *Notes on the State of Virginia* (1781-82).[9]

Jefferson's worst material on African-Americans, much of which follows, seems now to me an Asperger's-related elaboration of folk fiction in the guise of fact. Perhaps some of it was prattle he had overheard from young aristocrats with nothing better to do than swap absurdities while basking in imagined superiority. It was certainly not science. The starkly offensive material could have reflected his Asperger's naivete as well, for it poured forth almost as recorded hearsay. A tempting explanation is that he wished to offer testimony to conformity, particularly after he failed in early political efforts to condemn and even to modify slavery. But pandering was not Jefferson's style, just as the words that follow could not have remained among Jefferson's more thoroughly-considered views on race after Sally Hemings entered his life:

> The first difference which strikes us is that of colour. Whether the
> black of the negro resides in the reticular membrane between the skin and
> scarf-skin, or in the scarf-skin itself; whether it proceeds from the colour of
> the blood, the colour of the bile, or from that of some other secretion, the

difference is fixed in nature, and is as real as if its seat and cause were better known to us. And is this difference of no importance? Is it not the foundation of a greater or less share of beauty in the two races? Are not the fine mixtures of red and white, the expressions of every passion by greater or less suffusions of colour in the one, preferable to that eternal monotony, which reigns in the countenances, that immoveable veil of black which covers all the emotions of the other race? Add to these, flowing hair, a more elegant symmetry of form, their own judgment in favour of the whites, declared by their preference of them, as uniformly as is the preference of the Oranootan for the black women over those of his own species...

The reference to "Oranootan" (orangutan) was explained by Fawn M. Brodie as resulting from confusion in that time by natural historians and scientists over precisely what an orangutan was: A creature of mythology, a "man of the woods" but of another species, or a primate yet to be captured and examined? Historian Winthrop D. Jordan, who encouraged Professor Brodie in her work on Jefferson, wrote in *White Over Black: American Attitudes Toward the Negro, 1550-1812* (1968), that the "Oranootan" reference was intended to mean what we now know as a chimpanzee, humankind's nearest relative. Jefferson, while in Paris in 1788 and several years after he wrote the offending passage, ordered a book from London to learn more about orangutans. Continuing—

They have less hair on the face and body. They secrete less by the kidnies, and more by the glands of the skin, which gives them a very strong and disagreeable odour....They seem to require less sleep. A black, after hard labour through the day, will be induced by the slightest amusements to sit up till midnight, or later, though knowing he must be out with the first dawn of the morning. They are at least as brave, and more adventuresome. But this may perhaps proceed from a want of forethought, which prevents their seeing a danger till it be present. When present, they do not go through it with more coolness or steadiness than the whites. They are more ardent after their female: but love seems with them to be more an eager desire, than a tender delicate mixture of sentiment and sensation. Their griefs are transient. Those numberless afflictions, which render it doubtful whether heaven has given life to us in mercy or in wrath, are less felt, and sooner forgotten with them. In general, their existence appears to participate more of sensation than reflection. To this must be ascribed their disposition to sleep when abstracted from their diversions, and unemployed in labour. An animal whose body is at rest, and who does not reflect, must be disposed to sleep of course.

Jefferson's lack of clarity and his ambiguities on such points must also be placed side by side with an apparent self-contradiction: Note the earlier "require less sleep" in contrast with "their disposition to sleep." Once having seized upon notions such as those given here, an Asperger's person will sometimes seek to reinforce them, even at risk to his or her otherwise grand powers for logic and reasoning. Moving on—

Comparing them by their faculties of memory, reason, and imagination, it appears to me, that in memory they are equal to the whites; in reason much inferior, as I think one could scarcely be found capable of tracing and comprehending the investigations of Euclid; and that in imagination they are dull, tasteless, and anomalous. It would be unfair to follow them to Africa for this investigation. We will consider them here, on the same stage with the whites, and where the facts are not apocryphal on which a judgment is to be formed. It will be right to make great allowances for the difference of condition, of education, of conversation, of the sphere in which they move. Many millions of them have been brought to, and born in America. Most of them indeed have been confined to tillage, to their own homes, and their own society: yet many have been so situated, that they might have availed themselves of the conversation of their masters; many have been brought up to the handicraft arts, and from that circumstance have always been associated with the whites.

That Jefferson should have believed the best hope for blacks lay in association with whites is a compounding of his earlier scientific errors on this topic. The mistake was his belief in this portion of *Notes* that tracing black culture to its African roots, from which people were captured and torn for the slave trade, would have been pointless and somehow "unfair." Africa, birthplace of the human species, had yet to be explored by whites for its cultural significance to humankind. Rich discoveries such as highly-advanced civilizations and evidence of far-reaching maritime activity by Africans lay far ahead. Concluding—

> Some have been liberally educated, and all have lived in countries where the arts and sciences are cultivated to a considerable degree, and have had before their eyes samples of the best works from abroad...But never yet could I find that a black had uttered a thought above the level of plain narration; never see even an elementary trait of painting or sculpture. In music they are more generally gifted than the whites with accurate ears for tune and time, and they have been found capable of imagining a small catch (early guitar devised in Africa).[10]

Jefferson offered no sign of having made a scientific collection and analysis of data to support his generalizations. Historical biographer Merrill D. Peterson wrote that, on the subject of race, *Notes on the State of Virginia* contained "opinions that seriously embarrassed his philosophy."[11]

The only saving grace was Jefferson's admission of practicing science poorly in this area. "To our reproach it must be said," he added in *Notes*, "that though for a century and a half we have had under our eyes the races of black and of red men, they have never yet been viewed by us as subjects of natural history. I advance it therefore *as a suspicion only*, that the blacks, whether originally a distinct race, or made distinct by time and circumstances, are inferior to the whites in the endowments both of body and mind" (emphasis added).[12]

Jefferson's book of *Notes* was published in 1787 in England, around the time Sally Hemings arrived at the Adams's place in London on her way to Paris as the companion and servant of her blood-niece, Mary (Polly) Jefferson. The fact that further writings did not contain such harsh and inaccurate generalizations about people of color may be credited to his subsequent relationship with Sally, according to Professor Jordan. Thirty years before the DNA test of Jefferson and Hemings descendants, Jordan drew a relationship between Jefferson's apparently reformed views on race after Paris and his affair with Sally Hemings.

In *White Over Black* Jordan described Jefferson as ambivalent in several respects in his attitude about African-Americans. Then he speculated that, if there was such a Jefferson-Hemings affair, it was possible the "attachment with Sally represented a happy resolution of his inner conflict. This would account," he added, "for the absence after his return from Paris in 1789 of evidence pointing to continuing high tension concerning women and Negroes, an absence hardly to be explained by senility."[13]

Because Asperger's-affected people seldom shake off early beliefs, the change in Jefferson brought by association with Sally and by subsequent reflection must have been profound. The Asperger's literature does, however, accommodate such influence. By 1809 Jefferson invited and appeared ready to concede "complete refutation of the doubts" he had expressed earlier about the relative "grade of understanding allotted to them (to blacks) by nature." Though his response to the Abbe Henri Gregoire about the "literature of Negroes" made no explicit offer to renounce his earlier "suspicion" of physical and mental deficiencies, the letter touched such a possibility peripherally. Jefferson admitted his "personal observation" in *Notes* had been "limited." One could conclude from such a concession that he believed it had also been flawed.[14]

Why was Jefferson so conflicted on the point of race? No other public figure of his time seemed so bothered about it.

What did Jefferson the slaveowner do to offset his apparent self-torment?

What did Jefferson the public figure do about slavery?

Why did Jefferson not simply set all his slaves free?

To approach Jefferson's internal conflict requires some understanding of his concept of equality. According to Garry Wills, the Adjunct Humanities Professor at Johns Hopkins University and journalist who wrote *Inventing America: Jefferson's Declaration of Independence* (1978), Jefferson subscribed to "a literal equality more far-reaching than most educated people recognize today." The harsh observations by Jefferson in *Notes* were of "accidental differences of body or mind," Wills wrote, but the "all-important equality in the governing faculty of man" overshadowed such differences for Jefferson. Wills went on to show that Jefferson's view of slavery even at an early age was that the institution and practice were wrong.[15]

To answer the riddle of why Jefferson entered such a controversy at all we must rely in part if not wholly on the presence of Asperger's traits, as I will explain presently. While Jefferson acquired philosophical bases for his views from his reading of Enlightenment philosophers such as John Locke and David Hume, he chose also to go beyond them. He maintained a lingering belief in, and hope for, emancipation. Yet, because he feared that freeing blacks would lead to a race war over abuses they had suffered, he also believed in deportation or at least resettlement of African-Americans. On that point he was never able to theorize a practical way for such separation to be accomplished.

Less complicated as a factor in plumbing Jefferson's reasoning and his leaning toward manumission, however, is an observation available from the writings of Hans Asperger. The Austrian pediatrician observed that people with the condition eventually named for him "treat everyone as an equal as a matter of course." That is an observation that might be said to exceed, in quality and subtle implications, a disdain for social hierarchies. Of course, Jefferson also made differing judgments about the worth of individuals on grounds of their ethical conduct, sometimes relying on only a few observations or experiences with them in order to do so. But he still viewed each person as worthy of respect, regardless of his or her station in life and in some instances in forgiveness of the other person's transgressions.[16]

As the owner of a shifting number of slaves, depending on the point in his life when they are counted—in the mid-1790s when he was in his early fifties there were roughly 150 slaves in his keep—he offset his apparent uneasiness about slave ownership by treating slaves more responsibly than others were said to have done. If slaves were to be sold, for example, his rule was that family members were to be kept together. Their general health and well-being were to be given proper attention. Historian Jack McLaughlin in *Jefferson and Monticello* provided examples of how Jefferson sought care for his slaves as they required it. Jefferson also arranged to have a number of them taught trades, and he was known to have paid many for their labors.[17]

From his earliest written references, and continuing throughout his life, Jefferson called African-Americans "Negroes," which was then the current respectful reference. In specific terms he also referred to his slaves and those of others who worked in households and shops and farms as "servants." He wrote such designations in preference to any others and may be presumed to have spoken of blacks generally in the same way. His commitment to their acquiring new skills prompted Dumas Malone to notice Jefferson's references to "artisans and tradesmen, as he called them."[18]

The fortunate blending of recollections by a Monticello slave, Isaac Jefferson, and a white overseer, Edmund Bacon, into a valuable little book (*Jefferson at Monticello*, edited in 1967 by James A. Bear, Jr.) furnished us with separate and corroborating testimony of Jefferson's overriding concern for the treatment of his slaves. To guard against abuse he often kept one slave as overseer of the hands.

Dumas Malone wrote that he once replaced a white overseer he thought too "unkind to the workers," though the records fail to describe specifics of such treatment.[19]

"Mr. Jefferson was always very kind and indulgent to his servants," his overseer Bacon said. "He would not allow them to be at all overworked, and he would hardly ever allow one of them to be whipped....He could not bear to have a servant whipped, no odds how much he deserved it." As a matter of fact, Fawn M. Brodie pointed out, he actually forbade the use of the whip.[20]

A slave named Jupiter was the same age as Jefferson when he died in 1800 after having been hired out to a mason who had been dismantling parts of Monticello. Evidently the moving and hauling of rock exhausted Jupiter severely, and his condition was worse than suspected. His death prompted Jefferson to write of his concern during Jupiter's final days with him and of the outcome. The text was far more extensive than anything he had ever put on paper about the death of his own mother:

> I was extremely against his coming to Fredericksburg with me & had engaged Davy Bowles, but Jupiter was so much disturbed at this that I yielded. At the end of the second day's journey I saw how much he was worsted, & pressed him to wait at Hyde's, a very excellent house till the horses should return, & I got the promise of a servant from thence. But he would not hear of it. At Fredericksburg again I engaged the tavernkeeper to take care of him till he should be quite well enough to proceed. And it seems that immediately on his arrival at home, he took another journey to my brother's where he died. I am sorry for him.[21]

The description by Jefferson indicates also a far greater exercise of will by a slave than one would suppose was available to slaves in that period. But the more important interpretation to derive from it is the quality of Jefferson's sense of loss.

Somewhat as a reflection on his employer's attitude toward the downtrodden of any race, the overseer Edmund Bacon observed, "Mr. Jefferson was very liberal and kind to the poor." They learned when he was coming home and lined up at Monticello for handouts. Bacon thought many to be "lazy, good-for-nothing people" and said so to Jefferson. "He told me that when they came to him and told him their pitiful tales, he could not refuse them."[22]

A former slave at Monticello overheard the following exchange between the visiting Marquis de Lafayette and Thomas Jefferson in 1824. Israel Jefferson described the conversation in his reminiscence in 1873:

> Lafayette remarked that he thought that the slaves ought to be free; that no man could rightly hold ownership in his brother man; that he gave his best services to and spent his money in behalf of the Americans freely because he felt that they were fighting for a great and noble principle—the freedom of mankind; that instead of all being free a portion were held in bondage (which seemed to grieve his noble heart); that it would be mutually beneficial to masters and slaves if the latter were educated, and so on. Mr. Jefferson replied that he thought the time would come when the slaves would be free, but did not indicate when or in what manner they would get their freedom. He seemed to think that the time had not then arrived. To the latter proposition of Gen. Lafayette, Mr. Jefferson in part assented. He was in favor of teaching the slaves to learn to read print; that to teach them to write would enable them to forge papers, when they could no longer be kept in subjugation.
>
> This conversation was very gratifying to me, and I treasured it up in my heart.[23]

Jefferson's conduct as a benevolent slaveowner followed the rules that persons with Asperger's traits have accepted as principle. Clinician Dr. Tony Attwood has seen "their qualities of personality" as including a "sense of justice." That would help explain Jefferson's behavior as atypical—out of step with the attitudes of other plantation aristocrats, one who defied the defense of slavery by his contemporaries.[24]

As a political figure he strayed even more conspicuously from the norm. In his mid-twenties his first act as a member of the Virginia legislature in 1769 was to introduce a bill that would allow slaveholders to free their slaves as a matter of choice, not just as a reward for "meritorious services," a prerequisite set in law. Needless to say, that legislation was rejected. Five years later Jefferson called for abolition of slavery—nearly a year before the first abolition society was organized in Pennsylvania in 1775.[25]

Jefferson "set his heart on the eradication of slavery," Merrill D. Peterson wrote, as a priority next to establishment of a public education system. His effort in 1776 to write into the Declaration of Independence a condemnation of slavery and the slave trade went against the majority mood of the Continental Congress, but it was an act of incredible courage for him to have tried. Garry Wills said that Jefferson's drafted argument in that area was flawed, because his claim that Britain had forced the slave trade on the Colonies against their will was known to be contrary to prevailing opinion for the trade in such places as South Carolina and Georgia.[26]

Together with the final question, why Jefferson did not set all his slaves free instead of limiting that action to members of the Hemings family, we should weigh in an observation Temple Grandin made to me from a practical, logical, and principled perspective: "What he did about slavery was more important than his ownership of slaves."[27]

The ownership of slaves became inevitable when Jefferson's father died. Thomas was then fourteen years old. Young men schooled in the Virginia aristocracy knew they were dependent on the slave system. It is probable that when discussions of morality arose within families, understanding parents advised their maturing children not to permit erosion of, nor jeopardy to, the family's economic interests, particularly over a sense of guilt and never in support of rash political proposals.

Members of Jefferson's generation of Virginians, therefore, would not risk proposing limitations on slavery, such as liberalizing options for voluntary manumission of slaves or for ending the slave trade. But Jefferson did. No Southern whites of his time would seriously advocate emancipation. But Jefferson did that, too. Such ideals were closely related to his concept of "what ought to be." Joseph J. Ellis saw the contest between that ideal on the one hand and the truth of what was being tolerated on the other as Jefferson's "central dilemma" in nearly all political matters. At times he seemed affected by the dilemma over slavery acutely. At other times he seemed ready to entrust resolution of the slavery issue to a future generation.[28]

In Jefferson's time other reasons also governed slaveowners' holding fast to the family "property" represented by slaves. The Jeffersons took seriously their responsibility for the health, welfare, and security of their slaves. To free a plantation's slaves *en masse* and turn them loose in Virginia in the eighteenth or early nineteenth century would have been an inhumane and irresponsible act under the then existing laws and circumstances. Such an act would have resulted most certainly in their being hunted, captured, and claimed as property by other slaveowners without legal recourse. Most likely they would have been sold and separated from their families. Jefferson's relatively gentle and personal touch with slaves was appreciated and reciprocated. They greeted him with an outpouring of warmth upon his return from his five-year stay in Paris, and there is neither evidence nor reason to suspect the display was orchestrated.[29]

Criticism today of Jefferson's failure to have freed slaves at the approach of his death, except for a few in the favored Hemings family, does not take into account the fact that he was not always in clear possession of them. As his final days approached he owed so much money that even human "property" had to be held for the family's application of assets against creditors' claims. Because he was "always in debt," Garry Wills observed, for Jefferson to free more than a few slaves was "legally impossible."[30]

George Washington, on the other hand, was able to arrange that all his slaves would go free upon his widow's death. Historian Howard Zinn observed that Washington "was the richest man in America."[31]

In attempting to understand and explain separate realities as they affected Jefferson—one such set tied to his motives for independence and another connected to the contradictory problems of race for his mind to deal with—Professor Ellis concluded that "denial mechanisms" gave him some guidance and that "interior defenses" protected him from becoming unduly pressed. Ellis maintained there were "capsules or compartments" that had been "constructed" in Jefferson's "mind or soul" to stop conflicting thoughts on the slavery issue from colliding. The track Ellis was following parallels the Webster's dictionary definition of idealism—"the essential nature of reality lies in consciousness or reason." In other words what is real to some is what they think is real. It takes a special mental maneuver, which Asperger's people are equipped to use deliberately or involuntarily, in order to avoid observing and knowing what may truly be real.[32]

Notes

1   *Ellis*, 239, 36.

2   *Ibid.*, 32-33.

3   *Peterson*, 60; *Attwood*, 118.

4   *Burstein*, 31-35.

5   *Attwood*, 124-25.

6   *Ellis*, 53.

7   *Ibid*, 81-82.

8   *Ibid*, 128.

9   *Miller*, 64, 67.

10 "Notes on the State of Virginia," *Writings*, 264-67; *Brodie*, 232-33;
    Winthrop D. Jordan, *White Over Black: American Attitudes Toward the Negro,
    1550-1812* (Chapel Hill, N.C.: University of North Carolina Press, 1968),
    29, 32.

11 *Peterson*, 260.

12 *Writings*, 270.

13 *Jordan*, 467.

14 Digby Tantam, "Asperger syndrome in adulthood," *Frith*, 177; Jefferson to
    Henri Gregoire, February 25, 1809, *Writings*, 1202.

15 Garry Wills, *Inventing America: Jefferson's Declaration of Independence* (New
    York: Vintage Books, 1978) (pb), 228, 295.

16 *Asperger/Frith*, 82.

17 *Malone*, 3:207; *McLaughlin*, 141-42. How Jefferson's actions conformed
    with his attitudes about slaves is a topic covered in well-rounded fashion by
    Dumas Malone at the mid-point of Jefferson's life. *Malone*, 3:207-13.

18 Observed in the earliest entries and throughout *Memorandum Books* and
    other records and writings. *Malone*, 3:210.

19 *Monticello: Recollections*, 51; McLaughlin, 141; Malone, 3:211.

20 *Monticello: Recollections*, 97; Brodie, 35.

21 *McLaughlin*, 107-8.

22 *Monticello: Recollections*, 75.

23 "Reminiscences of Israel Jefferson," *Brodie*, 481.

24 *Attwood*, 179.

25 *Brodie*, 91.

26 *Peterson*, 152; *Wills*, 66-68.

27 Conversation between Temple Grandin and the author of this work December 12, 1998.

28 *Ellis*, 145.

29 *Malone*, 3:208, 2:246.

30 *Wills*, 296.

31 Howard Zinn, *A People's History of the United States: 1492 - Present* (New York: Harper Collins Publishers, 1980) HarperPerennial edition (pb), 84.

32 *Ellis*, 274, 149, 88.

CHAPTER FIVE

Magnificent Obsession

To understand Thomas Jefferson, one must appreciate Monticello.

To help us all understand the extent to which his life was so sharply affected by Asperger's traits we must observe factors involved in Jefferson's directing the construction and reconstruction of his home. It was not to be a fancy place that ordinarily would serve as the focal point of a large plantation. Rather it was planned as a place of eventual comfort that would give meaning to utilitarianism, with a concession or two purely to aesthetics.

Jefferson's dedication to the Monticello project met the *Diagnostic and Statistical Manual* criterion of "encompassing preoccupation with one or more stereotyped and restricted patterns of interest that is abnormal either in intensity or focus." Perhaps as many as a half-dozen separate Asperger's traits as well went into the long-term construction of the dwelling and into his use of the place that met so many of his exacting demands.

That the creation and construction of Monticello would cover fifty-four years of Jefferson's life from start to finish—and he was unwilling "to admit that it was ever finished"—is fair testimony to Monticello's being considered an interest of abnormal focus or an unusual fixation.[1]

That it helped bankrupt him classifies it as a costly distraction from priority consideration of whether he would leave his family anything but debt. In that latter regard we are taken back to the Asperger's diagnostic standard discussed in Chapters Three and Four—that of "significant impairment," and this time in "other important areas of functioning."

William Howard Adams in *Jefferson's Monticello* (1983) probably did not intend the phrase borrowed here in quite the way I am expanding its significance, for I am factoring in a Jefferson connection to the Asperger's condition. But Adams is on target for having referred to the place as "the quintessential example of the autobiographical house." Signs of that are everywhere, especially in the built-in gadgetry.[2]

More recently a *New Yorker* article drew contrasts between George Washington's approach to restructuring Mount Vernon and Jefferson's work at Monticello. Architecture critic Paul Goldberger wrote that "both conceptually and physically" the Jefferson intellect was central to the project. "Jefferson's psyche" gave meaning to an exceptional architecture (Goldberger found in it "nothing universal"), and the more deeply one might "penetrate that psyche" the more pleasure one should draw from the place.[3]

The involvement of Asperger's-related considerations is quite evident in the overall concept. The building represented a prime commitment by Jefferson not just to family but to the familiarity of place and to the comfort of plantation routine, or it might not have been a home he selected as his principal creative outlet. It might instead have been a museum, a library, or a school. As it is, his final burst of architectural creativity went into designing the buildings and campus of the University of Virginia. But he was too old by then to give them quite the hands-on style and the continually evolving refinements of design and detail that went into his mountaintop dwelling.[4]

Monticello also represented on a few planes his aesthetic sensibilities, perhaps more strongly and of wider scope because of his Asperger's capacity for "thinking in pictures." The beauty of Monticello that Jefferson visualized lay first in its exterior plan. Actually he visualized Monticello in that way twice, for it is a revised exterior that we see today. Over the course of the work he had much of the structure torn down and then rebuilt. He borrowed the basic design from those of Andreas Palladio, who had set a pattern two centuries earlier that was widely imitated in England and later adapted in Williamsburg. Jefferson kept in his library a copy of Palladio's manual.[5]

The factor of aesthetics lay also in its position atop the mountain he had often visited as a young man for its view. And that placed it in the realm of what Joseph J. Ellis called his "lifelong urge to withdraw" into privacy. It may be important to know that his original name for the place was "The Hermitage," very much the choice of a loner, but he opted for the more mellifluous Italian for "little mountain."[6]

The mountaintop choice also placed it in the realm of what Jack McLaughlin in *Jefferson and Monticello* saw as defiance of "common sense," for homes were customarily built along rivers as a practical matter. To have abjured that which worked for others as their "common-sense" choice was typical of Jefferson's independent manner and was a course tied closely to Asperger's behavior.[7]

The beauty of the place rested also in its eye-pleasing interior. The use of half-octagon forms to capture natural lighting through the windows defied conventional design that normally begins with a square or rectangle. That innovation proved also to be a remarkable aesthetic bonus, which can only be appreciated fully by a visit. Photographs do not do justice to the perspectives provided by the half-octagon forms. At times Jefferson's choices reflected a blending of function and aesthetic design, at other times his sacrifice of function to design, the latter a yielding by Jefferson again to uncommon sense. Beauty lay also in the details: the touches of interior-finish delicacy, the friezes, the effects of the natural light captured intentionally, the fold-away interior shutters, the furnishings, the amenities such as dumbwaiters, the ease of regulating ventilation by mechanically-operated panels in skylights that admit air and light but not rain, the surprises such as half-automatic interior double doors, all of which fit his visual thinking and some of which even reflected his social attitudes as a reluctant slaveowner.[8]

The details of Monticello allowed a limited self-dependency—pivoting doors with shelves that held additional self-servings for the dining room, dumbwaiters built into the side of the fireplace that made fresh bottles of wine more accessible to users relaxing before the fire in conversation or contemplation, individual serving tables placed strategically among guests—all to cut down on the number of servants moving about.

Such interior-design amenities were said by Margaret Bayard Smith, a frequent visitor, to have met two purposes for Jefferson and his guests—first, that they might discuss any topic without the eavesdropping of servants, an idea evidently picked up in Paris. Edwin T. Martin in *Thomas Jefferson: Scientist* (1952) quoted Mrs. Smith as having passed along a second and more considerate explanation by Jefferson for such devices: that he "did not wish to bother a servant."[9]

With regard to the latter, when we remember that the servants were inherited slaves whose well-being was his responsibility, our attention is pointed toward a Jefferson who seemed strongly focused on right vs. wrong, a strong Asperger's characteristic we will encounter several times in this study. Other slaveowners might simply have paraded their "possessions"—their household slaves (and legend has it that many did)—as footmen opening doors or as servers entering and leaving, no doubt with quiet efficiency but with a conspicuousness that spoke of wealth. That was not a course Jefferson wished to follow for, as we have learned, he maintained a lifelong abhorrence of slavery and was probably embarrassed by it from his first awareness of it.

Yet another way in which an Asperger's trait may be said to have shown itself in the Monticello enterprise is in the positioning of the "dependencies"—the kitchen, laundry, and other utility rooms as well as a limited number of the slave quarters. The arrangement reflected visual thinking on two planes, for such facilities were partly below ground to serve the needs of activity on the main level. While such home design may seem obvious for its functionalism today, it was not then. Jefferson may have borrowed some of it from the Romans, whose classical designs were as much a part of his planning as was Palladio's influence, but he must be given credit for advancing America's household functionalism.[10]

Also among Asperger's-related features of this enterprise was the relationship Jefferson saw between the materials needed for the building and the resources in the immediate environment on which to draw. Logical to the core, though his accounting practices lapsed too frequently, Jefferson understood that some savings might be effected by drawing upon the mountain to shape what would be its crown. Stone was already to be found in the ground and was then reset for the foundation by the stonemasons. The clay excavated in order to burrow space for below-surface "dependencies" went into the brickmaking. The cleared trees were turned into lumber. Such conversion of what lay all around seemed a logical obedience to natural laws.[11]

Logic of that kind was a key to Jefferson's thinking on all subjects. For him the application of logic was a more enriching exercise when natural or mechanical sciences captured his attention. It was challenging also when the opportunity to apply mathematical dimensions and design features caught his boyish enthusiasm. Historian Merrill D. Peterson noted, "Nature meant him to be a scientist, Jefferson had told himself many times." Biographer Fawn M. Brodie observed, "None of our presidents had so prodigious a scientific curiosity."[12]

As a tinkerer and inventor, he could hardly resist joining the workmen for brickmaking or carpentry. Measured against the kind of directing skills required to put together a home today, he was at once planner, architect ("He figured the specifications down to the last detail."), engineer, general contractor, interior designer, finishing foreman, decorator—and "excited more by the process itself," according to Peterson, "than by the ultimate product."[13]

In that context the word "intensity" in the criteria of the *Diagnostic and Statistical Manual* takes on a new dimension. Relative to Jefferson's fixation, I find Sigmund Freud's view of neurosis significant: "The result of a conflict between the ego and the id; the person is at war with himself." William Howard Adams in *Jefferson's Monticello* quoted Jefferson as having observed at the close of his Presidency, "The whole of my life has been a war with my natural tastes, feelings and wishes."[14]

When he was present at Monticello, the project moved along. While away, he seemed unready to entrust its supervision to anyone else. Therefore, the building and rebuilding of Monticello was done in spurts—a staggeringly major rebuilding because, when he realized the original plan required enlargement for his growing family, he had begun to favor also a separate Palladian exterior over the original.

The design at first was to be a two-storied affair by all intended appearances, with columned porticos above as well as below. While it is not known for certain whether the original design reached execution at the second level, it is doubtful that it did. The waste in tearing it down would have been horrendous, although it was awful enough when so much of the original structure was dismantled starting in the mid-1790s. In that time Jefferson thought he had retired from public service for good, only to be drawn out of retirement in 1797 by his assumption of the Vice-Presidency.[15]

The major exterior design shifts that obsessed him when he decided upon enlargement were, first, the addition of the octagonal dome—today Monticello's most distinguishing feature—and, second, an eye-deceiving use of rising first-floor windows, making the place appear to be a single-storied home. Actually, the upper portions of the rising windows illuminated second-floor rooms beginning at their floor level. The intended effect worked masterfully, for we are left with *three* levels, not including the below-ground dependencies, which from a distance appear to be all in one level.

The dismantling of much of the original building was nightmarish for the family and for visitors. From the perspective of our looking back tolerantly over a period of two centuries, the situation seemed rooted in the apparent fact that Jefferson was oblivious to the short-range discomfort of others. He was not a man of great empathy. Major portions of the original structure were being torn down while the house was in full use, and that included already-laid bricks. As a result, people he loved were placed in some peril, not to mention the danger to visitors who had gone there simply to regard him with awe.[16]

Regardless of intended benefit to family members by the expansion, the discomfort inflicted upon them by changes in the project was greater than most people would tolerate. During her honeymoon Jefferson's younger daughter Polly was immobilized because of an accident—not her first during the turn-around in construction—in which she had fallen out a door and sprained her ankle.[17]

That he was obsessed with the architectural commitment to a fresh start left no doubt. When he decided to restructure Monticello in order to install a dome, the entire roof in place up to that time had to be removed. Thankfully, that was done in sections. Before Jefferson started his two-term Presidency in 1801 the project had been in progress more than thirty years. The home was by then "in no more livable condition than it was at the beginning of the American Revolution," according to historian Jack McLaughlin.[18]

Jefferson's architectural goals simply overrode such practical concerns as the money to be found to pay for them. Consider what he did about the Virginia capitol at Richmond. From Paris he insisted that its construction be interrupted, that what had been finished be torn down and restarted on the basis of a plan he was forwarding.

As minister to France and very much caught up in European and classical culture, Jefferson had seen drawings of the Maison Carree at Nimes, a fifteen- or sixteen-centuries-old (or older) relic of Roman times that he had not yet visited. That plan, he believed, was perfect for the capitol building of Virginia. Nothing else would do, he insisted. The Virginia Assembly went along with all his notions about it, including the tearing down of the uncompleted new structure.[19]

Jefferson's persistence in such matters was unusual. Skilled workmen at Monticello were forced to encounter the Vice President and later the President of the United States directing their construction efforts. Such a relationship was even more intimidating when they found his drawings had been carried out to precise scale and measured to several decimal places, the work of a "compulsive personality." The workmen could scarcely stay within an inch of planned dimensions.[20]

Jefferson insisted on an edifice as well as a shelter in which "beauty and function were inseparable," according to Andrew Burstein in *The Inner Jefferson: Portrait of a Grieving Optimist* (1995). That was a principle not readily appreciated by construction workmen. And that was not all. Jefferson insisted also on an arrangement with his major construction people that probably no other personage in his time could have managed. In order to maintain a flow of ready capital for the Monticello project, he persuaded major workers to lend him back the wages they were due. Although the loans were appended to an already long list of his obligations, he did manage to repay them.[21]

When combining his age (which his appearance contradicted) with his position in government and his reputation as a Founding Father, those working alongside Jefferson were evidently awestruck. As they encountered both his childlike enthusiasm for innovation and his methodical exactness, it is understandable that they gave in to every feature of his quiet spirit of creation.

Jack McLaughlin analyzed the childlike quality that Jefferson showed when he toyed with or crafted mechanical devices. McLaughlin related it to times of similar activity shared with his father, Peter Jefferson. Anyone inclined toward hand work, whether domestic or mechanical or for hobby or vocation, will think back with pleasure about the times in which it was learned—and from whom. Temple Grandin said in the course of providing guidance for this book that, for her, Asperger's Syndrome is like "a prolonged childhood." She is also involved deeply in design and invention, having planned at least one-third of all the livestock-handling facilities in use in this country and much of what is used in other countries. Dr. Grandin added she could identify with the logic of Jefferson's crafting useful products with which to furnish Monticello. There was a practicality to it, creativity in it, and a relationship with the fact-based and picture-based way in which Asperger's-influenced minds operate—while coping with a world that thinks verbally and expresses itself emotionally.[22]

William Howard Adams's *Jefferson's Monticello* leads us through both the place and the process and makes arresting pictorial stops among Jefferson's exterior and interior creations. The range of creations is surprising. It includes Jefferson's positioning a compass in the soffit above the east entrance to show the wind direction monitored by the weathervane on the roof. Nearby is the outside face of a clock that has its counterpart face inside, the latter positioned closely to an indicator of the day of the week which was fashioned from descending weights.

Jefferson even became involved in the design of curtains. Some of the window dressings we see at Monticello are copies of his exacting design preferences. Even the askos, or pouring vessels, as well as urns, goblets, and cups were products of Jefferson's designs, although not all such items have remained in the possession of the Thomas

Jefferson Memorial Foundation which owns and maintains Monticello. Guides call attention to the mechanical window and door arrangements mentioned earlier and the dumbwaiters, serving tables, and pivoting doors designed by Jefferson for the convenience of his family, guests, and servants.[23]

A music stand designed with five rests to serve a quintet or smaller chamber group may be folded into a box for transport. The device reflected not only the importance Jefferson placed on the musicales enjoyed frequently at home, with his difficult post-injury participation on the violin, but the painstaking ingenuity he applied toward assuring that the needs of family or guest performers were served conveniently. This device was used also as a revolving book-stand, and is pictured in that manner in Foundation materials.[24]

One of several polygraphs or copying mechanisms kept by Jefferson is displayed in his bedchamber-study. Except for such an item refined by him, history might not have had the benefit of copies of his correspondence and other writings. In many cases the letters are more revealing of Jefferson than speculation about what lay behind the choices he made in his life—interpretations by countless writers over the past 175 years.

In private correspondence Jefferson attributed historical significance to the portable writing desk on which he drafted the Declaration of Independence. The desk was borrowed from descendants for the 1993 commemoration of his 250th birthday.[25]

In *Thomas Jefferson: Scientist* Edwin T. Martin described special interests as well as inventions by Jefferson, the latter including the farthest-reaching in influence—his widely-imitated moldboard plow. Because of its mathematically-computed optimum shape, it turned earth and sod far more effectively than had any predecessor plow. It continues to do so in parts of the world today where farm machinery is still too expensive for poor agricultural societies to obtain. Jefferson also proposed modifications for a number of such wide-ranging devices as threshing machines and dry docks. His interest in, tinkering with, and use of countless mechanical devices were among his amusements, his friend Margaret Bayard Smith said.[26]

The scientist in Jefferson influenced the Lewis and Clark expedition that followed his purchase of Louisiana Territory from Napoleon in 1803. The frontiersmen brought back records that enriched general knowledge about the plant and animal life of the continent then being claimed from Native Americans with an almost studied disregard of law and morality. Jefferson's hopes and dreams for development of the United States pitted him against the interests and claims of Indians. There can be no doubt that he coped with such issues in much the same way that he did with other conflicting matters, relegating them to separate tracks in his mind. Although he showed in his writings that he admired Indians in many ways, he would not surrender his expansionist ideals for them. Application of right-wrong judgment might have allowed him to see clearly the attendant injustices, but he was, first and foremost and like his father, a frontier Virginian who looked westward with singleminded purpose and superseding values.

Monticello had architectural echoes by way of Jefferson's involvement in other projects such as the design for Barboursville, a neighbor's home, and the design and building of his octagon-shaped retreat at Poplar Forest on land he owned roughly a day's carriage ride southwest. He escaped to that place when sightseers who were dropping in uninvited at Monticello made it impossible for him to concentrate.[27]

The University of Virginia design was Jefferson's "final encore," as historian Joseph J. Ellis put it, in which he continued to be the "meticulous master of detail" while carrying in his mind an overall vision of the result he was working toward. Still, the abstract concept and the particulars were never brought together satisfactorily to avoid cost overrruns. Monticello, however, was the work that gave Jefferson a "sense of purpose," according to Ellis.[28]

As an aside, I had written earlier that Jefferson's utilitarianism caved in to aesthetics in a couple of instances. The dome, as it turned out, proved practically useless as the housing for a room. But it certainly looked nice from the outside and even from the inside.

The interior stairways were and are difficult to negotiate, and they make Monticello guides sound nervous in their instructions to tourists about using them. But they were aesthetically inconspicuous by their squeezed-away placement. No *Gone with the Wind* grand staircases here. And that matched the unobtrusive effect Jefferson evidently wished to achieve.[29]

When I first noticed certain Monticello features in 1993, I found Jefferson's compromising over the stairways disturbing. Outside he had also flattened the posts of the balustrade—the balusters—where he could not fit their rounded shapes against the dome. Were they indications of some form of cheating in order to achieve aesthetic effects? In the context of what I now know about Asperger's influences, Jefferson's design compromises were probably more compelling for him to craft than they could ever be worrisome to a relatively uninventive person like me.

In carrying out such accommodations he demonstrated that his thinking moved from small details to a large effect, or from specific to general, just as it had when he chose half-octagons as a strong basis for the layout of Monticello. People whose minds move the opposite way, from general to specific, may believe such a detail as flat balusters to be anachronistic and bothersome, which is almost like saying they cannot see the woods for the trees. Visual thinkers such as Jefferson evidently have no such problem.

An Asperger's condition thus served Jefferson's functional disposition and his aesthetic sensibilities simultaneously. Logic prevailed for the one, and a search for overall beauty of form governed the other. The seeming conflict was reconciled in a mind equipped to join those often disparate principles.

Jefferson's short-term fixations having nothing to do with architecture were numerous and of remarkable variety. Examples of top-ics he pursued with differing degrees of intensity are given in an appendix. A number of the subjects were examined by Jefferson so extensively that, for any person not otherwise occupied, they might have led to special ties vocationally. In *Thinking in Pictures* the autis-tic Dr. Grandin wrote this comment about such fixations:

> Many children with autism become fixated on various subjects. Some teachers make the mistake of trying to stamp out the fixation. Instead, they should broaden it and channel it into constructive activities. For example, if a child becomes infatuated with boats, then use boats to motivate him to read and do math. Read books about boats and do arithmetic problems on calculating boat speed. Fixations provide great motivation. Leo Kanner (the pioneer psychiatrist of autism) stated that the path to success for some peo-ple with autism was to channel their fixation into a career.

Similarly, the London researcher Uta Frith wrote that "autistic repetitions and obsessions" are bothersome only to nonautistics, "not to the Asperger person." She indicated there could be potential for great achievement by someone able "to sustain strong interest in a par-ticular area and to be absorbed and even enraptured by its pursuit. [31]

Dr. Grandin's book included a chapter titled "Einstein's Second Cousin," in which she cited reasonable speculation about a few famous achievers. She quoted neurologist Oliver Sacks's work, *An Anthropologist on Mars* (1995), to describe Stephen Wiltshire, English autistic savant, who "draws fabulously detailed pictures of build-ings" and is gifted musically. When he sings, Grandin wrote of Wiltshire, "all signs of autism disappear," and then they reappear when he stops. I find it interesting that Jefferson was in the habit of finding relaxation by singing under his breath almost constantly, even while reading.[32]

Considering the achievements of people whom Grandin cited, along with more personal information she shared about Albert

Einstein, Charles Darwin, Vincent van Gogh, Gregor Mendel, and others, I find her conclusion compelling that "It is likely that genius is an abnormality."[33]

Depending on their orientation, people reading about Jefferson today will refer to him as a political theorist, or they will say that, basically, he was a lawyer whose avocation was architecture. As an afterthought they might say, no, we should rank him as a scientist, which is the way Jefferson enjoyed thinking of himself. He was most certainly an inventor and innovator. Personally, I refer to him as a writer because that is what I call myself.

Weighing such perceptions of his creative talent and recalling Professor Merrill D. Peterson's application of "historiometry" to grade him with an IQ of 150, there is no doubt Jefferson was a genius. But was his genius the result of an abnormality, as Einstein's brain has lately revealed about the basis for such special gifts? If it were possible, a brain scan of Jefferson might provide an answer in physical terms. In terms of consequences, however, we might conclude that, for a man so gifted and so variously talented, Jefferson's dying in a state of financial ruin was an eloquent sign that an abnormality of some nature was present.

Notes:

1 William Howard Adams, *Jefferson's Monticello* (New York: Abbeville Press, 1983), 231.

2 *Ibid.*, 2.

3 Paul Goldberger, "Why Washington Slept Here," *The New Yorker*, Vol. 74, February 15, 1999, 88.

4 *Grandin*, 93; *Attwood*, 99-100.

5 *Happe*, 48; *Attwood*, 125; *Grandin*, 19; *Burstein*, 18-19.

6 *Ellis*, 27.

7 *McLaughlin*, 34; The social bias seldom noticed about the phrase "common sense" raises the question, Common to whom? For Asperger's Syndrome scholars to use such a term without a qualifier might declare their unconditional endorsement of others' standards as the behavioral norms of choice—as the preferred way of doing things. Therefore, they hardly ever

use the term in quite the way it is customarily tossed about, usually by parents harking back to their own past imitative behavior (for which they may claim credit as some "common-sense" initiative). Tony Attwood maintained that Asperger's children do not "seem to be aware of the unwritten rules of social conduct." (Attwood, 31). So we are dealing with a "sense" for which there is not even a reliable standard, unless we get into such elementary guides as "Pick up what you drop." What cannot be ignored by those in the field of Asperger's Syndrome studies, and what should not be overlooked by others, is that persons with Asperger's become involved in social experiences with few if any concepts about what is "common" (as that term might be applied to available choices) and short of knowledge about what makes "sense" behaviorally. When others were receiving social cues and learning behavioral norms from infancy, they were not. As Hans Asperger has pointed out, autistics "can only be original, and mechanical learning is hard for them" (*Asperger/Frith*, 70), whether such learning is in academics or in the social environment. Again, there is no school that Asperger's Syndrome children might attend to learn "common sense" except that provided in social interaction. And their autistic brain disorder, which directs them into visual-based and fact-based thinking, makes them unequal to the challenge of society's mixed values and unprepared to comprehend meanings behind emotion-based verbalizing.

8 Guides at Monticello like to point out the utility of Jefferson's arranging for the second side of a double interior door to open automatically when one opens the first manually. But the wear and tear on the mechanisms to operate such devices have forced hesitation about demonstrating that.

9 *Adams/Monticello*, 207; Edward T. Martin, *Thomas Jefferson: Scientist* (New York: Henry Schuman, 1952), 85.

10 *Burstein*, 19.

11 *McLaughlin*, 70, 72, 84.

12 *Peterson*, 951; *Brodie*, 5.

13 *Peterson*, 541, 26.

14 Mark McCutcheon, *Roget's Super Thesaurus* (Cincinnati: Writer's Digest Books, 1995), 346; *Adams/Monticello*, 88.

15 *Adams/Monticello*, 63.

16 *Peterson*, 521.

17 *McLaughlin*, 258.

18 *Ibid*, 272.

19 Jefferson believed the new plan would actually effect a savings because the building was smaller than the one that had been started in Richmond. He wrote James Madison it was nevertheless roomier for the needs of Virginia officials than the one then under way. By the time he wrote William Buchanan and James Hay, he had revised his space estimate to one less

roomy. Because the Maison Carree was "superior in beauty to any thing in America," the change was compelling. (Jefferson to Madison, September 1,1785, *Republic*, 1:381). He advised Virginians Buchanan and Hay to salvage the bricks at Richmond. "Mortar never becomes so hard and adhesive to the bricks, in a few months, but that it may be easily chipped off." (Jefferson to William Buchanan and James Hay, January 26, 1786, *Writings*, 847.) "Here I am, Madam, gazing whole hours at the Maison quarree, like a lover at his mistress," Jefferson wrote to Madame deTesse, from Nimes, March 20,1787, *Writings*, 891; *Ellis*, 83.

20 *McLaughlin*, 58.

21 *Burstein*, 21; *McLaughlin*, 335-36.

22 *McLaughlin*, 373; Conversation between Temple Grandin and Norm Ledgin, December 12, 1998.

23 *Adams/Monticello*, 110, 196, 220, 212, 214, 206-7

24 *Ibid.*, 203; *Guidebook*, 49, 124.

25 *Adams/Monticello*, 233; "Most interesting of all Jefferson's desks" according to Edward T. Martin, was the portable one he used to write the Declaration of Independence. Jefferson called it a "writing box." It was a generally flat box and contained a drawer for writing materials. It featured a lid that could be lifted, then tilted slightly to form a handy surface. The writing desk was made from Jefferson's drawing by the Philadelphia cabinetmaker, Benjamin Randolph (alternately Randall), with whom he boarded in 1776. The year before Jefferson died, his granddaughter, Ellen Wayles Coolidge, lost all her baggage when the ship carrying it sank en route to Boston. Among items that went down with the ship was a desk made for Mrs. Coolidge by Jefferson's cabinetmaker, John Hemings. As consolation Jefferson sent her and her husband the portable writing desk, noting it "claims no merit of particular beauty. It is plain, neat, convenient, and, taking no more room on the writing table than a moderate quarto volume, it yet displays itself sufficiently for any writing. Mr. Coolidge must do me the favor of accepting this. Its imaginary value will increase with the years, and if he lives to my age, or another half century, he may see it carried in the procession of our nation's birthday, as the relics of the saints are in those of the church." *Martin*, 86-87.

26 *Martin*, 104-6, 74-76, 99-100, 85.

27 *Adams/Monticello*, 92-94; *Malone*, 6-.290-92; *Adams/Monticello*, 224-25.

28 *Ellis*, 282, 144.

29 *McLaughlin*, 250, 252; *Adams/Monticello*, 84.

30 *Grandin*, 100.

31 *Frith*, 14.

32 *Grandin*, 187; *Ellis*, 26.

33 *Grandin*, 178-79

CHAPTER SIX

"Disastrous Legacy"

T he Asperger's characteristic that appears to have contributed most directly to Thomas Jefferson's end-of-life financial insolvency was his faithfulness to pointless routines. The criterion of the *Diagnostic and Statistical Manual* that addresses the habit reads, "apparently inflexible adherence to specific nonfunctional routines or rituals." Before I describe the routine that may have proved malignant toward his family's long-term economic well-being, it may enhance understanding of the power of Asperger's traits if I describe a routine that was harmless.

For sixty or more of his eighty-three years Thomas Jefferson began each day by soaking his feet in cold and preferably icy water. Ice became readily available at Monticello, principally to preserve butter and meat, after the ice house was completed in 1803, and it was available in season from other sources. Jefferson claimed the foot-soaking decreased the number and severity of colds. Historian Dumas Malone translated that assertion into a fictional "lifelong freedom from colds." Actually Jefferson never claimed he did not catch cold, only that he could go eight or ten years without one.1

Jefferson was in generally good health for most of his life, strong as an ox, and careful about his diet, eating lots of fruit and vegetables. Those factors probably lowered the number of successful invasions by organisms. Though he swore by the foot-bathing, it was neverthe-less a routine without provable health benefit, one that he began as a young man in Williamsburg and continued to follow day-in and day-out for the rest of his life.[2]

Psychologist and Asperger's authority Tony Attwood attributed the establishment of such routines to the easing of people with the disorder through their periods of anxiety. For some these routines ward off anticipated unpleasantness by "ensuring consistency and reducing anxiety."[3]

Jefferson began his foot-bathing ritual when he started to prac-tice law, which by the very nature of the profession required court-room performance, and was a prospect that made him tense. Knowing what we have already learned of his apprehensions, one can accept that on waking one morning and realizing what lay ahead for the day, he fashioned an activity that would get him moving. It is likely he also rationalized for it an association with good feeling and good health.

The autistic scientist/designer Temple Grandin uses what she calls a "squeeze machine" to reduce anxiety. The apparatus is actu-ally a large mechanical box she devised into which she crawls and in which she is able to control the pressure its panels apply to parts of her body. Her use of the squeeze machine must be counted as com-forting routine, for it is therapy that produces selectively a calming pressure wherever required. The way it differs from Jefferson's ritu-al is that she is not inflexible about it, and it has a real purpose for her, not a rationalized one.[4]

To play out a possible comparison with Dr. Grandin's practice, we should consider whether Jefferson was also receiving local pres-sure to relieve tension by means of skin contraction from ice-water contact. Although he is known to have preferred to wear soft shoes or slippers while working indoors, thus escaping pressure on his feet, the possibility of alternative and perhaps real benefit of the icy foot bath begs for consideration.

Sitting with one's feet so restricted, there is not much else one can do than reflect or plan. That enforcing pause in itself is calming. To explore yet another possibility, could cold-water foot-bathing have proved so uncomfortable that the ending of it brought relief, like the silly legend of a man's hitting his head repeatedly because it felt good when he stopped? I do not mean to say Jefferson was in any manner an ascetic. Rather I offer the observation that temporary discomforts appear to serve Asperger's-related needs for physical pressure, needs which the scientific community has not yet elaborated fully.

Dr. Attwood indicated that the development of nonfunctional daily routine is related to superstitious actions—touching wood, for example. Such a practice "operates as a negative reinforcer" to end a bad feeling. Regardless of the fact he came down with occasional colds as well as the flu, Jefferson simply would not abandon his morning ritual.[5]

Of even greater significance and probably calamitous among Jefferson's nonfunctional routines was his persistent recording of financial transactions to the penny. Again, it was a daily practice he kept up for most of his life—actually fifty-nine years. However, he did not establish a method for referring back to recorded accounts nor did he reconcile his cash outlays. He did not total them to match them with his cash flow. On those few occasions when he did try to summarize his accounts he was taken by surprise. He found debts so staggering that he seemed afterward to avoid such auditing from fear of what new calamity the tallies might disclose.[6]

"Whatever Jefferson's reasons for keeping them," wrote editors James A. Bear, Jr., and Lucia C. Stanton in their introduction of the 1997 two-volume *Memorandum Books* collection, they were the "first flowering" of his "passion for making daily records" that spread to weather, plantings, law activity, and other interests occupying him. But the routinized recording "may actually have contributed to the disastrous legacy of debt," editors Bear and Stanton maintained, for it gave Jefferson a sense of control that, in reality, he did not know how to exercise.[7]

Jefferson developed very early the habit of carrying account books wherever he went, jotting down transactions as soon as they were completed. Annually—or with less frequency and uncertain consistency—he went back to them to index transactions by persons' names. That only buoyed his confidence that he was on top of everything having to do with personal finances. Of course, he was not.

After the 1770 fire in the home of his boyhood and early adulthood, Shadwell, he became *"par excellence* a keeper of records," Dumas Malone observed. The biographer described the collection of data as "documentary treasures such as have rarely been amassed by any man." Not for a moment discounting the value that such records have proved to be for historians and biographers, the Jefferson historian Merrill D. Peterson nonetheless saw them also as a "profusion of minutiae."[8]

The imagined benefit that the recording of payments daily might allow him for meaningful data retrieval was a reflection of Jefferson's naivete. He simply did not know how to do cost accounting. What he did know how to do and what he seemed to enjoy doing, with or without great purpose, was just to keep writing everything down.

Furthermore, he was penny-wise and pound-foolish, or as Professor Peterson put it, "Prudent in small expenditures...lavish in large ones." The expense of his Paris quarters exceeded his salary. His $25,000 annual Presidential pay (worth half a million dollars or more today, which exceeds President William Clinton's salary and perquisites) should have covered direct expenses of the office. But with one-tenth or more of that spent on wine alone, it is hard to say whether it did. The expenses were such that none of his pay was left over to relieve his worsening personal financial condition.[9]

Fond of wine, Jefferson consumed by his own account three to four-plus glasses a day, or about half a bottle, maintaining the wines were "the weak ones only," or half the strength of "ardent wines." But they often followed mealtime beer and cider, the latter probably also fermented. So he must have had, at times, a walking-around buzz. In the current fashion of subjecting Presidents to closer examination than warranted for determining executive fitness, the question follows naturally, Did Jefferson become tipsy? Biographer Jack McLaughlin wrote that on the basis of his known consumption he was bound to have grown euphoric and convivial—and more talkative as a result.[10]

Quite interested in the European wines he ran across while abroad, he became something of an expert and kept records on that subject, too. As a matter of fact he kept records on a great variety of subjects. There seemed to be no point to the variety and volume of Jefferson's notetaking and recordkeeping, except that they satisfied an interest and a need and, in his so doing, comforted him. But when we recall the many reasons he required some relief from tension, that was possibly point enough.

Almost from the start his jottings included in minutest detail a record of his expenditures. He described his casework as a lawyer, showing also the smallest outlays of money for food, tips, material and personal-service wants and needs, charities, and loans in Williamsburg or other capitals and places he lived temporarily. At home there were house and plantation expenses to be written down, the garden planting and ripening dates for everything grown and aimed for the table, wind directions and wind shifts en route to Europe, as well as unusual bird and fish sightings during the voyage. Then came European expenses in exacting detail, daily temperature highs and lows as well as the humidity, and incoming letters posted to a journal by dates and sources.

There were also records of blankets and clothing issued to slaves, miles traveled between major points of long overland journeys, sources and major features of all Virginia's rivers worthy of note, livestock lists that included weights, feeding specifications, and dung outputs of the animals, relative merits of liquid-fuel lamps versus candles, weights and measures and coinage standards—and those covered only a portion of topics. Each of the subject areas represented, in varying scope and intensity, a fixation of short or long attention or duration. (See "100 topics" Appendix.)

The range of Thomas Jefferson's notes and writings is so broad that some people follow his work to its farthest extremes because they are more fascinated by what the scope of interests said about the man than what Jefferson actually wrote. In most instances his work reflected an application of his keenest faculties for analysis. Usually it was, for its subject, rather precise and revealing. Consider this excerpt from his lengthy piece on English prosody written in Paris in October, 1786, for the Marquis de Chastellux, the French intellectual who had served in the American Revolutionary War under the leadership of the Count de Rochambeau:

> That the accent shall never be displaced from the syllable whereon usage hath established it is the fundamental law of English verse. There are but three arrangements into which these accents can be thrown in the English language which entitled the composition to be distinguished by the name of verse. That is, 1. Where the accent falls on all the odd syllables; 2. Where it falls on all the even syllables; 3. When it falls on every third syllable. If the reason of this be asked, no other can be assigned but that it results from the nature of the sounds which compose the English language and from the construction of the human ear. So, in the infinite gradations of sounds from the lowest to the highest in the musical scale, those only give pleasure to the ear which are at the intervals we call whole tones and semi-tones. The reason is that it has pleased God to make us so. The English poet then must so arrange his words that their established accents shall fall regularly in one of these three orders. To aid him in this he has at his command the whole army of monosyllables which in the English language is a very numerous one. These he may accent or not, as he pleases.

And from the same work consider the extent to which one of Jefferson's conclusions is profound:

> What proves the excellence of blank verse is that the taste lasts longer than that for rhyme. The fondness for the jingle leaves us with that for the rattles and baubles of childhood, and if we continue to read rhymed verse at a later period of life it is such only where the poet has had force enough to bring great beauties of thought and diction into this form. When young any composition pleases which unites a little sense, some imagination, and some rhythm, in doses however small. But as we advance in life these things fall off one by one, and I suspect we are left at last with only Homer and Virgil, perhaps with Homer alone. He like
>
> Hope travels on nor quits us when we die.[11]

Jefferson's temporary fixation on this subject appeared so compelling that he brushed aside the pain and inconvenience incurred because of his broken right wrist. He produced this work for his friend Chastellux in the month following the spill he took showing off for Maria Cosway.

By contrast there are works showing similar intensity of focus or fixation upon subjects with considerably less need for analysis and little or none for wisdom." At times his writing could appear—to all but close followers of the topic—as dry as toast. Take as an example this description of lead resources from *Notes on the State of Virginia* (1781-82):

> On the Great Kanhaway, opposite to the mouth of Cripple creek, and about twenty-five miles from our southern boundary, in the county of Montgomery, are mines of lead. The metal is mixed, sometimes with earth, and sometimes with rock, which requires the force of gunpowder to open it; and is accompanied with a portion of silver, too small to be worth separation under any process hitherto attempted there. The proportion yielded is from 50 to 80 lb. of pure metal from 100 lb. of washed ore. The most common is

that of 60 to the 100 lb. The veins are at sometimes most flattering; at others they disappear suddenly and totally. They enter the side of the hill, and proceed horizontally. Two of them are wrought at present by the public, the best of which is 100 yards under the hill. These would employ about 50 labourers to advantage. We have not, however, more than 30 generally, and these cultivate their own corn. They have produced 60 tons of lead in the year; but the general quantity is from 20 to 25 tons. The present furnace is a mile from the ore-bank, and on the opposite side of the river. The ore is first waggoned to the river, a quarter of a mile, then laden on board of canoes and carried across the river, which is there about 200 yards wide, and then again taken into waggons and carried to the furnace. This mode was originally adopted, that they might avail themselves of a good situation on a creek, for a pounding mill: but it would be easy to have the furnace and pounding mill on the same side of the river, which would yield water, without any dam, by a canal of about half a mile in length....

Always the innovator, Jefferson moved from suggesting alternate placement of a furnace and mill to proposing an alternate means for carrying the lead from the Kanhaway. That river contained falls downstream that "may be laid open for useful navigation" to the James River, he suggested, the James being a principal estuary of commerce for Virginia.[12]

Jefferson's focusing for such writing can only have been possible as a result of thorough research. One can imagine the material he spread before him—books and charts or tables and notes and scribbled-on scraps of paper, all draped on shelves or his bed or the floor. For Jefferson to have attended to such detail in his works of geography and natural history required a store of records that appears to have escaped the notice of his biographers. It is doubtful Jefferson took part personally in digging to extract lead from the ground, though he probably observed it. And we must factor in his never having visited most of the rivers he described in Notes. But on whose examinations did Jefferson rely? Were they at least partly those of his father, Peter, who was more the hands-on field person than

Thomas? The method and materials used by such a prolific writer as Jefferson can be as interesting and potentially revealing as the consequential output and scope, for they disclose Asperger's tendencies for collecting and examining the kind of details most people would find boring and useless. Yet historians have given us little to go on about the resources of that nature that Jefferson used for self-education in practical areas, subjects to which he gave as great attention as he did to language and philosophy.

The evident patterns of scholarship in nearly all Jefferson's work of enormous breadth, and his repeated overfocusing on those topics, are consistent with what we see in Asperger's behavior. Some people may argue that Jefferson's interests were far more significant to higher human concerns than are the interests of autistics who collect and copy from catalogs of endless data. But they overlook the reality that Jefferson's intellect expanded also from his early collecting and copying.

While it is true that the collection young Jefferson called his "Literary Bible" was of copied excerpts from philosophy and literature, biographers have paid less notice to data that must have been closely available in substantial form and quantity to fortify his knowledge of the natural world. The historians do not dispute his having digested by the age of five all his father's books. But they seem to have forgotten that his father's books would have included works tied to Peter Jefferson's largely pragmatic and, I would wager, often commonplace interests.[13]

Lorna Wing, who was greatly responsible for bringing Hans Asperger's once-forgotten work to worldwide attention and who serves in the Social Psychiatry Unit of the Medical Research Council, London, illustrated briefly the variety of interests by persons with Asperger's Syndrome. Common among them were "railway timetables, calendars, chemistry, complex arithmetical calculations." The Australian clinician Tony Attwood, who has worked with Dr. Wing, wrote of a variety of interests and collections that included bottle labels, key rings, flags, maps, train information, dinosaur data, other science subjects, and quite a bent among Asperger's children for computers and electronics. Dr. Attwood and others observed that such "repetitive pursuits" allowed Asperger's-affected people to avoid the stress brought by social contact. Their ritualized behavior, over matters that most people would find mundane, furnished them a way "to relax in the security of routine."[14]

As is made clear in the biographies, Jefferson often sought escape from the combative area of politics. From such conflict he made his way to the place where he could cope more comfortably with ideas and arguments, his writing desk. But on his way out of the public arena he could have stopped to refine his drawing of a cornice for Monticello. He also could have glanced from a window to read a thermometer and then entered the temperature in his pocket Memorandum Book. He might have written that he had just given five dollars to charity, as well as record the precise amount of pocket change he had just handed one of his daughters. For a man of quiet temperament and neurologically-induced inscrutability, it was the sort of routine that relaxed him.

Notes:

1   *Malone,* 1:57; *Guidebook,* 62; Jefferson to Dr. Vine Utley, March 21, 1819, *Writings,* 1416-17. Also, "My dear Martha, I am at length got well of a terrible cold..." Jefferson to Martha Jefferson Randolph, December 27,1797, *Family Letters,* 150.

2   "He had a machine for measuring strength (a dynamometer). There were very few men that I have seen try it that were as strong in the arms as his son-in-law, Colonel Thomas Mann Randolph, but Mr. Jefferson was stronger than he." *Monticello: Recollections,* Edmund Bacon, 71.

3   *Attwood,* 100.

4   *Grandin,* 79-81.

5   *Attwood,* 100.

6   *Memorandum Books,* l:xviii-xix.

7   *Ibid*, xix.

8   *Malone*, 1:127; *Peterson*, 30.

9   *Peterson*, 533; *Ellis*, 70; *Peterson*, lll).

10 Jefferson to Dr. Utley, *Writings*, 1416; *McLaughlin*, 235.

11 "Thoughts on English Prosody," *Writings*, 596, 619.

12 "Notes on the State of Virginia," *Writings*, 150.

13 *Malone*, 1:104

14 Lorna Wing, "The relationship between Asperger's syndrome and Kanner's autism," *Frith*, 109; *Attwood*, 94.

CHAPTER SEVEN

"Glacial Exterior"

Two years after Thomas Jefferson died, his family surrendered Monticello to settle part of his accumulated debts. They were not fully settled for another fifty years. Toward the end of his life Jefferson was reduced to the humiliation (Dumas Malone called it "over-pleading") of asking the Virginia legislature to allow the lottery for his lands described in Chapter Two, hoping by that means to wipe out his debts and keep the home in the family. Because the lottery ticket sales were disappointing, the dying Jefferson was uncertain whether or not his beloved Monticello would be destined for the auction block.[1]

Though a satisfactorily thorough analysis of the decline of Jefferson's fortunes is still awaited by the large audience that finds all features of his life fascinating, I must take a separate view of it in the context of the elements of Asperger's Syndrome. Why did Jefferson, who put his family above all other concerns of his life, fail to give his daughter Martha and his grown grandchildren and close friends a timely signal of approaching disaster? While that question carries an assumption they might have been able to turn things around with sufficient warning, speculation that they might not have succeeded has some validity as well.[2]

Had she realized the possibility of what lay ahead, Martha

Jefferson Randolph might have wished first to turn to her husband for advice about remedying the situation the best they could. But if Jefferson's handling of accounts was bad, that of his reportedly disordered and often-depressed son-in-law, Thomas Mann Randolph, was either as bad or worse. As strong and accomplished a person as history has recognized Jefferson's daughter Martha to have been, she nevertheless found herself in the worst conceivable trap with regard to future financial well-being that circumstances might have fashioned for a woman of Virginia gentry.[3]

Guarded as Jefferson was about discussing such personal matters or concerns, he might have shown on his face, however, enough worry so family members could have taken a cue. They might have sat down with him to address the problem. With the help of their closest family friends and that of advisors on the subject of plantation operations—regardless whether such dependency would have been a confession of surrendered initiative—they might have engineered some creative turnaround.

Vital to this situation were problems about what anyone could see in Jefferson's face. Evidence points to his having been unable to project by facial expression the worries that must have burdened him over his economic straits well in advance of the attempted lottery rescue. Jefferson was headed for financial ruin because of his putting too great a trust in the wrong places, because of plain bad luck as well as his downright extravagance, and owing to a "constitutional inability to live within a budget."[4]

Jefferson's relatively stony-faced reserve was a classic Asperger's trait. The diagnostic criteria of the American Psychiatric Association calls attention to the following: "Qualitative impairment in social interaction, as manifested by...marked impairment in the use of multiple nonverbal behaviors such as eye-to-eye gaze, facial expression, body postures, and gestures to regulate social interaction." In laymen's terms the statement could read, *Weakened social skills as revealed by impaired eye gaze, facial expression, posturing, and gesturing.*

Of the four nonverbal impairments listed, Jefferson by several accounts exhibited the whole range in varying degrees.

Much of what we learn is picked up by what we see, or by what we *recognize* in what we see. This includes knowledge that children gather (and knowledge that adults continue to refine) about how people respond nonverbally and through body language. The information evolves into norms of accepted social behavior.

Because of brain signals that are misdirecting, many high-functioning autistics are restricted in how much of this particular type of learning they can absorb. By not looking directly into the eyes or at the faces of those with whom they are communicating, they deprive themselves of certain signs. They may miss a sudden glint of understanding in the other person's eyes, or recognition of a truth or joy to be shared, or a fleeting glance upward in supplication, or a lowered and sideways turn in embarrassment or avoidance. Non-eye gazers miss useful social cues.

Hans Asperger said that among the high-functioning autistic children he examined he could not be sure whether their glance was going into the far distance or was a sign of momentary introspection. "The disturbance is particularly clear when they are in conversation with others," he wrote. In conversation we not only "answer" others with words but with our look, tone, and the interplay of face and hands. He noted, "A large part of social relationships is conducted through eye gaze."[5]

Examining her own problem with eye gaze, Temple Grandin added that some of the eye-contact problems "may be nothing more than an intolerance for the movement of the other person's eyes." A damaged portion of the brain makes an annoyance of it. Overall there is a problem with others' intentions, she said, and an inability "to recognize subtle changes in facial expression."[6]

A fully attentive gaze is not to be expected during the entire length of many conversations. Distractions occur, or the parties may be discussing an object or document at hand, at times not looking at each other. They may walk together, which activity also limits eye contact. And depending on the topic, either laughter or pauses for collecting thoughts will interrupt a meeting of the eyes. On the other hand, a shared tone of seriousness will lock the gaze at least temporarily. These are illustrations that reading the signs of others is difficult enough without the involuntary blocks so common to autism.

After dialogue, if for some reason the eye contact is thought to have been worthy of comment by one of the parties, it will be described with such words as "steady," "firm," "fixed," "stable," or even "unwavering." The person exercising steady eye contact will learn to read and convey unspoken social cues, and this is as close to "mind-reading" as most of us get.

In presenting contemporary descriptions of Jefferson, biographer Dumas Malone observed first that one of the President's admirers described his "clear and penetrating eye." While that is far off other descriptions from Malone s collection on this single item, it could still fall within the context of Asperger's Syndrome. Clinician Tony Attwood passed along an interesting comment from a case study. The subject said she has trouble looking into people's eyes and must make a conscious effort to do so, and she can only hold that eye contact for a second. If she looks for a longer time, "they usually claim that I seem to be just looking through them rather than at them."[7]

"Penetrating" and "looking through" are, to me, close to being two sides of an equation. There is also the possibility that Jefferson's eye penetrated while there was no conversation at all, that he was in fact staring. Asperger's writers Brenda Smith Myles and Richard L. Simpson noted that "intensely staring at another person for long periods" is common to persons with the syndrome.[8]

Other reports and descriptions agree that Jefferson's eye contact was anything but steady. Partisan foes, if not Alexander Hamilton himself, said he had a "shifty glance," which bordered on an incredible choice of insult if there were not a shared observation that

Jefferson's eyes moved noticeably in conversation. Hamilton observed Jefferson frequently when both served President Washington. In view of their ideological conflicts it is understandable that Hamilton would perceive conversational eye movement as evasiveness. Others spoke of Jefferson's "free and intelligent eye" or, as the artist and dramatist William Dunlap put it, his "very animated" eye and his conversing "with ease & vivacity," which last reference fits comfortably with eye movement.[9]

The descriptions of "free," "very animated," and even "shifty" make a believable match. And further evidence of the elusiveness of Jefferson's eye gaze is the wide disagreement among observers over the color of his eyes, which was hazel. *American Sphinx* author Joseph J. Ellis wrote that this topic was a matter of some controversy, for the early colors "hazel or green" seemed to have evolved to "clear blue" later in Jefferson's life, at any rate by description. Ellis speculated the light in which they were seen could have made a difference.[10]

Edmund Bacon, Jefferson's farm manager during his presidency and for some time afterward, observed him closely and over long periods almost daily. He said Jefferson "had blue eyes." At the same time Bacon saw blue, portrait artists Rembrandt Peale and Gilbert Stuart were painting Jefferson's eyes a brownish hazel. Six years into Jefferson's retirement (in 1815) a visitor to Monticello, Francis C. Gray, reported after spending three days with Jefferson that they were "light gray."[11]

Plainly my judgment must be that there was more eye movement by Jefferson—and difficulty in fixing on his eyes—than there was steady eye contact with him in conversation. Professionals or experienced lay persons observing signs of high-functioning autism might very well assess such evidence as that which I offer here to mean there was distracted and possibly impaired eye gaze.

Often a facial expression comes over a person with Asperger's Syndrome that projects a "far-away" look. Such an appearance masks that person's attention to whatever new thing is occurring and may give the impression he or she is in another place mentally. Parents sometimes see this lack of recognition mistakenly as their child's "insensitivity." And compounding the poker-face problem is the marked inability by many with the Asperger's condition (not necessarily all) to read the facial expressions or the reactions of others.[12]

Facial expression, as with eye gaze, is a two-sided affair. While contrasting normal or nonautistic development with that of Fritz, a patient, Hans Asperger wrote that the learning of appropriate behavior cannot depend primarily on the learner's intellectual understanding. Before a child can understand what is being said "he learns to comply" and responds to his mother's glances, tone, look, and gestures rather than her words. "In short," Asperger noted, "he learns to respond to the infinitely rich display of human expressive phenomena.[13]

Not having learned to vary facial expressions to fit the occasion, a person with Asperger's Syndrome will often enter situations wearing a look that defies understanding by others, or as Drs. Myles and Simpson have offered, "displaying an inexpressive face." Behind such a face there is, of course, mental activity and there may be a thought stimulated previously that will lead shortly to a response, but that part of the exchange is hardly ever readable. Even long experience with an inexpressive face will prove a poor guide, for a parent may only speculate, *That's either his What's-for-dinner look, or it means, Ma, the cat threw up in my room again.*[14]

Impairment of facial expression is not a sign of intellectual deficiency. Such impairment indicates that the person with this Asperger's trait is navigating a course of social engagement blindly and unsteadily. Can a person with a dead-pan face be persuaded that people find such habits extremely annoying? That it is time to work on changing those habits? Yes, but to alter such a demeanor is difficult and requires enormous patience, if it is even concluded to be truly worth the effort.

"Intervention strategies" are available today from professionals for improving autistics' understanding of social cues projected by the eyes, faces, or body language of others. Furthermore, self-correcting steps are often taken by high-functioning autistic youngsters on their own as they begin to emerge into adulthood and understand more completely what they are missing. With age and experience the Asperger's individual may search memories of social misfirings for signs that will lead to successful adaptation. "Most children with autism," the London research scientist Francesca Happe wrote, "make some progress as they grow older, whatever the (therapeutic) provision made for them."[15]

In a related context and stepping back to consider Dumas Malone's six-volume story of *Jefferson and His Time*, one notices that with retirements both imagined (1794) and real (1809) Jefferson seemed to grow more cheerful and more relaxed in social engagement. At minimum there were fewer reports of a stoic demeanor. Relative ease and informality of interaction was reported. While homesickness had plagued him often during his public career, one could conclude Jefferson was relieved to be with his loved ones in their accustomed settings.

What we should be careful not to discount, however, is that he was also more comfortable returning to routines, a definite reassurance to people with Asperger's traits. At Monticello, where he saw familiar faces in the course of doing familiar work, Jefferson's sense of well-being was served also by such activities as the planning for gardens and crops, the keeping of lists, the designing and execution of mechanical projects.[16]

If I were to select a single word from the great mass of Jefferson literature as most representative of Jefferson's perceived overall style, that word would be "reserved"—and, as it was put by his colleague Edmund Randolph at the time they practiced law before the same courts, "reserved toward the world at large."[17]

If a single phrase could be selected to stand as a modern evaluation of the Jefferson demeanor, it might be Professor Ellis's reference to the "ever-elusive Virginian with the glacial exterior and almost eerie serenity." Having established that, I will confront a more intimate description of Jefferson that piqued Dumas Malone and biographer Andrew Burstein.[18]

Senator William Maclay from the hinterlands of Pennsylvania described Jefferson as having an "air of stiffness in his manner," as well as a "loose, shackling air" about his figure. The latter phrase by construction and definition means appearing in body movement to be partly fettered or slightly handicapped. Malone, ignoring the word "shackling," saw the description by Senator Maclay (from the "backwoods," as Malone put it) to be self-contradictory at minimum, loose versus stiff.

Most significant in his description was Maclay's reference to "a rambling, vacant look." Unsure what to do with one of the farthest-reaching word portraits of Jefferson that history has provided, however, Malone wrote that if Jefferson had such a look about him "he belied his systematic habits and masked his deeply purposeful character." In other words, it was not that Maclay was mistaken necessarily about what he saw, or thought he saw, in Secretary of State Jefferson. What mattered more to Malone was that Maclay failed to appreciate the motivations and industriousness that lay behind Jefferson's unrevealing visage.[19]

This occasional tack taken by the biographer—spinning away from testimony by sources he did not trust because they came from a humbler class or region—is one reason for greater awareness that there has existed for too long a "rose-colored glasses" school of Jefferson studies. Fortunately, coming into notice as a welcome counterbalance, there appears to be a developing nucleus of thoughtfully investigative writers.

Andrew Burstein handled the classic Maclay description somewhat differently in *The Inner Jefferson*. First he took the gushing words of nineteenth-century biographer Henry S. Randall—of a Jefferson who moved in an "unrestrained, swinging and bold" manner, who held "calm authority" in his eye, who was the very picture of "great firmness and gentleness" as well as "powerful energy in perfect repose"—and he wrote that portrait did not quite "come to life."[20]

When he took up Maclay's observations Burstein gave them relatively free rein. But he faulted the Senator, just as Malone had done, for not seeing what lay behind Jefferson's "undemonstrative veneer." According to Burstein, the Senator missed "the fastness of his (Jefferson's) inner constitution" and the "intensity of his mental exertions." The pre-Freudian Maclay saw Jefferson merely as what he appeared to be, not as a sphinx projecting such a challenge as, *Please make a guess about the inner me.*

That "loose, shackling air," wrote biographer Burstein, "is hard to gauge today." Well, not really, but Burstein did not get into the business of diagnosing. He could not have known that Jefferson's moving as though his limbs were held by a loose tether, or puppet string, which is a fair translation of "shackling," is characteristic of some people with traits of Asperger's Syndrome. There may simply be little or no arm swinging during locomotion.[21]

Biographer and lecturer Alf J. Mapp, Jr., in *Thomas Jefferson: Passionate Pilgrim* (1991) saw conflict between what he read as a "slouch" in the Maclay description and later testimony by Bacon, the farm overseer. Bacon described Jefferson as "six feet two and a half inches high, well proportioned, and straight as a gun barrel. He was like a fine horse—he had no surplus flesh." Professor Mapp wondered whether Jefferson had begun to stand straighter in the Presidential years approximating Bacon's recollections than he had stood in Maclay's presence a decade or two earlier. Whether self-conscious in posture or not, Jefferson managed at eighty—about the time Bacon last saw him—to look like a man of sixty.[22]

Two descriptions containing references to Jefferson's smiling are interesting, one for its guarded assessment by the observer, the other for Dumas Malone's overall treatment. Senator Samuel L. Mitchill, New York, wrote his wife after meeting Jefferson that "he is grave, or rather sedate, but...occasionally can smile." In modern times anyone writing that might be called sarcastic, but it is doubtful Mitchill intended such meaning. Of course Jefferson could smile! Just about anybody "can" smile. My reasoned guess about the purpose of the comment, however, is that Mitchill, who was also a physician with a broad scientific background, observed something few others saw. He apparently noticed that this characteristically "grave" man was capable of setting aside what Mitchill may have speculated to be an innate composure in order to put together a smile—thus "can smile."[23]

Malone took on the role of editor in relating observations of a casually-dressed Jefferson by Joseph Story, of Massachusetts, who would later become a Supreme Court justice. Referring to the "out of order" slippers and old-fashioned clothes Jefferson wore, Story added that Virginians pride themselves in wearing "simple habiliments" and prefer to call others' attention to characteristics of mind and manners.

While Jefferson was "a little awkward in his first address," all of that soon eased nicely. His manners, smile, and familiarity were "tempered with great calmness" and with "becoming propriety." Unexplainably, Malone felt it necessary to italicize the following closing by Story: "*Open to all, he (Jefferson) seems willing to stand the test of inquiry and to be weighed in the balance only by his merit and attainments.*"[24]

Rather than highlight that comment as a summary of Story's unclear conclusion, it would have proved more illuminating if Malone the historian had explained what the future Supreme Court justice meant by "becoming propriety"—especially after the man took notice of Jefferson's "out of order" slippers. The future member of the Court offered the twisted logic of including Jefferson's noticeable impropriety (wearing bedroom slippers for such a reception) in his overall judgment of "propriety."

If nothing else, the description by Story reinforced the belief

that, despite his stature and his presumed knowledge of public protocol, Jefferson was capable of ignoring (or at bottom was neither
constantly nor strongly aware of) social convention. Disregarding
such niceties is what many people with Asperger's characteristics
very often do without intending any social insult. They can only
hope that any complaint of impropriety will be similarly forgiven
and described as "becoming propriety."[25]

For someone with Asperger's traits, relatively consistent facial
inexpressiveness does not necessarily mean being stony-faced morning till night. For some people with the disorder the face has been
noticed to exhibit often a frozen half-smile, to a degree just short of
the Mona Lisa. It is as though the person on the Asperger's continuum has at least persuaded himself toward practice: *One step up
from what others have described as my irritating reserve, perhaps this look
will get me by.*

Alexander Hamilton, writing under a pseudonym as a critic of
Jefferson, mentioned a "visor of stoicism"—a mask of indifference or
insensibility—as typical of the look projected by his political foe. Of
course, partisanship was involved. Yet the observation of facial inexpressiveness was consistent with observations from other sources.[26]

Studying observations contemporary with Jefferson's retirement
years after his Presidency, Joseph J. Ellis reported in *American Sphinx*
that Jefferson continued to display a "nonchalant demeanor," or an
image and manner that lacked warmth and showed casual indifference. Other observers said he looked "cynical," or even that his face
reflected "hypocrisy."[27]

Because posterity has decent painted portraits of Thomas
Jefferson to refer to, there seems little compulsion for anyone to be
discussing the physical arrangement or bearing in his face. Yet the
biographers have left us such wide disagreement, we cannot simply
dismiss the subject of his facial look. He had hazel eyes that offset
reddish hair, strong nose and chin, and a possibly ruddy complexion
(1815 visitor Francis C. Gray said it was "streaked and speckled with

red"). Is there anything left to say? Apparently there is more to say or biographers would not have become so confused trying to say it. All of this goes back to Senator Maclay's 1790 observation. My own admittedly shaky finding is that Maclay wrote in his journal about Jefferson, "His face has a scruny (or scrany) aspect," whatever that meant.[28]

Using various printings and editions of Maclay's journal to arrive at the elusive word that would tell us what kind of "aspect" Maclay intended to describe, nine biographers came up with five separate adjectives. "Sunny" was the most popular, selected by Fawn M. Brodie, Andrew Burstein, Dumas Malone, andAlf J. Mapp, Jr. But Merrill D. Peterson chose "crany," which might have given me another Asperger's clue, for neck-and-face-craning as though looking into the far distance is a feature I have noticed among some with the syndrome.[29]

Both William Howard Adams and Garry Wills selected "scranny," and Wills tried to be helpful by adding that "scranny" means "scrawny," for "Maclay was a Scot." Willard Sterne Randall went straight for "scrawny." Noble E. Cunningham, Jr., came closest to the shaky result of my own inquiries with "scrany," which eludes definition equally with "scruny." Notice, however, that varying interpretations—such as those by chroniclers of Maclay and historical researchers—may throw us off the trail to truth, and we are left to one side in that quest for long periods. The Hemings denials were a more important case in point, and most of Jefferson's modern biographers were culpable.[30]

The significant evidence in historical works about Jefferson, however, adds up to customary unreadability or vacancy of facial expression. At most the perception leaned often to gravity within his aura of reserve. And though he had a capacity for purposeful adjustment of his look, he relied on that quite selectively, hardly with the reflexive freedom and spontaneity available to most people. When varying, by all accounts, the expressions on Jefferson's face touched only lightly and never appeared to sweep fully the range of faces available through learned or "second-nature" cues for subtle social engagement. As a result Jefferson was *not read* and was misunderstood by many of his contemporaries, even his family.

As for the most drastic consequence of such broken communication, I find it impossible to suppose he consciously caught his family off guard over the deterioration of his financial affairs. If anything at least partly within his control can be blamed, it would be his separate sense of reality—his romantic internalizing that somehow, something would make things right—and *that* served to combine with a demeanor that left others clueless for so long. Both his catastrophic naivete and his unreadable bearing are common traits found along the Asperger's continuum. A Dutch visitor, G.K. van Hogendorp, is quoted by Dumas Malone effectively to illustrate the enigmatic qualities of Jefferson at middle age. "I grew fond of your benevolent character, as much as I admired your extensive learning, your strength of judgment. I pitied your situation, for I thought you unhappy. Why, I did not know...."[31]

The remaining nonverbal contributors to social impairment to consider are inappropriate gestures and postures. Might they be the source of descriptions that Jefferson was "more awkward than graceful" at age seventeen? Or was that problem simply due to his rapid growth to a full six feet two and a half inches in height—and that tall persons seldom appear graceful to any except other tall persons? If awkwardness had been a pronounced factor in his life, and if he had also recognized and resigned himself to it grudgingly, that might account for the evident shyness so widely observed. It might even account for his flights into solitude. There does not seem to have been enough specific awkwardness, however, to have mattered greatly. Yet Jefferson's desire to play the violin could have reflected his will to overcome any small awkwardness he saw in himself or was teased for.[32]

Carrying it to another plane, a boyish awkwardness, however

slight, may have increased the charm of the intellect he shared in salons with ladies of Paris, where he had gone in 1784 with daughter Patsy to serve as trade commissioner. The ladies found the widower Jefferson as fascinating in *tete-a-tetes* as he found them coquettish and intruiging. He could concentrate on practicing with them his abominably broken French. The practicing kept Jefferson too busy with mechanics of language and with explanations of literal meaning for him to feel lost about his missing social cues.[33]

The way in which psychiatrists have included "posture" and "gesture" in the Asperger's Syndrome criteria makes it appear possible to examine each clinically on its own. To a curious layman the terms differ so minutely as to elude clear distinguishment. To satisfy criteria, however, some separation must be attempted. Posture is usually defined as the position of the body or of parts of the body in the sense of an overall bearing. The definition of gesture is movement of the body or of a part of the body to express ideas or emotions.

Biographer Joseph J. Ellis considered significant the eyewitness account by Isaac Jefferson, a slave who observed Thomas Jefferson over a period of about forty years. As Ellis noted, Jefferson bowed to each person he met, then folded his arms across his chest, "defining his own private space and warding off intruders." The slave Isaac's description is eloquent testimony to Jefferson's guarded style and is all the more reliable for its source and its long-term observation.[34]

Implied in the bowing is, *I offer you my respect*, and implied in the action of folding his arms is, *Now I am going to offer you my attention.* That he stood there and talked or listened in that posture has implications such as, *No need to come closer. This talk can be carried on without your placing a hand on me to be assured of my continued attention. I will signal that the conversation is over by unfolding my arms.* The stance is significant because it contained some of the few signals in conversation Jefferson seemed capable of sending, negative though they may have been.

Despite Jefferson's active eye movement in place of customary conversational eye gaze and his usual facial immobility over the course of dialogue, one must ask whether his habit of folding his arms by itself impeded social interaction. To the extent this habit barred any motion the other person might have considered—say to deepen or broaden the listener Jefferson's understanding with a touch on the arm signaling encouragement or sincerity—and to the extent Jefferson locked out his own possible reciprocation, then interaction was restricted. Furthermore, because Jefferson's conversational pose put the other person on notice that venturing closer was forbidden, it must have lessened the conversational partner s wish to employ his or her full range of expression. And it was bound to have lowered expectations of receiving nonverbal signals from Jefferson in return.

Should not the brilliant Jefferson have been capable of catching the full meaning solely from words and their vocal emphases and intonations, regardless of whether he missed social cues and despite his stance that blocked them further? As good an ear and memory as he had for significant elements of proceedings in larger meetings (remember, he was also a dedicated note-taker), it is doubtful he could have decoded by hearing alone very many of the subtleties more common in one-to-one conversation. Dumas Malone testified to that deficiency—that "he did not learn through the ear but through the eye" and "put all important things down on paper."[35]

In your own next experience watching a televised or movie drama, notice an actor or actress will say—or he or she will project by a look—the equivalent of, *What did I say that offended or puzzled you? Why are you looking at me that way?* Such responses to the other's nonverbal cue are not scripted for effect, necessarily, but reflect realities of social engagement. They also remind us of the ever-present potential for shortness of understanding.

People standing in face-to-face conversation move about slightly, reach or touch one another occasionally, scratch their own foreheads or chins, pull at their own earlobes, rear back or double over to laugh, throw out arms or clap once to indicate appreciation of the humor just shared. And Jefferson must have been caught up in a small measure of that sort of behavior, but only minimally, because testimony to any such responses by him is quite limited.

Does that represent, as Professor Ellis has commented about Jefferson, a longstanding "distracted manner that was sometimes mistaken for arrogance"? Did the folded arms that signaled stand-offishness make Jefferson a bad or insufficiently attentive listener in such chats? Beyond the polite bow, such gestures and posturing, along with everything else we know of his nonverbal habits, could not possibly have made him a good one. And of course social inter-action was impaired.[36]

Visitors during his retirement to Monticello reported that dia-logues tended to become largely one-sided guided tours. Probably Jefferson had not intended them to turn out that way. He had no rea-son to try to dominate a conversation, but he had plenty of reason to share his building and gardening achievements (and not all with Asperger's traits can do that well, but *he* could). He was proud of what he had managed to bring to life or completion.[37]

Long-term evidence shows he would much rather have been the listener, as he was most often in groups of any size. The force of his great intellect, however, and the compulsion that was part of his traits apparently directed a number of his conversations toward skewed outcomes. By the same token, who would not have enjoyed having Jefferson for a natural history or horticultural or architec-tural lecturer?[38]

The sitting posture described by Senator Maclay does not quite match the way in which people of height normally arrange them-selves:

> ...he sits in a lounging manner, on one hip commonly, and with one of his shoulders elevated much above the other...

Others could have perceived Jefferson thus seated for talk as disregarding poise and convention, as lacking consideration. That, too, could have impaired social interaction and probably did.[39]

Were all four nonverbal habits of the criteria in play during private family moments, when warmth and candor were warranted? A father or grandfather listening and responding with arms habitually folded is difficult for me to picture, but it is disturbingly possible, and indirect support for such a possibility is reserved for Chapter Eight.

Isaac Jefferson did not distinguish between people whom his master met for the first time and people he simply "met" or ran into, whether family members or friends and acquaintances. It seems harsh to assume Thomas Jefferson could have carried out the same acts of apparent stiffness indiscriminately toward everyone. Yet his known reserve brings that assumption also within the range of the possible. My conclusion here is based upon historian Ellis's observation about Jefferson's relationship with his daughters. Jefferson appeared restrained about showing certain forms of affection toward them publicly, and perhaps privately. And because his family regarded him as quite amiable, his children and later his apparently less-restricted grandchildren might have taken innocent delight in his bowing and arm-crossing as a silly amusement or a recurring game that, for them, fed happily on itself.[40]

Jefferson was not a cold man. Not at all. He loved and was loved. Margaret Bayard Smith, who along with her publisher-husband, Samuel Harrison Smith, were among Jefferson's dearest friends, wrote in general terms, "He could not live without something to love" (though she was inspired to that comment by his pet mockingbird).[41]

However, it is clear from historians' and biographers' research that he lacked the ability to understand and follow accepted practices of loving at certain levels of his family relationships, notably toward his mother and, perhaps more sadly, toward his daughters. While we have yet to learn everything about what lies behind the barrier against affectionate display among members of many families, we have at least a key in a trait of Asperger's Syndrome next to be analyzed.

Notes:

1 *Malone*, 6:474.

2 The topic begs for separate study, but recommended readings include Ellis, Peterson, and Malone. It should be noted that three of Martha Randolph Jefferson's children, Anne, Thomas (Jeff), and Ellen, were adults before 1819—a year of countrywide financial panic. After that, according to Ellis, Jefferson's financial rescue was no longer possible. *Ellis*, 273.

3 *Brodie*, 281. See also *Malone*, 6:472.

4 *Ellis*, 137.

5 *Asperger/Frith*, 68-69.

6 *Grandin*, 73, 90.

7 *Malone*, 4:373-74; *Attwood*, 55.

8 *Myles/Simpson*, 6.

9 *Malone*, 4:373-74, 5:122.

10 *Ellis*, 25.

11 *Monticello: Recollections*, 71; *Malone*, 4:439, 6:470; Alf J. Mapp, Jr., *Thomas Jefferson: Passionate Pilgrim* (Lanham, Md.: Madison Books, 1991), 248-49.

12 *Tantam/Frith*, 158.

13 *Asperger/Frith*, 46.

14 *Myles/Simpson*, 6. Also, *Attwood* (195-201) in his appendices offers four sets of diagnostic criteria, Gillberg and Gillberg, 1989; Szatmari, Bremner and Nagy, 1989; World Health Organization, 1993, and DSM-IV of the American Psychiatric Association, 1994. Limited facial expression is common to all four sets.

15 See *Attwood* and *Myles/Simpson*; *Happe*, 111.

16 "Experience in boarding schools for autistic children over many years confirms that severe homesickness can occur but is not particularly common. (Hans) Asperger...suggests a reason for the type of homesickness he observed: the missing of daily routines." *Asperger/Frith*, 73n.

17 Willard Sterne Randall, *Thomas Jefferson: A Life* (New York: HarperPerennial, 1993) (pb), 100.

18 *Ellis*, 74.

19 *Malone*, 2:258-59.

20 *Burstein*, 150.

21 *Ibid*, 151; *Attwood*, 104.

22 *Mapp*, 193-94; *Ellis*, 231.

23 *Malone*, 4:94.

24 *Ibid.*,4:373.

25 *Attwood*, 31.

26 *Malone*, 2:471.

27 *Ellis*, 231; *Malone*, 4:374: Louisa Catherine Adams, wife of John Quincy (and no doubt faithful to her father-in-law, John Adams, who was rankled at the time over Jefferson's comments on issues of Adams's Presidency), wrote that Jefferson's face "indicated strongly the hypocrisy of his nature." But that reference was made in a period preceding what was to become longstanding reconciliation and a time of brilliant and cordial correspondence between Adams and Jefferson that eased their final fifteen years. They died the same day, July 4,1826, the fiftieth anniversary of the Declaration of Independence for which they had closely teamed their efforts in the Continental Congress.

28 *Mapp*, 287; The fluidity of interpreting handwriting in Maclay's journal entries governed caution about citing the printed edition used here. Maclay's chroniclers ranged widely in their faithfulness to his original text or there would not be such disparity by conscientious biographers over a single word. For this book a scholarly University of Virginia observer made a studied guess, and the yield of that guess was the obscure word "scruny."

29 *Brodie*, 27; *Burstein*, 151; *Malone*, 2:258; Alf J. Mapp, Jr., *Thomas Jefferson: A Strange Case of Mistaken Identity* (Lanham, Md.: Madison Books, 1987) (pb), 287; *Peterson*, 399.

30 *Adams/Paris*, 18; *Wills*, 15; *Randall*, 497; *Cunningham*, 139.

31 *Malone*, 1:420.

32 *Peterson*, 10.

33 *Malone*, 2:70; *Ellis*, 84.

34 *Ellis*, 26.

35 *Malone*, 1:126.

36 *Ellis*, 28.

37 *Ibid*, 230-31.

38 *Attwood*, 85-86. In such "verbal fluency" as that cited by Attwood, there is unfortunate potential that an Asperger's person will simply fail to learn "the cues when to be quiet." In the ubiquitous Maclay account there is reference to Jefferson's speaking "almost without ceasing" (*Adams/Paris*, 18).

39 *Burstein*, 150-51.

40 *Ellis*, 92-93.

41 *Burstein*, 40.

CHAPTER EIGHT

Relative Insensitivity

In Chapters Three and Four I drew a parallel between one of the five *Diagnostic and Statistical Manual* criteria applicable to Thomas Jefferson and descriptions of his behavior that were contained in biographies of the past half century. The links were evident in vital areas, for Jefferson's Asperger's traits generated social and other impairments that led him toward certain critical choices. As it turned out, some of those choices worked well for him, and some did not.

In each of Chapters Five, Six, and Seven I applied separate criteria from the manual that supported his tendency to fixate or obsess, his adherence to routines that did not always serve him well, and his confronting others with the demeanor of a "sphinx," as Joseph J. Ellis has called him.

In this chapter I plan to cover the last of the five *Diagnostic and Statistical Manual* criteria that apply to Jefferson. It is the one that addresses a "lack of social or emotional reciprocity," with particular emphasis on the emotional, as biographers have observed such a problem for Jefferson with members of his immediate family.

Thomas Jefferson's mother, Jane, was a Randolph, one of the most prominent families of Virginia. While Jefferson's biographers have not dwelled or speculated on the following information, they have provided partial family trees so that we might draw our own conclusions:

Jane's nephew, Charles Lewis, married Jane's daughter, Lucy.

Jane's niece, Anne Lewis, married Jane's other surviving son, Randolph.

Jane's granddaughter, Martha (Thomas's oldest child), married Jane's cousin's grandson.

Although such family intermarriages were common in that period and continued among aristocrats well into the twentieth century, the jury is still out on how well they served the species. Furthermore, the kinds of alliances described above were likely to have occurred during Jane's generation or earlier generations in a number of gentrified families, whether to preserve imagined purity of a line or for whatever reasons such matches received encouragement. But it was the Randolphs at that time who appeared to be carrying a strain of problems we should acknowledge, for those problems affected Randolph kinsmen of Thomas Jefferson both near and distant.

Dumas Malone footnoted a partial Randolph family tree with an escape phrase, that he had not attempted to "trace the vast ramifications" of the Randolphs' genealogy. What ramifications could the late Professor Malone have had in mind? "Was there something worth knowing that might have given us more significant information about Thomas Jefferson by way of genetic connections? I am not suggesting close breeding might trigger Asperger's traits. Instead I am suggesting that, in a family known to exhibit such traits, close intermarriage could have spread the incidence more intensely in that time, when such a marriage pattern was prevalent and before a preference for introducing the "new blood" of external alliances took hold. Genetic links have long been suspected and are now being found by researchers of Asperger's Syndrome to be among causes of the disorder.[1]

For purposes of diagnosing Jefferson by that which may be found in the family's gene pool we have a few significant observations and anecdotes. First there is Jefferson's son-in-law and second cousin once removed, Thomas Mann Randolph, Jr., whose politics carried him to the Virginia Governorship, among other posts. Historian Ellis maintained Randolph "became afflicted with a mysterious nervous disorder" shortly after Jefferson left service in Washington's administration at the end of 1793 and returned as head of the household at Monticello.[2]

More likely, based partly on a separate description by a later overseer, Edmund Bacon, the disorder had not appeared suddenly but was in place and manifesting itself throughout Randolph's life in periods of anxiety. Still, believable connections were made by the biographers between the son-in-law's lapses and the close presence of Jefferson, whom his daughter, Martha Jefferson Randolph, clearly idolized above all other men. The troubled younger man, Randolph, took long trips to shake off his disturbances, but those did not help. He picked up a drinking habit that did not help either. Ellis reported there were rumors that Randolph had inherited "a streak of the eccentric behavior...that stalked the Randolph line."[3]

Biographer Malone remarked similarly on this family's singularity by speculating that Thomas Mann Randolph's "depression" was somehow tied to problems "which had beset him *as a Randolph*" (emphasis added).[4]

From Bacon, the overseer, came a report that Randolph "was a very eccentric man." Bacon told of accompanying Jefferson's son-in-law to Edgehill, Randolph's plantation. When Randolph noticed wheat shocks "were not put up to suit him," he rode his horse through them angrily to scatter them every which way. Later they talked with the Edgehill overseer. Randolph commented to the Edgehill manager that "the old bull must have been in the lot," for many of the shocks were "torn down and scattered." The overseer and Bacon swapped knowing looks.

Randolph dressed indifferently and "was very queer." In fact, all the Randolphs were "strange people," Bacon added. He compared Thomas Mann Randolph to John Randolph of Roanoke, but that was an exaggeration because their manifestations of strange behavior were acutely dissimilar in several respects.[5]

There were doubdess others in the family about whom tales could be told and from whose behavior inferences could be drawn. Beyond pausing to observe John as possibly exhibiting a classic feature of high-functioning autism—savant abilities—we must shortly quit the Randolphs.

Biographer Alf J. Mapp, Jr., wrote that Jefferson's distant cousin John, a prominent Republican Congressman soon to become majority leader, challenged administration secrecy in negotiations that were leading to the eventual Louisiana Purchase. John Randolph had a style of getting the attention of the House of Representatives that was so purposely dramatic it would have done credit to a period Hollywood production. The "understated performance" by this strange kinsman of Jefferson included "striding alone into the chamber, booted and spurred," then leaning his tall, thin body against a column, where he began "idly toying with his riding crop."

When John began to speak, however, his soprano voice was so incongruous with the macho entrance that an audience less acquainted with him might have hooted and howled rudely. But no one wanted to upset John Randolph. According to Professor Mapp it was rumored that childhood scarlet fever had made John impotent, and it was further reported he once chased a man on horseback firing a pistol in each hand because the fellow had suggested "he was a eunuch."

John Randolph of Roanoke quoted the classics to support his arguments in the House, and if anyone accused him of taking anything out of context "he was quite capable of quoting accurately page after page." Before he was twelve he had absorbed the works of Plutarch, Cervantes, Shakespeare, and others and later formalized his education at three prestigious colleges.[6]

Although examples of Asperger s-like behavior in the Randolph family are helpful toward our tracing likely genetic ties in that time, we need not go beyond the Jefferson household to find a strong indicator of the condition, given what we know of the relationship between Jane Randolph Jefferson and her son Thomas.

Dumas Malone speculated about their relationship on the bright side but conceded that the only known reference Jefferson made to his mothers influence on him "was negative," and it is probable he "did not value her counsel very highly."[7]

Joseph J. Ellis added the "strained" relationship was evident after his father died, when young Jefferson did his best to "remove himself from her supervision." Thomas was fourteen when Peter Jefferson died. Much that happened afterward points to that loss as the most significant source of his sense of unease and vulnerability. Andrew Burstein, author of *The Inner Jefferson*, described Jane as a woman whose talent for mothering evidently failed to exude "great warmth." Merrill D. Peterson wrote she was a "zero quantity in his life" by all interpretations from Jefferson himself.[8]

Although it had been thought by many people, even into the 1990s, that being raised by a cold parent can lead to autism in children, researchers have rejected that view. In no way known to science would a cold substitution for positive nurturing initiate a developmental disorder rooted in the brain. British researcher Francesca Happe has said flatly, "Autism is not caused by refrigerator parenting," and all the latest literature on the subject appears to confirm that position.[9]

Still, Jefferson's zero or negative attitude toward his mother is only half the puzzle of that relationship. The other half, frozen wordlessly in time, raises such questions as, What was Jane Randolph Jefferson's attitude? What was her problem?

Jane could see developmental deficiencies plainly in her daughter Elizabeth. According to Malone, Elizabeth was "subnormal." Jane must have experienced disappointments over that circumstance. She must have had notions about where blame lay, worries about what would show up among any children yet to be brought into the world with Peter Jefferson. (With Thomas and Elizabeth there had been a total of four children so far, and there would be six more.) She could see disorder less plainly in Thomas, but she could see traces of it nevertheless.[10]

After all—and I must place some emphasis on this point—if historians have been able to call to our attention enigmas, puzzles, and sphinx-like qualities of Jefferson for a century and three-quarters after his death, surely Jane saw them while her son Thomas was living under the same roof with her the first twenty-seven years of his life.

Was Jane receiving from her children the loving warmth most mothers believe is their due? From Elizabeth and Thomas the affection may not have been of the same quality as that from her two oldest daughters or from the rest of her surviving children (two died in infancy). If there was such a difference, did she simply take that difference in her stride? To give this issue another perspective, was she giving *any* of them the affection on which children thrive? If so, was she doing that equally for the idiosyncratic as well as the normal? And if Jane was unequal about it, how did the apparently disordered exceptions fare when they lacked the comforting regularity of a mother's hugs? Again, that question is not to imply a *cause* of Asperger's. I intend it to broaden the base of understanding and to suggest also possible consequences of the disorder.

Where else may the barrier between Jane the mother and Thomas the son have been situated? Did something awful happen for which she blamed him or he blamed her, prompting a confrontation and an everlastingly ruptured relationship? Later on, Jefferson was remembered well by his own children and his grandchildren for his amiability. Surely that characteristic would have included a capacity to forgive anything harsh he may have endured in his own upbringing.

Or, between Thomas Jefferson and his mother, perhaps there was nothing to forgive. His lifelong lack of honoring her memory would then turn out to have been little more than a variation of his own habitually undemonstrative behavior—a seeming aloofness toward family members with whom he was otherwise presumed to have had a strong emotional bond.

Of historians' observations about Jefferson's mother, perhaps the analytical writer Burstein's comes closest to understated accuracy—that she simply did not radiate "great warmth." But that conclusion must be matched with shortcomings found in Jefferson, such as the one that Ellis cited—an inability "to convey affection" even to his own children.[11]

Logic suggests a balance to the "lack of emotional reciprocity"— on the one side a mother showing traits of what we now know of Asperger's, which traits it is reasonable to conclude were transmitted genetically through the Randolph clan, and on the other side a son with a now-identifiable set of Asperger's characteristics, not forgetting a daughter who was very possibly on the lower portion of the autistic continuum.

Ellis was correct that we lack "explicit evidence" to explain the chilly mother-son relationship. But we also lack any other explanation that conforms so well with such historical evidence as we have and meets the tests of logic as Asperger's does.[12]

There is one other possibility that could have had a bearing on the emotional problems of Jefferson with family women of the generation before and the generation after, and that is a fear of incest— not actual incest but accusations or suspicions. Again, he was not a paranoid person. But we should consider the possibility of an underlying fear. My supposition that this is worth considering is based partly on evidence and partly on experience with other unusual fears that plague Asperger's individuals.

As a witness to close intermarriage within the aristocratic families of Virginia, Jefferson might well have become alarmed by some of the closeness he observed through life that he thought inappropriate. Still he was quite tolerant, for his own daughter Polly married his late wife's half-sister's son, John Wayles Eppes, therefore Polly's first cousin—not an uncommon type of alliance then.[13]

Yet he might have harbored the same honest fears that closely intermarrying families in those days could not have avoided considering and discussing, problems Jefferson might have observed, such as widower uncles lusting after nieces. Could such apprehensions have placed an Asperger's-affected individual at greater emotional distance from immediate family members than was warranted for avoiding suspicion? Could fears have compounded an emotional problem already present because of Asperger's Syndrome? Yes, they certainly could have, and they do within the range of my own observations today. But the *root* of the emotional problems lies in the way the brain of high-functioning autistics differs from others.

The power of a compounding fear and the power of a notion seized and clung to are worth considering nonetheless. When my Asperger's son Fred was small I lectured him on the importance of getting rid of germs that we all pick up in the course of the day, simply by washing his hands carefully before coming to the dinner table. I happened to give the handling of money as an example of how germs can be spread. For a few years afterward he refused to accept coins in his hands, treating them instead as objects so foul as to require another person's help depositing them in a piggy bank.

Did such early fears and imaginings—of potential sexual temptations in a family's intergenerational love—drive Jefferson and his mother farther from each other than autistic traits already had? And did they later affect his relationship with his daughters? What of his relationships with his sisters? The quality of their bonds is simply not known to us completely, except that he felt and expressed great loss when his older sister Jane Jefferson died unmarried at the age of twenty-five.

Whatever ingredients may have gone into a blend of Jefferson's deficiencies for emotional reciprocity with females of his family, the best suggestion about where it was rooted is that the problem was basically another characteristic of Asperger's Syndrome. And the apparent early emotional barrier between him and Jane Randolph Jefferson carried over into fatherhood. It stayed in place to the bafflement of others in his time and ours to affect his daughters Patsy and Polly.

After Jefferson took Patsy to France in 1784, his youngest daughter Lucy Elizabeth died of whooping cough in Virginia when she was a toddler not yet three years of age. Jefferson then sent for his other daughter Polly, who had recovered from the ailment, to join him in Paris. But the arrangements were painfully slow to carry out in those days. The long-distance planning and fulfillment of his goal took more than two years. When Polly finally stopped off at the quarters of John and Abigail Adams in London on the way to France in the summer of 1787, Jefferson's romance with Maria Cosway had already run its course, and his recuperating travels in Europe that followed his wrist fracture were ended.

Yet Jefferson did not go to London to meet Polly, who was then approaching nine years of age and who was accompanied by Sally Hemings. Instead he sent Adrien Petit, *maitre d'hotel* of his Paris quarters, to guide his daughter and Sally to his home in France. Abigail Adams wrote Jefferson that Polly "told me this morning, that as she had left all her friends in Virginia to come over the ocean to see you, she did think you would have taken the pains to have come here for her, and not have sent a man whom she cannot understand. I express her own words."[14]

Joseph J. Ellis referred to the sending of a third party by Jefferson as an example of "his failures as a father." Abigail Adams continued to show testiness years later over the incident after Jefferson had succeeded her husband as President. In the spring of 1804 Polly, at age twenty-five, died of complications of childbirth as her mother had. Abigail Adams's letter of condolence contained recollections of the child's being sent "to a strange land amongst strangers," which she said had been Polly's words at the time.[15]

By referring to Jefferson's "arm's-length parenting" in France, where he kept both girls in a convent ostensibly to shield them from excitements of Parisian life and from hazards of the blossoming revolution, Ellis reinforced the image of a father uneasy with displaying or reciprocating emotions. As signs of this distancing, Jefferson's letters to his daughters in this period were sermonizing in the extreme. In his letters he addressed the girls by their correct names of Martha and Mary (later Maria) rather than by their nicknames of Patsy and Polly. Ellis highlighted examples of insensitivity, such as an inappropriate passage to a child of impressionable age in which Jefferson cautioned Polly that his love was conditional on her guarding her good looks.[16]

As a pre-teenager prior to her stay in Paris, Patsy also received letters from Jefferson that were extraordinary for their lack of consideration. Biographer Peterson wrote that Jefferson's letters showed him to be simultaneously solicitous and demanding of her. "I have placed my happiness on seeing you good and accomplished," Jefferson wrote his older daughter Patsy, "and no distress which this world can now bring on me could equal that of your disappointing my hopes." Peterson observed that challenge as constituting "a dreadful onus to place on a child."[17]

The same letter spelled out a regimen not necessarily insisted upon but, as Jefferson wrote her, one that represented a routine that he would certainly "approve." From 8 to 10 a.m. she was to practice music, from 10 to 1 "dance one day, draw another," and from 1 to 2 "draw on the day you dance, and write a letter the next day." The time of 3 to 4 p.m. was to be given over to reading French, 4 to 5 "exercise yourself in music," 5 until bedtime read English and write.[18]

Why were such letters at the most impressionable and formative times of Jefferson's daughters' lives so interesting to Peterson and more recently to Ellis? They inspired wonder over Jefferson's proposing overstructured routines and sometimes unattainable goals for his children. The letters revealed a part of his peculiar perception of paternal love. They (with the replies and follow-up) recorded the extent to which he succeeded in winning conformity, and, at times failing in that, how he put aside his proposals quietly. Jefferson proved a nagging father but also a forgiving one.

If he could have understood his own overreaching through the eyes of others and ultimately through his own, he may also have wished to be forgiving of himself. Prompt second thoughts about his expectations from Patsy and Polly never surfaced, at any rate not prominently in his writings if at all. The letters attracting biographers' attention, then, reflected Jefferson's inability to grasp what Asperger's researchers call a "theory of mind"—a "good understanding of others' minds."[19]

Related to an apparent lifelong inability to spot social cues, much less weigh their importance for crafting easy and relevant verbal responses, this consequent lack of a theory of mind dominated his early correspondence with his daughters. Writing should be thought to have served his need to get past some of his social misunderstandings, but it did not at this level. The only advantage of the written words was the opportunity to record affection on paper, something it is doubtful he handled very well in person with Patsy and Polly.

That old trap of social and emotional impairment, which Jefferson seemed unable to overcome fully, though he appears on occasion to have tried, is what made him seem unfeeling and made him behave didactically during critical moments in the lives of his daughters. As the sole parent Jefferson took a stance he believed most appropriate to their upbringing, never realizing how prepubescent girls viewed his advice when they were on the edge of more compelling anxieties. He lacked the ability to recognize their perceptions and beliefs. Perhaps he also overlooked their right to separate beliefs. His daughters showed their opposition not by arguing the point but by failing quietly to meet his demands.

Jefferson's "carrot and stick" approach—balancing his love in return for their conformity—was evidence of a mechanistic perception of how the minds of others worked. It was about as graceless a tool of parenting as anyone might ever have stumbled upon.

Before we leave the letters there is a post-Paris exchange with his daughter Polly when she was twelve years of age that deserves mention. Jefferson wrote her when he was in New York in the Washington administration. Besides the usual reproaches for Polly's failure to be a good correspondent and the implications of conditional love, Jefferson offered primitive debit and credit accounting to show her that she owed him four letters. But within a year the child apparently remembered her father's earlier charting and later wrote: "It is three weeks my Dear Papa since I have had a letter from you however as it is now my turn I shall not be ceremonious."[20]

As is characteristic of Asperger's individuals who welcome the chance to avoid frequent social encounters, Jefferson appeared to be relieved over the prospect of retirement from public life early in 1794. He had just left the role of Secretary of State in the Washington administration at the end of the previous year. But his optimism was to be short-lived. Crop failures, financial setbacks, family strains brought about by his son-in-law's condition, his own temporary ill health and that of others reversed the promise of paradise. Sally had her deep disappointments as well with two more of their babies' dying, one after approximately two years and the next in infancy, both daughters.[21]

Fawn M. Brodie called the three-year period before his assumption of the Vice Presidency in February, 1797, "the most mysterious" of his life. He went from high spirits to dashed hopes, only to bounce ultimately to a place somewhere in between, which showed an improved outlook overall. Whatever insight Jefferson drew from this period of imagined release from public obligations, that lesson, combined with personal disappointments, appeared to have changed him lastingly.[22]

Friendships formerly taken for granted, and which had appeared to be passive or lacking in co-dependency, seemed at last to be growing more reciprocal. Instead of shutting himself away as he had done most of the first fifty years of his life, he appeared more relaxed about visiting the homes of others and lingering a while. And instead of relying on his poor instincts in matters of personal and social relationships, he began to depend on James Madison's counsel.

A possible lesson here is that while passiveness in friendships is an early-stage feature not uncommon in people on the Asperger's continuum, a late-stage turn in such a characteristic can occur because of a strong emotional influence, according to Digby Tantam, a psychologist specializing in Asperger's studies at the University of Warwick, England. The variable in the picture, of course, was Sally Hemings. Add to that the combined joys and woes they had been sharing over the equivalent period he had been married to his late wife Martha.[23]

In one of his most candid moments, in a letter to the adult Polly when he was President, Jefferson recounted the lessons he learned in that three-year interlude and turned the reflection into what was, for him, a remarkable social statement:

> I think I discover in you a willingness to withdraw from society more than is prudent. I am convinced our own happiness requires that we should continue to mix with the world, and to keep pace with it as it goes; and that every person who retires from free communication with it is severely punished afterwards by the state of mind into which they get, and which can only be prevented by feeding our sociable principles. I can speak from experience on this subject. From 1793 to 1797 I remained closely at home, saw none but those who came there, and at length became very sensible of the ill effect it had upon my own mind, and of it's direct and irresistible tendency to render me unfit for society, and uneasy when necessarily engaged in it. I felt enough of the effect of withdrawing from the world then, to see that it led to an antisocial and misanthropic state of mind, which severely punishes him who gives in to it: and it will be a lesson I never shall forget as to myself.[24]

Notes:

1   *Malone*, 1:428n; Attwood wrote three "potential causes" of autism are recognized—"genetic factors, unfavorable obstetric events, and infections during pregnancy or early infancy that affect the brain." *Attwood*, 143. See also Christopher Gillberg, "Six family studies," *Frith*, 122-46.

2   *Ellis*, 136.

3   *Ibid.*

4   *Malone*, 3:175.

5   *Monticello: Recollections*, 89-90.

6   *Mapp*, 40-41.

7   *Malone*, 1:37.

8   *Ellis*, 27; *Burstein*, 281; *Peterson*, 9.

9   *Happe*, 5.

10   *Malone*, 1:38.

11   *Ellis*, 92.

12   *Ibid*, 27.

13   *Malone*, 1:432. The historian did not say John and Polly were cousins but left a trail for his readers to figure that out.

14   Abigail Adams to Jefferson, July 6, 1787, *Adams-Jefferson*, 183.

15   *Ellis*, 73; Abigail Adams to Jefferson, May 20,1804, *Adams-Jefferson*, 268-69.

16   *Ellis*, 92-93.

17   *Peterson*, 268.

18   Jefferson to Martha, November 28,1783, *The Family Letters of Thomas Jefferson*, Edwin Morris Betts and James Adam Bear, Jr., editors (Charlottesville, Va.: The University Press of Virginia, 1966), 19-20.

19   Francesca G.E. Happe, "The autobiographical writings of three Asperger syndrome adults: problems of interpretation and implications for theory," *Frith*, 218

20   Jefferson to Mary, July 25,1790, *Family Letters*, 62; Mary to Jefferson, March 26, 1791, *Family Letters*, 77.

21   *Brodie*, 277, 279.

22   *Ibid.*, 276.

23   *Gillberg/Frith*, 129; *Tantam/Frith*, 177.

24   Jefferson to Mary Jefferson Eppes, March 3, 1802, *Family Letters*, 218-20.

CHAPTER NINE

The Man in the Red Vest

Thomas Jefferson was intolerant of loud or disturbing vocal sounds, and that intolerance contributed to a perception that he was shy. His inability to endure such sounds is a common Asperger's characteristic rooted in sensory problems.

Jefferson shrank from noisy chatter or argument. And, whether or not because of an intolerance for his own voice in projection, he was conspicuously without talent for public speaking. Rather than project his great thoughts from the podium in speech, he simply ruled himself out of oratory altogether. Notable exceptions were his two efforts at making Presidential inaugural addresses—which he delivered too quietly for most in the audience to hear and without apparent concern over that—and his introductory moves in behalf of the Virginia Statute for Religious Freedom.

Writers have made Jefferson's being annoyed by voice volume and dissonance appear to be signs that he was shy, never realizing that apparent shyness and sound intolerance might stand independently as signs of something else. Only because both are Asperger's-related traits does it seem to me reasonable to connect them, but not necessarily as one growing out of the other.

The time is approaching when we will see sensory factors make their way into future editions of the *Diagnostic and Statistical Manual.*

They are already beginning to be recognized in the criteria for Asperger's Syndrome of the World Health Organization.[1]

Tony Attwood has cited sound and touch as the "most common sensitivities" among persons with Asperger's. Sensitive responses to taste, light, smell, pain levels, and temperature follow behind those two as factors found in case studies.[2]

Sound and touch sensitivities to the near-exclusion of any other sensory problems have come up repeatedly in historians' descriptions of Jefferson and his habits. Because Jefferson sought "a darkened room for days" to recover from headaches, it is possible that bright sunlight also gave him anxieties.[3]

From the evidence it is also clear Jefferson could not tolerate certain levels or mixes of speaking voices, yet in selected instances of noise he could tune out even harsher sounds that must have assaulted others' hearing, such as those in his nail shop at Monticello. What bothered him most were voices crossing one another in conversations or bickering and voices raised because of argument to levels he found intolerable.[4]

This evident discrepancy in the toleration of sounds was a topic of discussion I had with Temple Grandin on December 12, 1998. She said, "Sound sensitivity problems are not the same across all frequencies—across the entire sound spectrum." She added, "High-pitched voices are usually the most disturbing." I shared an experience in which I noticed that my son winced near an activated bullhorn. But it was not the volume of the voice coming through the device that was the problem for him, Fred told me later. It was the piercing noise the bullhorn had emitted when being turned on.

To guard against either dissonance or volatility when guests vented their political passions, Jefferson ruled out political conversation at the dinner table. He also hosted separately the representatives of opposing political factions. On the chance his cabinet secretaries might become too contentious, he did away with their meetings and conferred with them individually.[5]

The voices whose higher volumes and pitches he sought to avoid or regulate most probably included his own. "It was impossible for him to bellow," Dumas Malone observed. He was "unable to raise his voice above the loudness of ordinary conversation," Andrew Burstein quoted nineteenth-century biographer Henry S. Randall as having observed. When Jefferson tried to speak loudly his voice "would 'sink in his throat' and render him inarticulate."[6]

After watching Patrick Henry at full tilt during his time in Williamsburg, Jefferson knew what it took to command an audience. Any notion of using his lung power to project such enthralling rhetoric or histrionics, however, was out of the question. Besides, Jefferson was too genuine. While he could tell a joke or a tall story and enjoy drama and comedy, he could never place his ideology under rules of staging or lecturing for successful oratory and debate, so he never did. Even beyond his failure to project his voice for the benefit of others, historians have described (usually as unaccountable shyness) a deep-seated aversion by Jefferson in approximately the first half of his life to speaking *at all*.

Jefferson moved from being almost disturbingly laconic, especially while a young man, to occasional loquaciousness in middle and advanced age. In fact, his rare bursts of verbosity bordered on stream-of-consciousness by Senator Maclay's account of him during the Washington administration. "He spoke almost without ceasing. But even his discourse partook of his personal demeanor. It was loose and rambling and yet he scattered information wherever he went, and some even brilliant sentiments sparkled from him."[7]

Turning from a quiet man into one who, at times, could run on, Jefferson made a wider-than-normal pendulum swing and one that Dr. Attwood has acknowledged as common to people with Asperger's traits. "Probably more interested in the study of law than in practice," according to Dumas Malone, Jefferson exhibited early the taciturn pattern that would be the habit of a good part of his life. Joseph J. Ellis called him a "listener and observer" who shrank from the spotlight.[8]

One would think Jefferson might have used the buttonholing talents for persuasion for which successful political party leaders are famous. After all, he was the acknowledged founder of the Democratic Party, which underwent name changes in his lifetime from Republican to Democratic-Republican. Historians have given us no evidence, however, that Jefferson had such abilities. Ellis wrote that Jefferson was hindered against easy give-and-take "in the corridors" by his shyness and his preference for staying out of sight.[9]

If Jefferson possessed a stunningly superior intellect, keen powers of observation and insight, an enthusiasm for the liberating adventure on which the colonists had embarked, and a rare power of language making him one of the most prolific writers of his time, what blocked the connection between his mind and his mouth? Purely because he retreated habitually to his writing desk I am tempted toward speculating he may have had a problem similar to that described by Temple Grandin: "There is a process of using my intellect and logical decision-making for every social decision. Emotion does not guide my decision; it is pure computing," she wrote.[10]

In political debate, in which Ellis said Jefferson avoided participation, it is not uncommon to listen to a speaker's personal values and opinions, to his sense of irony, sarcasm, innuendo, double meanings, even to his intonations for effect—all to elicit an emotional rather than intellectual identification with the speaker's side of the issue.[11]

Such rhetorical tools and political propaganda that were expected to rally partisans did not appear always to elicit ready response from Jefferson. Furthermore, Malone observed, Jefferson put everything important on paper, "and without notes he was lost." From note-taking for his own clear understanding and decision-making to world-class letter-writing for everyone's understanding was a logical progression.[12]

Jefferson's mind seemed most at ease with imagery and mathematics. What his mind craved for comfort and best understanding had to be logical, rhythmic, and orderly. His early drawings showed "a compulsiveness in mechanical effort and a fascination with numbers," according to Burstein. As we learned in Chapter Five, in the course of designing features of Monticello and other projects he carried measurements to four or five decimal places. Carpenters and bricklayers of the time could barely "keep to the inch, let alone fractions."[13]

In music there is a broad mathematical basis beyond rhythm or beat, and there is logical arrangement. In Jefferson's day of the baroque and the classical, perhaps also the early romantic, music was patterned. The thematic turns were almost predictable. His taste need not have confined itself to sweet sounds alone. His appreciation might also have included his own mental pictures of harmonic sound images and geometrical shapes, similar to those portrayed closer to our time in the Bach portion of Walt Disney's *Fantasia*. In that 1940 movie the narrator asked us to link the music with our wide-eyed imagination.

With or without a violin, though he usually kept one handy before the Paris disablement, and he owned at least three, Jefferson let music become his functional, comforting ally in a world whose artifices and ambiguities he would always have trouble fathoming. Distressed as he was over the demands his roles thrust on him, he relaxed by giving his voice to song.[14]

"Mr. Jefferson always singing," the slave Isaac Jefferson recounted, "when ridin' or walkin'; hardly see him anywhar outdoors but what he was a-singin. Had a fine clear voice; sung minnits (minuets) and sich; fiddled in the parlor."[15]

Dr. Grandin made the observation that "In some people the brain circuits used for singing may be more normal than the circuits used for speech." She speculated that the song rhythm may help "stabilize auditory processing and block out intruding sounds."[16]

In another and more conspicuous area reflecting Jefferson's sensory discomforts his manner of dressing was a significant sign of Asperger's traits. Hamiltonians lashed at his casual wardrobe with negative interpretation, branding it an "affectation of simplicity" and an "assumed cloak of humility" intended to hide all manner of Republican nefariousness.[17]

Jefferson's conspicuously informal way of dressing, except on rare occasions such as the times he tried to look sharp for his inaugurations, had three classic Asperger's features: First, avoidance of a sensory discomfort over materials coming in contact with certain parts of his body; second, if a key piece of obliquely-corroborated evidence is accurate, deliberate placement of calming pressure by means of selectively-applied tight clothing, and third, a common disregard for conventional style or fashion except in rare instances.

Jefferson wore a particular red vest that comes up again and again in one historical fashion statement after another about him. In a significant reference offered by historian Malone we learn the garment was designed originally as an "under-waistcoat." Jefferson appeared instead to have worn it for a different purpose. According to English diplomat Augustus J. Foster, as quoted by Malone, Jefferson wore it "lapped over" (wrapping or enveloping) a thicker vest of a grey, "hairy" material, the softer of the two vests being closer to his skin.[18]

Others such as Senator Maclay, noticing his "cloaths seem too small for him," were apparently describing a tightness or binding quality of his chest coverings. Had they meant that his limbs were sticking out of pants legs or sleeves, or that his trousers were splitting in the seat, those vivid pictures would have been too outstanding to ignore. That view does not appear except for Garry Wills's speculation. He wrote Maclay "must have thought Jefferson's clothes too small because his thin wrists were so prominent." Daniel Webster offered a contradictory description of Jefferson's appendages. David Leon Chandler quoted Webster in *The Jefferson Conspiracies* (1994) as having written to describe Jefferson, "Limbs uncommonly long; his hands and feet very large, and his wrists of an extraordinary size."[19]

Biographer Alf J. Mapp, Jr., gave helpful attention to Jefferson's manner of dressing, an outstanding feature of his odd behavior. Describing visits to Grandpapa by Francis Eppes and the teenage youths friends, Mapp wrote that the boys were amused by his eccentricities, especially when "he would wear the same garment over and over." When he showed up repeatedly in his red vest, they could not help but notice. A pair of red knee breeches he wore day after day was even more conspicuous. It was said the breeches were held over from his time in France. Because Mapp was describing the boys' reactions in 1819, the breeches were at least thirty years in Jefferson's keep and must have been comfortably softened by washings over time.[20]

Soft materials for the legs ran also to corduroy, as described by others. And then, of course, there were those slippers—bedroom slippers, alternately slippers "down at the heels," slippers that were "old," Jefferson "*en dishabille* (sic) and slippered," and on went the descriptions of his preferred footwear. By that it is safe to say his feet were discomforted by shoes. However, Jefferson ignored protocol by wearing slippers at occasions of *state* (two of the people who provided these descriptions were diplomats), which indicates the extent to which regular shoes were uncomfortable for him.[21]

Sensory problems of sound, which Jefferson overcame by his social engineering of dinners and conferences, and of touch, which he handled by wearing soft leather on his feet and by other adjustments, are believed to affect upwards of forty percent of persons with Asperger's traits. At times the problems occur in combination with a need for pressure by tight clothing or accessories in selected places.[22]

Temple Grandin cited personal problems with skin sensitivity on the scalp and legs, the latter affected by a scratchy petticoat in the same manner as "sandpaper scraping away at raw nerve endings." Sometimes she would accustom herself to long pants and not be able to wear a skirt. At other times she became used to shorts and "could-n't tolerate long pants." She wrote that new bras go through "no fewer than ten washings to make them comfortable."[23]

Tight accessories such as watchbands and belts—even converted wet suits—were described by Grandin as a calming choice by some people with Asperger's. "One man wore very tight belts and shoes, and a woman reported that pressure applied to certain parts of her body helped her senses to work better."[24]

In Chapter Six I described a "squeeze machine" Dr. Grandin invented. She crawls into it in order to squeeze panels against parts of her body to relieve anxieties. She can regulate the amount of pressure required for the desired effect, and she uses the machine often. From descriptions of the innovative manner in which Jefferson dressed himself, uncaring about raised eyebrows or amusement over it by children at Monticello or anyone else, he had obviously devised a form of regulation. He put pressure where he liked—across his chest—and he arranged for looseness and softness where he wished to guard against acute irritation.[25]

A report that he was in a state of "utter slovenliness" must be taken with a grain of salt, considering the source. Anthony Merry, a very formal British minister, found little to enjoy in Jefferson's company after he became confused by the President's disregard for rank or ceremony—which disregard may or may not have been a political statement by Jefferson.[26]

It may seem paradoxical that Jefferson would wear clothes both loosely and extra tightly, depending what part of his body we are describing. And it may seem strange as well that he could be present for what must have been a noisy manufacturing of nails in the Monticello nailery, one of his pet projects, while being unable to tolerate voices in argument. People linked to Asperger's just happen to have seemingly contradictory tolerances and intolerances in such matters. Hans Asperger discussed as paradoxical, but as fact nevertheless, a phenomenon of combined "hypersensitivy and hyposensitivity to sound, light and touch" among his young patients. More recent studies by British scientists Uta Frith and Francesca Happe deal with the unusual combination as well. Hypersensitivity is excessive sensitivity to such sensory factors as sound or touch. Hyposensitivity means being exceptionally tolerant in such areas.[27]

Asperger added this about hypersensitivity to noise:

> ...the same children who are often distinctly hypersensitive to noise in particular situations, in other situations may appear to be hyposensitive. They may appear to be switched off even to loud noises.[28]

Notes:

1   *Attwood*, 200-1.

2   *Ibid*, 129.

3   *Burstein*, 245.

4   Episodes of his supervising the noisy nailery at Monticello were frequent, prolonged, and spread over many years. That Jefferson could tolerate the sound of nails being cut and shaped, but not loud voices, indicates he carried an efficient tuning-out mechanism in his brain. It enabled him to oversee one of the few areas of temporary profitability that were directed from his mountaintop. *Malone*, 3:217-20. Attwood described this tuning-out capability. *Attwood*, 83-84, 132. *Ellis*, 44. Also Jefferson to Dr. Vine Utley, March 21, 1819 in *Writings*, 1417.

5   *Writings*, 191; *Malone*, 4:61 -62.

6   *Malone*, 1:119; *Burstein*, 150.

7   *Peterson*, 399-400.

8   *Attwood*, 85; *Malone*, 1:113; *Ellis*, 28.

9   *Ellis*, 38.

10 *Grandin*, 103.

11 *Ellis*, 44.

12 *Malone*, 1:126.

13 *Burstein*, 18-19.

14 He carried a "kit" on his early travels—a small fiddle—which he played "at odd moments with a minimum of annoyance to his hosts." *Malone*, 1:159.

15 *Monticello: Recollections*, 13.

16 *Grandin*, 72-73.

17 The criticism was from an anonymous pamphlet, *The Politicks and Views of a Certain Party Displayed*, which Malone identified as the work of William Loughton Smith, a Hamiltonian. *Malone*, 2:473-74.

18 *Ibid*, 4:371.

19 *Peterson*, 399; *Wills*, 15; David Leon Chandler, *The Jefferson Conspiracies* (New York: William Morrow and Company, Inc., 1994), 26-27.

20 *Mapp*, 289-90.

21 *Malone*, 6:166; *Peterson*, 731; *Malone*, 4:371, 5:124.

22 "Soft leather" shoes have also been mentioned. *Malone*, 6:166; *Attwood*, 129.

23 *Grandin*, 66.

24 *Ibid*, 65.

25 *Ibid*, 63-64.

26 *Peterson*, 731-32.

27 *Asperger/Frith*, 80n.

28 *Ibid*, 80.

CHAPTER TEN

Moving Past Coincidence

Any reader who knows one or two Asperger's-diagnosed children or adults—and who is also in understandable awe of Thomas Jefferson—may hesitate to make comparisons. My explanation of Jefferson's eccentricities could be in jeopardy for such a reader if the examples of Asperger's-affected persons that leap to mind are radically different from Jefferson in significant ways. Again it is necessary to remind readers that no two high-functioning autistics will exhibit exactly the same collection of traits, nor will they show precisely the same intensities of those traits that they may have in common. "Each child," the clinician Tony Attwood wrote, "is an individual in terms of the degree of expression in each of the areas (of diagnostic characteristics)."[1]

We will benefit from understanding there is a vast variety of Asperger's traits, that they combine randomly in such individuals, and that some traits will be prominent as we shift our observation from case to case while others will take mild forms.

I am in awe of Jefferson for the staggering volume and the rich quality of his achievements and by the way he generally comported himself innocently, admirably, and at times courageously in a life marked by one tragic circumstance after another. From my having lived with an Asperger's-affected person, however, I recognize that my family and the Jefferson family were lucky. Neither in my son nor in Jefferson did autism restrict intelligence, and it may have enhanced it. I see a number of differences between my son Fred and Thomas Jefferson, but I see more Asperger's-related similarities of behavior and attitude than differences. I have every confidence there are other parents who will have that kind of experience as well.

A conclusion that there could be some gain in intellectual capacity from autism has recently become easier for me to reach. As I noted earlier, during 1999 we were given information from a long-overdue analysis of Albert Einstein's preserved brain. Scientists discovered abnormalities in the physicist's brain structure that they concluded were probably the basis for Einstein's superior intellectual powers. The finding substantiated what I had learned to suspect, for it supported a view that people who are prominent in the field of autism studies had been advancing—that genius may be an abnormality.

There is another side to that coin, which is that not all high-functioning autistics who are geniuses behave in the same benign way Jefferson is described as having behaved. For reasons not yet known to science, some conduct themselves in ways causing them to be judged "behaviorally disordered," or borderline delinquent. Others who do not exhibit antisocial behavior in school or in public may show problems at home that only the family must grapple with quietly, perhaps heartbreakingly. Many with Asperger's, on the other hand, are generally steady and even-tempered in their relationships, as Jefferson appeared to have been. They show little if any behavior toward others that is inappropriate and irreconcilable, and they bring considerably more pride to their families than they do burdens.

Temple Grandin insists on calling attention to an autism-Asperger's continuum from normal to abnormal because there is such a wide range of characteristics among people diagnosed with the syndrome. One cannot describe the condition in a way that would offer a prototype for everyone to see and recognize at a glance. Those who seek to understand the disorder must accept that no two persons with Asperger's will ever be found completely alike, and each may be a highly complex individual. In a similar connection scientists involved with studying the problems of aging now realize that even so-called identical twins are not truly alike. They will age in appearance differently, depending on separate attitudes and lifestyles.

My Asperger's-diagnosed son has observed other teens who have been similarly diagnosed, and he has remarked that he does not resemble them, that he does not have their problems. The negative synthesis and abiding hope that grew from his observation was that those who diagnosed him as having Asperger's Syndrome may have been mistaken. Lately, however, and as a result of deeper study and reflection, Fred has become more accepting.

The futile search for a model of Asperger's that simply does not exist is a contributor to denial. The concept of a continuum, together with the various mixtures of traits among individuals belonging on that continuum, is difficult for some people to grasp. Yet such factors serve most reliably the conclusion I offer in this study. Potentially the continuum and the blend of traits are bases also for full understanding of experiences that many of us will encounter when we are engaged with high-functioning autistics.

The fact remains—and persists—that there is strong compatibility between traits of Asperger's and traits of Thomas Jefferson. And, again, no one has come forward with any other explanation for his idiosyncratic behavior.

Readers may benefit from my describing situations in Jefferson's life not previously mentioned, or only briefly touched upon, and my offering further parallels to Asperger's behavior. A number of the parallels emerge in the area of physical characteristics:

❑ When reading biographies so thorough as to give the reader the impression it was possible to track Jefferson's activity day by day for much of his life, I noticed two recurring afflictions plagued him, headaches and diarrhea. That happens to be the same combination that torments a number of people with Asperger's Syndrome.

As early as 1764 Jefferson complained of a "periodical headach." He would spend days in a darkened room to await relief, according to biographer Andrew Burstein. When Jefferson assumed the office of President in 1801, according to Merrill D. Peterson, he began to experience "a persistent diarrhea, occasionally violent." Joseph J. Ellis wrote that "recurrent diarrhea and intestinal disorders... eventually killed him." If we look for the late-in-life anxiety that may have contributed most to such a condition, we should remember that toward the end he finally understood the effect that his woeful financial condition was to have upon his family. We have comparable reports of the same ailments from personal experiences of the autistic Dr. Grandin, whose doctors "found no physical cause for the headaches that accompanied my anxiety" and who had "anxiety-induced... bouts of colitis that lasted for months."[2]

❏ Vocal problems may have contributed to Jefferson's inhibitions about public speaking. He had vocal difficulties common among Asperger's individuals. For instance, when he was a law student of twenty he decided to announce his deeply affectionate feelings to Rebecca Burwell, an orphaned girl of sixteen whose father had known or at least met his own father. Approaching her with a memorized text, he delivered much of what he had planned to say in a "disordered" manner with long, frequent pauses. She was unimpressed, and shortly she became engaged to another young man. Dumas Malone observed that young Thomas should have relied upon sending something in writing rather than trust "his stammering speech." Burstein made a separate observation of a speaking problem.

He revealed from nineteenth-century accounts by biographer Henry S. Randall that Jefferson's efforts to speak louder than normal—at a volume he was unused to—would cause his voice to sink and make him "inarticulate."

We have testimony about stammering from clinician Tony Attwood—that "the effect of emotion on the ability to speak" will cause some with Asperger's to stutter. In the matter of a "swallowed" tone, Dr. Attwood also passed along a case study of a woman whose vocal pitch was alternately normal and at times "deep like I was doing an Elvis impersonation."[3]

❑ In the area of intolerance regarding others' speaking, there is another connection to Asperger's experiences. Jefferson wrote to physician Vine Utley in 1819 that his "hearing is distinct in particular conversation, but confused when several voices cross each other, which unfits me for the society of the table." Although high-functioning autistics appear to have remarkable qualities for ignoring certain types of loud and persistent noises, some appear to draw the line at the dissonance of two or more people speaking at once. As for what may be tolerated, I have observed an obliviousness by my son to the shrill barking of small dogs very close by. Other shrill sounds may affect him acutely. Many with Asperger's (and possibly Jefferson, for he was very hostile toward dogs) find such barking to be intolerable and, according to Dr. Attwood, "have spent their lives avoiding dogs."

When individuals with Asperger's must concentrate, however, in order to understand what another person is saying in conversation, any tolerance they may have had for surrounding voices abandons them. For Dr. Grandin, as an example, conflicting voices enter her hearing with equal intensities. She wrote in her autobiography, "When two people are talking at once, it is difficult for me to screen out one voice and listen to the other."[4]

❑ Moving to another form of Jefferson's physical expression, he was said to be somewhat awkward in the manner of gesturing he sometimes used to go with his speaking, especially during the period of retirement that followed his presidency. Ellis wrote of Jefferson's "emphatic shrugging" of his shoulders and using his "long arms and large hands" while chatting with visitors at Monticello.

Such animation supplemented what we learned earlier about Jefferson's folded-arms stance when in one-to-one conversation. But it is natural for gesturing to accompany speech to a visiting group as a guide might do, to punctuate one's delivery as professors will, during lectures in which they are carried away with enthusiasm. The key consideration seems to be whether Jefferson was smooth about it or awkward.

Ellis's references to "emphatic" and "long" and "large" indicate that listeners may have found the gesturing delivery by the Sage of Monticello somewhat unusual in that respect, thus awkward. From the bowing described earlier to the stance with folded arms and on to the movements which Ellis also found noteworthy, I am compelled to cite a diagnostic criterion offered by the Asperger's research team of P. Szatmari, R. Bremner, and J. Nagy. In their pointedly-phrased 1989 range of criteria for diagnosis of Asperger's Syndrome which Attwood carried in his 1998 book there is this reference: "Gestures are large and clumsy."[5]

❑ Biographer Peterson wrote Jefferson was "more awkward than graceful" in youth. That may have mattered to such a sensitive young man, for he could have been teased over that. But to examine teasing—if it occurred, and that appears likely—we should turn from physical issues we have identified with Jefferson in this and earlier chapters toward those idiosyncrasies that fall more easily into the social realm. What seems likely to have been the problem between Jefferson and his contemporaries more than his "fresh country lad" awkwardness was his extreme devotion to study and books. He "studied first and played later."

Malone wrote that Jefferson devoted fifteen hours a day to studying and spent three-quarters of his vacation time in studies. Such a regimen and dedication would have denied him many privileges of mixing with his peers, including those peers who regarded themselves as his "dearest friends." Jefferson "could tear himself away" from them in order to "fly to his studies," in the words of John Page, a close and early companion at the College of William and Mary, Williamsburg. Another college chum, Francis Gilmer, observed that Jefferson was seen often carrying his Greek grammar book while his friends were "enjoying relaxation in the interval of school hours."

While such glimpses do not treat Jefferson negatively, they raise important questions: Why did Jefferson find it necessary to spend more time at his studies than was warranted for a teenage youth of superior intelligence wanting to get through college? Was he without any desire to lead a balanced life that would have allowed more time for simple pleasures of camaraderie? (He entered college just before turning seventeen and moved on to law studies at about the time he turned nineteen.) What was the effect on Jefferson of any such face-to-face observations by Page or Gilmer or other young men? While we may never have answers, we do have insights to lead us to answers.

One insight is from the landmark study by Hans Asperger, who observed that high-functioning autistics were far more comfortable with self-education than they were in meeting the rigid demands of instructors. Autistic children can only be original or spontaneous, according to Dr. Asperger. "Mechanical learning is hard for them," and they would rather "follow their own ideas" than be directed by teachers toward whatever goals a school demands of them. Earlier I mentioned that Jefferson confessed to being a "hard student," and it is possible that his shortcomings for learning by hearing motivated him toward deep study in isolation, in order to grasp the full meaning of lectures from which he had taken notes.

As for the way in which others responded to his self-isolation, Page gave us a clue in the phrase, "fly to his studies," and Gilmer saw intervals as the time for "relaxation." It would be stretching credulity to assume they or others did not tease Jefferson over his choices, for that is what young men do in such situations. Chiding remarks may well have stung the sensitive Jefferson. What is probable is that he applied his gift for separating the two conflicting realities—his friends' perceptions of his Spartan studiousness on the one hand, his need to understand his lessons and his subjects thoroughly on the other.

According to all of his historical biographers, from this point of his life onward—including his time as a sometimes gracious host at Monticello—we have a picture of a man who fled the company of others more often than not. And he did that in order to read or to write "in splendid isolation," to borrow a phrase from Professor Ellis. Perhaps more than any other habit, that is the hallmark behavior of a person who carries and exhibits traits linking him or her to Asperger's Syndrome.[6]

❑ How, then, may we account for the fact that Jefferson appeared to have so many friends? Was his lack of emotional reciprocity with members of his family offset by a normal social reciprocity? If we study his letters to friends with whom he maintained his strongest bonds, such as James Madison, we will notice that Jefferson may have been hospitable but he was also one-sided in his friendships. His letters convey the impression that it was appropriate for them to come to him, but missing from such exchanges were offers that he might go to them. Biographer Peterson remarked that he had a talent "for drawing men to him."[7]

❑ By the nature of Jefferson's work in behalf of the people, he was required to entertain and to preside at countless gatherings, and the less formal or official the better. He was said to be a good storyteller and was amiable toward his guests before retiring to the privacy of his study and the company of his library and writing desk. But Ellis has given us a more vivid picture of Jefferson's style at social gatherings. He noted that contemporaries saw Jefferson as a "hovering" presence, like a foreign guest at a dinner party who moves about and acknowledges others politely but never lets on whether he can speak or understand English. The autistic Dr. Grandin made a comparable observation about herself when she wrote, "All my life I have...felt like someone who watches from the outside."[8]

❑ Professor Peterson wrote of British Minister Anthony Merry's experience at a Jefferson dinner party in 1803. Merry assumed that as a newly-arrived diplomat he would be the honored guest. He was annoyed by the presence of a French diplomatic official, for tensions between Britain and France had resumed by then, but personal circumstances were to worsen.

When it was time to move to the dinner table, Jefferson offered his arm to Dolley Madison. He ignored her frantic whispering, "Take Mrs. Merry," and seated Mrs. Madison to his right. Mrs.

Merry was upstaged by several seating places, and "her poor husband scurried to find any seat at all." None of Jefferson's actions in the incident appeared to have been intended to slight the Merry couple, but they took offense because they did not know that Jefferson "gave no official dinners (and) eschewed rank."

The London psychiatric scholar Lorna Wing touched upon such matters when she wrote that autistics cannot understand why nonautistics give recognition to social hierarchies and do not simply treat all people alike. It should be noted also that by ignoring Dolley Madison's whispered protest, Jefferson exhibited the same kind of Asperger's trait of indifference to pressures by peers or close acquaintances that he showed with his schoolmates in Williamsburg.[9]

❑ Issues of Jefferson's style for dealing with others arose early in his life of public service, and his actions and attitudes baffled people at times. During the administration of President George Washington, British Minister George Hammond said he preferred dealing with Secretary of the Treasury Alexander Hamilton because he could "speak more freely to him." Hammond's complaint regarding Jefferson, according to Professor Malone, was that the Secretary of State put him "at a distance." Jefferson, Hammond lamented, "prefers writing to conversing."

Professor Ellis added that while Hamilton's critics saw him as the "American Machiavelli," Jefferson's cast him as the naive and vulnerable "Candide."

Because of his sensitivity to criticism, which Jefferson was unable to accept in the way John Adams or Benjamin Franklin withstood attacks, Ellis added that retirement from the Washington administration at the end of 1793 resolved a fear of

Jefferson's: That as a man repeatedly in the public eye "he had always been miscast."

From an Asperger's point of view, part of the problem lay in social deficits which did not fit a public figure, and part lay in his quiet naivete. Both factors might have placed him at greater risk politically had he not mastered persuasion through his writing skills. Had he ventured into public service without such a gift, he would likely have fallen at the outset. "During the whole time I sat with him in Congress," Ellis quoted John Adams as reporting of Jefferson, "I never heard him utter three sentences together." Assign Jefferson such a task as writing the Declaration of Independence, however, and the outcome for all would be quite different.[10]

❑ Ellis drew yet another significant contrast between Jefferson and a public figure—the kinsman with whom he differed philosophically and politically, Chief Justice John Marshall. In disagreements over the presumed power of the Supreme Court to review acts of the legislative and executive branches and declare them null and void, and in all matters requiring Jefferson's choices on moral grounds, the "primal categories of right and wrong" were Jefferson's principal guide. Marshall, on the other hand, was comfortable exploring and even exploiting the middle ground.

Historian Winthrop D. Jordan, too, made the point of Jefferson's "thinking of the world in terms of...black or white" and his "inability to admit a possible middle ground." A black-and-white disposition by individuals with the Asperger's disorder is typical. A dichotomous rigidity such as Jefferson's parallels Dr. Grandin's explanations about autistics' choices, whether moral or pragmatic. Autistics are guided, she wrote, by explicit rules to meet a simple and straightforward need for knowing "how things are done." Middle-ground choices become a confusing quagmire.[11]

☐ Except for his lapse with Betsey Walker in 1768 and the irresponsible nature of his scholarship for describing African-Americans in 1781-82, Jefferson took the high ground in all areas. But that principle denied him, to an indeterminable extent, the comforts of financial gain. Before and then during his service as Secretary of State in the early 1790s he developed a new design for a moldboard plow. Its mathematically calculated configuration was superior to that of any groundbreaking agricultural tool yet developed. It lifted earth away for a deep furrow rather than simply split and push aside the ground as plows had done for many years.

Because the State Department in the Washington administration had oversight of patents, however, Jefferson saw potential conflict over the principle against using one's office for personal gain. Royalties would have accrued to him if he had patented the new moldboard plow. Therefore, in an appearance before the American Philosophical Association in 1798, when he had by then become Vice President, he simply made a gift of the design for his invention to the public at large. That allowed its copying by anyone who cared to use it.

Jefferson's gift was a choice of action very much in keeping with ethics that are characteristic of Asperger's individuals. It was based in rules of doing things properly, and he carried it to a level more self-ennobling than self-enriching, perhaps past the point of so-called "common sense." He may have anticipated the scientific glory in it and was in fact rewarded on that front with praise and a medal. But had he been a more practical person in matters of self-interest—whether or not visionary about the possibility of financial disaster later to devastate him—Jefferson the attorney might have arranged instead for patenting along with a trust to receive royalties on which he would decline to draw while holding office.[12]

❑ One more example of a parallel between Jefferson's behavior and Asperger's behavior was his obsessive activity in creating the University of Virginia. Of that institution he saw himself as "Father." In that role he was naturally concerned about the effect that absence from their homes and families would have on young men in the strange environment of this "academical village." No doubt he remembered temptations to which he and his schoolmates were drawn occasionally in bustling Williamsburg, where young men were accustomed to coming and going freely, where they frequented taverns and mixed with young women of either high or uncertain reputation.

Perhaps to safeguard the purity of his design—which went beyond the campus and buildings, beyond the choice of faculty and curricula—Jefferson and others with whom he launched the university specified that students should be quartered with "quasi-parents," as biographer Ellis called the instructors whose responsibilities were thus expanded. In that protective way the students would be supervised in their off-hours activities. A student rebellion took place in 1825, resulting in extensive vandalism and threats of harm to two professors. Eighty-two-year-old Jefferson was shaken by that incident, visibly so in the board inquiry that followed. It is doubtful, however, that he recognized clearly how his close-supervision quartering plan for students precipitated the setback.

Again, Jefferson's persistent naivete in matters of human relationships robbed him of the chance to anticipate the trouble that lay ahead. To attract young men from home was a giant step for them. To place before them requirements of attending class and then of demonstrating their scholarship by after-class study was yet another. But to deny them freedom to enjoy whatever hospitality the small community of Charlottesville might furnish in their off-hours, placing them under the watchful eyes of the same faculty members with whom they had already spent much of each day, was simply too much.

Jefferson the educational theoretician demonstrated his lack of knowledge about the way social relationships and especially stratified relationships might actually work in practice. It was a classic failure in a plan that Ellis believed to be wobbly in other respects. By my view the quartering mistake was rooted in Jefferson's inability to venture into the minds of other people. As discussed earlier, that deficiency is a strong characteristic among Asperger's-influenced individuals. Jefferson was a humanitarian idealist with no effective experience for gauging beforehand the way his rules might affect the attitudes of those he hoped to guide.[13]

If we supposed the foregoing parallels to be coincidences and nothing more, then we would be shutting the door against an opportunity to take a closer look at the issues I have raised. Perhaps there are young scholars more committed to deep research than I who will find direct evidence verifying strongly the connections I have gleaned from the secondary literature about Jefferson. I believe such future study to be worth the effort, if for no other reason than to pursue the challenging possibility that, as Dr. Grandin has contended, genius may be an abnormality. My stronger hope, however, is that Thomas Jefferson will now be accepted for what he was, based on the evidence—a rare individual guided toward great achievement by a high-functioning autistic condition. And I hope that acceptance will lead to a better understanding of both Jefferson and that condition.

Notes:

1   *Attwood*, 21-22.

2   *Burstein*, 244-45; *Peterson*, 722; *Ellis*, 230; *Grandin*, 112-13.

3   *Malone*, 1:83; *Burstein*, 150; *Attwood*, 86, 79.

4   *Writings*, 1417; *Brodie*, 22; *Attwood*, 132; *Grandin*, 68.

5   *Ellis*, 230; *Attwood*, 197.

6   *Peterson*, 9-10; *Malone*, 1:56-58; *Asperger/Frith*, 70, 75-76; *Ellis*, 193.

7   *Republic*, 1:297; *Peterson*, 29.

8   *Ellis*, 28; *Grandin*, 132.

9   *Peterson*, 731-32; Lorna Wing in preface, *Attwood*, 9.

10   *Malone*, 2:413; *Ellis*, 129-30, 120, 38

11   *Ellis*, 175-76; *Jordan*, 475-76; *Grandin*, 103.

12   *Malone*, 3:216.

13   *Ellis*, 281,286-87.

CHAPTER ELEVEN

"A More Universal Acquaintance"

A predictable consequence of this work is parents' attempting to apply it in some way to children with characteristics of high-functioning autism, particularly if there have been diagnoses of Asperger's Syndrome by such professionals as developmental pediatricians and psychologists. "See?" they may say to their youngsters. "All along we suspected that you have greatness in you. This book puts you in a class with Thomas Jefferson!"

Their sensitive children may be freshly returned from weekday battles with poorly-prepared teachers, uncaring and power-bloated school administrators, and predatory peers. So some among those young people may fire back the question, "What does it say in there about how Jefferson survived school?"

As a matter of fact, there is a clue Jefferson left us. It is a letter he wrote at the age of sixteen to John Harvie, who was the working executor of his late father's will. In that brief letter young Jefferson asked to be allowed to move on early to college. A kinsman and also an executor, Peter Randolph, had suggested the change of educational environment, according to Thomas.

Too many distractions "by Company's coming here & detaining me from School" caused him to lose one-fourth of the time he was spending at home that he needed for study, he wrote Harvie. That

"Company" included his friends from James Maury's small school that he had been attending for two years, because Jefferson said housekeeping expenses would be saved by his absence and a resulting "Stop to so much Company." Unlike many young people with Asperger's characteristics who have difficulty establishing friendships, Jefferson through his magnetic intellect and generous nature appeared to draw others to him. It should be noted, however, that his adult correspondence often revealed a one-sidedness about such friendships—or, to put it another way, an unspoken assumption that the circle revolved about him. In the letter to John Harvie he revealed the start of a pattern for removing himself from their midst.

At college, Thomas wrote, he would "get a more universal Acquaintance," a more serious or studious milieu in which to nourish his intellect. We have little to rely on in order to determine whether Jefferson's stated wish was his own idea—the exchange of playmates for what he hoped would be intellectually-enriching and stimulating associations in college—or whether Randolph's observations inspired it. We do know that the young scholar Jefferson had become well-grounded in Greek and Latin at Maury's and wished to continue the classics, but he now craved mathematics as well.[1]

It was Jefferson's good fortune during his time at William and Mary in Williamsburg to become part of a foursome that met regularly at the Governor's Mansion for intellectual exchange. His mentoring by older men of culture and learning is now part of a portrait of a young man with a very special condition. The picture grows clearer when we add to it the excessively long hours he spent poring over texts and notes. It takes even sharper focus when we factor in Jefferson's untimely flights from the off-hours company of college classmates to return to studies. Significant in this image also was his conspicuous discomfort with young women who lived in or were visiting the lively college town and busy colonial capital. We must include in that picture that he was an avid collector of others' thoughts in special notebooks for future reference. We must recall that he was an apparently awkward young man and that his range of interests had already spanned at one end his father's mapmaking field studies and, at the other, the profound teachings of the sages. We must remember, sadly, that in this time of only occasional visits to his home at Shadwell, Thomas was by all evidence a lad without any recognizable bond with his mother. Without doubt, he was a student with special talents and, considering all features of this portrait combined with features of later years described by contemporaries and historians, a student with special needs and idiosyncrasies we associate today with Asperger's Syndrome.

An answer has now come due to the imagined question, "What does it say in there about how Jefferson survived school?" Jefferson had been attending a small private school. The generalized term "school" in such a question about his survival or adjustment would undoubtedly spring from present-day concepts about middle or high schools, whether in public systems or private or parochial. Really, though, there is little basis for perfect comparison. To cut to the heart of the matter, though, the answer is, *When his schooling and attendant circumstances made him uncomfortable, Jefferson was fortunate enough to be able to move on to a more serious educational setting.*

In this final chapter I intend to apply Jefferson's example to present-day situations that young people of special needs are confronting, and I will recommend courses of action that I believe will work. Before I do, however, I should reenter the minds of loving parents in order to help them with related questions I know from personal experience must be nagging if not tormenting them:

- What kind of career can my special son or daughter look forward to, given the demands for social adjustment the child has so much trouble meeting?
- Will he or she ever find the kind of loving companionship that might make us grandparents?
- What can we do right now to help our special child, especially in the vital area of his or her schooling?

We are learning to observe and rely upon the Asperger's-affected child for clues to future occupation. Any one of the seemingly quirky interests with which an Asperger's youngster surprises us could turn into a lifelong commitment for the mutual benefit of society and our specially-talented offspring. The proudly autistic animal scientist Temple Grandin sets an example and offers advice. "Fixations provide great motivation," she has reminded us. In general the lessons a worried parent may learn from her are invaluable and comforting, and I recommend her book, *Thinking in Pictures*, for its messages of optimism.[2]

My teenage son Fred's curiosity and observations have given him encyclopedic knowledge in a broad variety of subject areas, a few of them surprising. He is interested chiefly in the design of automobiles and their functional power features; the design, practical location, and administration of motels; video games and the history of their development and refinement; elements of personal computers; traffic engineering signs, signals, and markings and issues of traffic flow; urban geography and consequent planning needs; music theory, and functional residential and commercial architecture. Do I have grounds for worry about his vocational prospects? In a way I do, primarily because he may not appreciate fully the negotiable value of any one among those interests.

The adult work environment is changing continually. While white-collar cubicles permit productive concentration, the home computer in combination with Internet access and fax machines carries even more of such advantages. Yes, it is important to develop social skills in Asperger's youngsters, but that development is becoming less and less critical to their future occupational placement. With such connections to the "outside world" now available as those which computers and ubiquitous cell phones provide, we could not be living in a more promising time for young people who have a limited grasp of social skills. A parent may transform worry into productive assistance (even into a partnership making good use of the *parent's* pragmatic knowledge) by supporting as fully as reasonable the youngster's needs in this world of new technology.

The area of teenage dating and eventual loving partnerships involving young people with Asperger's Syndrome is somewhat more difficult to speculate with assurance but not impossible to rationalize with hope. I must confess that the firmly-diagnosed high-functioning autistic adults I know are successful occupationally but are also unmarried. I hasten to add, however, that I know a number of undiagnosed adults with a rather full array of Asperger's traits, and several are in apparently successful marital relationships. What makes such relationships succeed, of course, is that they have found mates who carry their own special sets of quirks or differences from society's so-called norms. Both parties among these couples have identified common ground while also being highly motivated to respect each other's areas of autonomy.

I know a few Asperger's-affected youngsters who, I believe, would make great parents. I also know a few for whom such a prospect or fact of parenthood might put them and others at some emotional risk. But in many cases it would seem that the simple element of Time may provide a key to success. I recall a conversation with an unmarried man approaching his middle years in Spain. He asked a small group of visiting Americans whether they knew why so many Spaniards married late. A few searched aloud unsuccessfully for a believable answer, so he explained, "We want to give ourselves as much time as possible. We can't afford to be unsure." Then we realized how easy it is for people of non-Catholic societies to carry into marriage unconsciously what they see as the safeguard of divorce. That is hardly a positive alternative in devout cultures.

Thomas Jefferson waited until he was a few months short of his twenty-ninth birthday before marrying Martha Wayles Skelton. Why so late? Was he so busy lawyering and supervising the beginning stages of building Monticello that he had no time to cultivate a good relationship? Hardly, for we know from his notes and his subsequent admissions that even in his teenage years and continuing through his twenties he longed for a loving commitment with a young woman. When he was twenty-five Jefferson either had an affair or tried to have an affair with his neighbor Mrs. Walker.

Why did Jefferson allow so much time to elapse between the first arousal of his urges for women and his choosing a woman to wed? Was his hesitancy rooted in a practical need to be financially independent enough to support a wife and family? Again, hardly, for he behaved as though little concerned about such matters and in later life seemed habitually to be living beyond his means. Clearly he had simply not yet established with anyone until Martha the kind of rapport he believed could sustain a marriage. Specifically for him that would include a mutual interest in children (though the limitations of Jefferson's affectionate display toward his children are legendary and closely tied to his condition) and a strong sharing of music. The reader may recall that the widow Martha had a son who died during their courtship, a boy whom Jefferson appeared to look forward to parenting. Furthermore, biographers' descriptions of the musically-accented courtship by Thomas of Martha resembled scripted light opera.

Whether intentionally or accidentally, by allowing enough time to pass while he acquired greater emotional maturity in such matters, Jefferson no doubt established within himself firmer bases for—more responsible attitudes toward—the loving commitment necessary in marriage. Let us say it took him a little longer than most to find the right woman and to "find himself" in that respect. Similarly any Asperger's youngster today who looks ahead to such a companionable relationship would be wise, and should be so counseled, to avoid forging ahead compulsively. It would be better to wait until he or she is certain that no purely sentimental inclinations nor lingering postpubescent longings are governing the decision, that instead sustainable elements of mutuality are strong and the outpourings of tolerance that will be necessary are sourced by a deep well. Time, patience, and practiced observation become allies of those in a special condition that has been inhibiting their social aptitude.

Readers who do not know a young person with an Asperger's diagnosis should understand some of the extra burdens such a person and his family carry before we transfer discussion to the educational setting. The youth has already been through periods of self-doubt, perhaps years of wondering, "What's wrong with me?"—a recognition that somehow he or she is different in ways drawing unwanted attention and unwarranted disapproval. Perhaps the most conspicuous problems are stuttering and unwillingness to take part in the games of other children. The child may not recognize others' facial signals of impatience, but soon someone will say something that will sting the child. Then add to a lack of acceptance the inevitable teasing by peers that will push the youngster's self-esteem through the floor.

The family burden includes internal misfiring of understanding over simple matters. It includes the frustration of trying to recover from expensive professional consultations leading to the diagnosis—a process that probably spanned several years. Then, of course, there is the expense of medication to reduce anxieties or lift the youngster from depression. And there is the occasional nightmarish side effect of such medicines upon the child for parents to witness, during which period of prescribed medicinal trial and error he or she may have inflicted self-injury.

I knew about the private misfortunes that such families go through in general. But I was shocked to learn also in 1996 that the school problems for my Asperger's son were uniformly multiplied throughout the United States for young people of that condition. I had assumed we in our family were running into harsh circumstances that were only local. In a late-summer meeting in the Chicago area that year Fred and I heard a panel of teenagers lamenting their treatment at school by administrators, by peers, and by teachers, especially substitute teachers.

Parents and children who have been through these trials expect to receive some sort of patient, human understanding from those responsible for carrying out a Congressionally-mandated public education program aimed at meeting the special needs of disabled children. Will they receive that understanding? The chances are close to 100 percent that they will not. They are in for a bumpy ride. And at the moment of their discovering just how bumpy that ride will be, many will conclude also there is no immediate escape. The situation has drained family resources to a point where tuition-based private schooling is probably out of the question. Besides, very few private schools are in a position to guarantee better circumstances for an Asperger's-affected child than those encountered in public school.

In general it seems a mark of our culture that anything less than perfection or near-perfection of face, form, and condition does not register on the public approval scale reflected by advertising and entertainment. Unless used as bases for comedic ridicule, individual eccentricities do not fit well into the picture most people have of society as a whole. We may argue that we crave individuality and personal liberty and would go to combat to make such rights universal. But deep down and for the sake of convenience and personal security we insist on a general sameness and conformity by those around us. We expect faithfulness to behavioral standards that such lifestyle-guiding media as magazines and soap operas teach us to expect in relationships.

At the levels below serious college study, those who run schools or those who teach in them or attend them are no different with respect to their holding that general attitude which values conformity. It is simply easier for school administrators to manage a program in which there are no special exceptions. Few educators have the breadth and depth of commitment that would inspire them to confront helpfully such exceptions as may arise among their students. Worse yet, most educators will look for ways to avoid having to deal with exceptions at all. A few will even become so mean-spirited about being forced by law and parental pressure to help special-needs children that they will respond with harmful retaliation.

I know now that in such observations I am not offering parents of Asperger's children anything new, anything that they have not already learned to their dismay. But I hope to propose alternative courses of action they may not yet have considered.

Congress intended the 1997 Individuals with Disabilities Education Act (IDEA) and predecessor laws going back to 1975 to bring equality to educational opportunities for young people with disabilities. Public schools were to meet the "unique needs" of each child and to assure a "free and appropriate public education" to each child, regardless of the nature and extent of the disability. Congress intended also to allow "mainstreaming" of disabled youngsters as much as possible while in school and to help them in their transition toward productive lives as they complete basic schooling. Clearly these have been humane and lofty commitments, a hopeful means for ending discrimination against the disabled.

The IDEA, however, has turned into a dismal failure. That is probably because the public educational system in place to serve the features of that law—a system designed substantially by Thomas Jefferson as a hope for the nation's future—is also badly frayed and failing. Part of the problem is the mentality of anarchy represented in Proposition 13, a California model that captured the national imagination beginning in the late 1970s. Its effect has been to trash the notion that governments may be required to levy new taxes for necessary services. Raising revenues to improve schools or to pay teachers at a level that will attract the best-trained people are goals that have also fallen in value, thanks to the current anti-tax mindset. So we get what we pay for and, in a sense, no more than we deserve— but not what disabled children need.

The gap is so wide between IDEA commitment and actual performance that the National Council on Disability reported in

January, 2000, not a single state complies with the law, according to *The Special Ed Advocate*, an online newsletter. Such a fact of state-level failure has the effect of stripping local school districts of motivation to obey the law, setting aside the ethic that local compliance in behalf of disabled children would be the right thing to do. The "burden of enforcement" of the IDEA falls on parents of disabled children who must turn to attorneys or advocates skilled in dealing with recalcitrant school districts. Parents must fight in due process proceedings or courts for those educational entitlements the law says the schools already owe their children.[3]

An apathy that reflects a public with no clear conscience in this area is cheating millions of disabled young people of the educational development they require. My congressman, Rep. Dennis Moore (D-Kans.), on February 8, 2000, commended President William Clinton for his recommendation to increase IDEA funding in fiscal 2001. But he called the President's attention to an overall and continuing underfunding of the program, "far below the promise Congress made in 1975."

Families of disabled children are entitled to a minimum level of decent behavior from their public school officials, with or without money. What would it cost, for example, for special education teachers and building administrators who come in contact with Asperger's youngsters to read a short book or even a few articles about Asperger's Syndrome? Material of that kind is already in school libraries and public libraries.

School personnel ignorance about basic problems of the condition is legendary. Take as an example two separate situations I know about involving Asperger's children with sensory problems, students who recoil from uninvited touching. Their peers taunted and molested them in the tolerating presence of teachers and caused classroom crises. The schools called the police. Can anyone guess whom the school people blamed? When an Asperger's child of thirteen with sensory difficulties reacted impulsively to an adult's inappropriate grabbing of him, school personnel handcuffed him and had him arrested. In the other case the principal announced the Asperger's boy would be suspended for his angry reaction to being molested. The schools ordered no disciplining for the offending students.

These are relatively recent incidents within my knowledge, but there are worse ones affecting students with disabilities that have become grounds for lawsuits. The weekly newsletter, *The Special Ed Advocate*, often provides horrifying descriptions of what is going on in public schools throughout the United States.[4]

Schools should identify students who prey on disabled children in school and shame them before their parents into turning their attitudes around. The students can be taught to be helpful instead of hateful. Such a program would require parental cooperation and monitoring by school counselors. As the problem of preying upon the disabled at school persists and grows worse, however, administrators who have been offered help for initiating such a recovery program refuse to respond, reacting only with the bureaucratic equivalent of a yawn. Again, this vital relief for the disabled requires virtually no expenditure of public funds.

An Asperger's child may be conspicuous for stuttering, or wearing a blank expression, or walking awkwardly, or for having such tics as incessant throat-clearing or ungainly and spontaneous arm-stretching or loud nose-blowing. The youngster may set himself or herself apart by being a conscientious study freak, by overfocusing on topics of little interest to anyone else, or by rebelling in one manner or another against overstructured teaching methods.

Perhaps the Asperger's student has felt it necessary to engage a teacher in a discussion that has "perseverating" features—repetition of certain phrases in the belief the teacher has not heard or does not understand. Such episodes call classmates' attention to a stark difference in the Asperger's student's methods of reasoning and negotiating. Or perhaps an Asperger's student has observed a racial or religious or economic-class injustice against another person and feels obliged to right that wrong, whether or not he or she even knows the slighted victim. Such championing seems also starkly different, unfortunately, from today's norms.

Those characteristics and behavioral features do not endear young people with the Asperger's condition to peers, nor to impatient teachers. Moreover, few authority figures in a school are trained to understand, accept, and redirect painlessly the behavioral expressions that emanate from the condition.

Why should children in middle or high school with Asperger's Syndrome continue to indulge the indignities their harmless differences prompt day after day?

I suggest parents *end* the children's discomfort as quickly and as smoothly as possible, that they spend less time arguing for justice and more in seeking alternate relief. A parent may work with the young person closely toward that magic day when he or she will turn sixteen. On that day the child may take two legal steps toward emancipation from further public school indignity: quit school and register for a General Education Development (GED) test.

The secret to passing the GED exam, by the way, is to study sample questions over a period of several weeks and to notice that, in most subject areas, the answers are contained in the questions. That pattern makes the correct choice among multiple choices quite evident in nearly all cases. A young person's qualification for work or college could then follow the passing of a GED exam, for it is the safety-valve equivalent to surviving and graduating from high school.

There is an earlier, partial escape opportunity to freedom, but that requires a slower approach. Schools often base *gifted* status on readings of the intelligence quotient (IQ). and there may be a variance among qualifying gifted levels from school district to school district. Yet early preparation for giftedness testing through conscientious study in core subjects, even as early as sixth grade, may be helpful and perhaps critical to the gaining of a few IQ points later when they are needed. Such gains do occur occasionally.

Some Asperger's children simply do not test well, and it may be necessary for parents to find a way to coax the youngsters past that block. It is worth the effort. The prize of giftedness can qualify students in their early teens for shared time at a nearby community college. That allows the student to be away from the hostile environment of middle or high school about half the school day. If he or she is harmlessly quirky in college, chances are no one there will take sharp notice and no one will care.

When the sixteenth birthday rolls around, the youngster should consider the steps suggested for the GED test. But the student must first be *confident of success* in that exam before quitting high school and surrendering gifted status, which enabled early college study in the first place. Community college admissions people seem reasonable and easy to work with for smoothing the way in those situations.

Consider the view of Leon Botstein, musical director of the American Symphony Orchestra and president of Bard College, Annandale-on-Hudson, N.Y. He took the helm of Bard at the age of twenty-three in 1975 and was the youngest person ever to become an American college president. Dr. Botstein wrote in *Jefferson's Children: Education and the Promise of American Culture* (1997), essentially, that the last two years of high school are a waste of time. I admit that I have oversimplified the theme of his section titled "Replacing the American High School," but as I have noted, that is the essence.

Dr. Botstein suggests that in recognition of earlier physical maturity by teenagers, which has become both noticeable and problematic in recent decades, we should free them at the present midpoint of high school. They may either go on to a community college or directly to a place of four-year higher education. Or they may enter the work force as qualified by our public education system, not necessarily as it is but as it could become under proposals by Dr. Botstein, proposals that my summarizing would not do justice. He has come up with a magnificent plan, not only for the disabled but for everyone. Oprah Winfrey gave her support by devoting a show to it.[5]

Discussion of early entrance into college for young people with Asperger's Syndrome, and even for some without the condition, is in step with action taken by Thomas Jefferson when he wrote to John Harvie at age sixteen. He, too, recognized a problem. On the one hand, he had outgrown the education he was receiving and was tiring of the relative lack of scholarly commitment among those with whom he was receiving it. On the other hand lay an opportunity for him to advance his knowledge and at the same time enter an environment of "a more universal acquaintance" that he believed he required.

There is yet another Jefferson connection to present educational issues worth mentioning. It involves remedies available in order to secure a better break for students covered by the Individuals with Disabilities Education Act. Although the situation at present seems nearly altogether hopeless, even with so-called improvements in 1997 by Congress that were signed by the president, there is still a small opening through which heroic parents may squeeze in order to effect reform.

First I should explain that the "procedural safeguards" provided in the law—safeguards intended to assure disabled students maximally-effective educational plans, services, and placements—are seriously flawed. The Individualized Educational Programs (IEPs), the rock foundation of the program, are customarily a cruel hoax in their execution. School people simply do not write them in full compliance with the law. The language entered in the IEPs by most school people is intended solely to dazzle parents and mask the real needs of disabled students. School officials seldom follow procedures governing requests for new or changed services, so parents arguing for them may never know why the school turned them down. Dissent by the parent for any reason is meaningless, for school personnel will outvote the parent—if there is even a structured vote or "decision" at all.

The law requires parent participation in "decisions" about the annually updated IEP document as part of a "team" process, but in my several years' experience I have never heard a call for "yes" or "no" or general consensus. Many parents suspect that school people make the decisions before the process begins, that the rest is mostly for show. Many administrators later believe the parent has approved the IEP if he or she signs it, but the law makes that alleged approval a moot point when there is anything in the oft-coded document that the parent does not understand.

Informal negotiation between parents and special education teachers, school counselors, the school psychologist, or the school district's special education director is normally unproductive when there is any disagreement over children's programs that the "teams" are considering or have decided upon. The 1997 revision of the law encourages mediation strongly as an alternative, but many school oflficials (who know parents' positions may be more reasonable than theirs) will simply refuse. The law implies they should not refuse, but they will anyway because mediation is "voluntary."

What many school officials hope to do with strongly dissenting parents is to lure them into an extreme "safeguard"—due process— because that is customarily a "win-win" situation for the schools. They will use an attorney whose meter runs at the expense of the tax- payers, and taxpaying parents of disabled children in turn must come up with fees to pay their own special education lawyers. Even if par- ents succeed at first in due process, school districts may turn the sit- uation around by finding a reason to bring due process against the parents, or appeal in order to seek reversal.

Due process brought in behalf of a disabled child under the IDEA may not only become his or her parents' worst nightmare but also a new form of quicksand.

Parents may complain to their state education officials, and there is a formal procedure for that. But they should not expect, real- istically, that anything will ever be done about their complaint. All fifty states are out of compliance with the IDEA, which often makes the complaint procedure a frustrating dead-end.

Higher up is the U.S. Department of Education, which runs an Office for Civil Rights (OCR) ostensibly to determine whether students' or parents' rights were violated in the administration of the IDEA. However, special education lawyers Peter W.D. Wright and Pamela Darr Wright have described cases in which teachers abused disabled children physically and cruelly in schools that had been "under OCR supervision" for years.[6]

That leaves the courts, if parents can afford to move in that direction and have the sustaining power to endure the experience. Most courts still insist on parents' exhausting their "safeguards" in the law first, but that may be changing. Generally, unless we are hearing only about landmark victories, parent appeals arising from early setbacks indicate a fair record of success.

I have shared with Congressman Moore, whom I cited earlier, another remedy that I believe is worth trying. That is to rely on the accountability features of representative government and work with local boards of education for reform, district by district. School administrators will contend it is no policymaker's business to be involved in the administrative features of the IDEA, but I am not interested in board members' intervening in disputes over specific children. What we should all bring to local school board members' attention is information about whether their administrators know and are obeying the law requiring the appropriate education of the disabled.

School administrators send directives to students cautioning them in language such as this: "Neither school rules nor the laws of the larger society work unless everyone knows and obeys them." Therefore, parents and patrons of the district are entitled to expect that teachers and administrators will set law-abiding examples in an area so vital to human development as the IDEA. Board members deserve to feel comfortable that the educators they employ to educate the disabled are doing so by meeting all requirements of the IDEA, a federal law, or they must reassign or dismiss those who are not.[7]

Related issues for school board members to consider—in the interest of accountability toward their constituencies—is whether the people they employ to work in special education are doing that effectively. Periodic objective testing of students in the program should provide a standard for measuring effectiveness and *meaningful benefit* to the children. Board members—who are, after all, people of the local community giving neighbors their time and talents voluntarily—should also consider whether those educators display a deeply caring attitude toward the disabled children of their neighbors, children who are supposed to benefit from teachers' close and informed assistance.

Local board of education members should seek assurances that administrators and teachers understand the various disabilities of the students for whose educational development the professionals are responsible. Unless they do, innocent people will fall victim or be hurt physically or become scarred emotionally by ignorance-induced crises.

Board of education members should be concerned also whether their administrators and professional advisers such as attorneys are truthful in describing what is really going on in the program for the disabled. Is the law being followed or broken?

They should look as well into the mean-spirited practice of retaliatory punishment inflicted upon disabled students. Administrators will at times withdraw or withhold a student's earned privileges, or they will issue notice of a negative change in student status, if his or her parents are outspoken about the poor way the special education program is administered. Such revenge, which jeopardizes the emotional well-being of the already disabled child, is a low and despicable form of abuse, yet even doctoral-level administrators practice it. Board members should call the adult bullies to account for that, or the practice will certainly continue.

If parents confront school board members, and the latter prove unresponsive or insufficiently attentive to the need for lawful behavior, the parents should simply replace the board members at the ballot box after attendant publicity is given board members' inexcusable failure. Publicity and even picketing would not be out of order as alternative measures. But such showdowns require that courageous parents ready themselves with complete and accurate records and with supporting parent allies. Then they can bring about changes in school districts corrupted by administrative arrogance, by the usual "circle the wagons" advice of imperious school attorneys, and by school board members who have grown woefully timid.

This suggested grass-roots reliance upon the potential strengths and safeguards of representative government is the connection to Jeffersonian principles I referred to earlier. I subscribe to such a system wholeheartedly. I believe it is the best chance for success available today in behalf of a beleaguered population of children with disabilities.

Notes:

1   *Malone*, 1:32; Jefferson to John Harvie, January 14, 1760, *Writings*, 733.

2   *Grandin*, 100.

3   Peter W.D. Wright and Pamela Darr Wright, *The Special Ed Advocate*, Vol. 3, No. 14, April 18, 2000, 2.

4   Website http://www.wrightslaw.com

5   Leon Botstein, *Jefferson's Children: Education and the Promise of American Culture* (New York: Doubleday, 1997), "Replacing the American High School," 79-130.

6   *The Special Ed Advocate*, Vol. 2, No. 31, December 7, 1999, 3.

7   *Student Rights and Responsibilities*, Blue Valley School District #229, Overland Park, Kans., 1999, 11.

Conclusion

I have already encountered stony silence from several people prominent in what may be called the "Jefferson establishment" with whom I had either shared early drafts of this work or brief descriptions of my thesis. Therefore, I expect *Diagnosing Jefferson* will be somewhat controversial when released. After all, I have written here that one of the greatest thinkers Western civilization has ever produced, an American icon and a Founding Father, was—by all evidence that historical biographers have provided—an autistic or brain-damaged person. Nobody is going to say "thank you" for that, regardless of whether it explains everything about him that has been puzzling his most committed disciples.

The problem is not whether I have done my homework in order to support a theory of Jefferson's autism-Asperger's connection. The problem is that autism frightens most people. We fear that which is unfamiliar, and we shrink from that which may seem a little too complicated to understand, unless it is accompanied by a bold-faced, ten-word summary. And saying that Albert Einstein was possibly autistic will scarcely help us move beyond such a fear. Only a broader and more accepting knowledge of autism will allow us to relax with the kind of material I have presented here. If left solely to researchers and parents of autistics to promote, an understanding of autism in full spectrum may not receive the public consideration I think it deserves, not for some time to come. But this book could change that.

The probability that nearly one million Americans have the Asperger's condition is a circumstance that would not necessarily lead us into full and frank discussion either. Many of them do not accept that they are different, much less care to learn the source of characteristics that others find odd. Too few have actually received a diagnosis. Only relatively recently have psychiatrists, neurologists, and researchers uncovered the phenomenon first suggested in wartime Vienna by Hans Asperger that autistics, professionals, and the rest of us are now dealing with.

Roughly a quarter-million children are involved in that Asperger's number for the United States. That is something a man like Jefferson would have wanted us to be concerned about, for the condition will affect their performance in school. The condition affects the way they are treated by teachers and peers who are poorly prepared to understand such children. Notwithstanding laws designed to serve and protect the disabled in public school, as described in Chapter Eleven, educators generally have remained ignorant of such topics and, worse, have resisted lawful accommodation to the special needs of the disabled minority. The performance by educators generally in that regard is a national disgrace.

I hope sincerely that this book will inspire much-needed and helpful dialogue about autism and Asperger's Syndrome and bring about a change in attitudes.

Returning to the image of Thomas Jefferson, I am not at all uncomfortable believing him to have been autistic and describing him in that way. That is because personal experience has led me to understand and accept the features of Asperger's behavior. Without that personal contact and the relatively new knowledge of Asperger's Syndrome, I might have lived out my life only vaguely aware of such a subject. Knowledge of autism has enriched many people like me. But equally enriching could be a well-reasoned consideration of what autism may have done for Jefferson, given the related facts and recent findings of the Einstein brain analysis. If such a factor as brain abnormality is found to be an important element of genius and human progress, we who are interested in this subject may have helped open a door, though I as a layman have only the sketchiest idea where that door might lead us.

In this book I have also tried to give Jefferson more personal consideration than he has received in most biographies. Most writers made judgments denying him in retrospect the freedom to have made basic, human choices. I will never understand their mental block against admission of the Sally Hemings evidence. For me such evidence held a key to a great area of Jefferson's human side. Subsurface racist attitudes tend to blur people's reasoning and undermine a frank examination of black-white relationships. I remember a maintenance man in a Louisiana public building where I worked in the 1950s. He was a very personable African-American nicknamed "Doc" with whom I felt free to discuss any topic. As we touched upon race-mixing one day he leaned toward me and asked, "How do you think I got these?" while pointing to his blue eyes.

To talk about close mixing among people of various colors is something many of us are uneasy doing, but such mixing is an activity people engage in every day without much talk and in a very natural way. Perhaps we are imitating unconsciously a practice that historian Joseph J. Ellis indicated was also a habit of Jefferson's—trying to keep a secret from ourselves by not discussing it. I do not expect to be present for the arrival of "one nation, indivisible" with respect to race or as a result of race-mixing. I wish I could be. And Thomas Jefferson, faithful to a sacred promise to his wife not to marry—and normally in self-exile socially—initiated some of that mixing in the late 1780s and must also have foreseen such a potential outcome.

A nineteenth-century biographer, James Parton, offered us a summary of Thomas Jefferson as a man who "could calculate an eclipse, survey an estate, tie an artery, plan an edifice, try a cause, break a horse, dance a minuet, and play a violin."

My Jefferson study reveals a brilliant and talented man who made love to women, tippled his wine, wore funny clothes, abhorred making speeches, fled to seclusion, brooded and wept, sidestepped disputes, waffled on race, obeyed dumb routines, believed fiction real, endured painful losses, and finally went broke.

Jefferson could not avoid being what he was. By his chosen alternative lifestyle he avoided trying to be what he was not—the socially-integrated person his Asperger's condition kept him from learning how to be. There are lessons in such honesty.

Comments

By Temple Grandin, Ph.D.
Assistant Professor, Department of Animal Science,
Colorado State University
and author of
*Thinking in Pictures—and Other Reports
from My Life with Autism* (1995)
Copyright T. Grandin, 1999

I have autism, and after I read Norm Ledgin's manuscript I became convinced that Thomas Jefferson was on the autism-Asperger's continuum because he had many traits and characteristics that I have.

Jefferson had a remarkable memory that served his enormous knowledge in many different subjects. He was socially awkward. Like me, he had trouble with eye contact, and he had sensitivities to noise and touch. I could relate to descriptions of Jefferson's clothes. He wore soft fabrics that would not feel scratchy against sensitive skin. When I was a child I hated scratchy petticoats because they felt like sandpaper on raw nerve endings.

Like many people with high-functioning autism or Asperger's, Jefferson was eccentric. He carried an account book and was constantly making entries, and he compulsively measured the distance his carriage travelled.

I could also relate to the descriptions of building Monticello. He was involved in every detail, and he constructed elaborate dumbwaiter systems. I could identify with that feature because when I was a child I was fascinated by the old dumbwaiter in my grandmother's apartment building. (Sometimes when I had been good she would run the dumbwaiter for me.) Other autistic-Asperger's traits in Jefferson were his overfocusing on pet projects, making lists on many topics, and having daily routines he adhered to.

I was most interested to read the appendix about Jefferson's writings and collection of data. His curiosity led him toward detailed knowledge in a great variety of areas. Making lists and gathering information on selected subjects is a favorite activity of many people with autism or Asperger's Syndrome. They make endless lists on subjects such as baseball statistics or weather information. When I was younger I collected brochures from every company that made cattle squeeze chutes. Collecting and cataloging piles of information is an activity people with autism and Asperger's spend many hours engaging in.

Autistic-Asperger's Thinking

People on the autism-Asperger's continuum are very detail oriented. They look at a lot of small details. When I read Norm Ledgin's manuscript I looked for details about Jefferson that would indicate his belonging on the continuum. Any one detail is meaningless, but a slew of details together paints a picture of Asperger's. While reading the manuscript I marked such details. Would there be enough to show Jefferson had Asperger's? Unfortunately documents about Jefferson's childhood were destroyed in a fire. Even with a lack of childhood information, however, I found there were enough details to show, clearly to my satisfaction, that Jefferson was definitely on the autism-Asperger's continuum.

The "100 topics" summaries of Jefferson's writings at the end of the book also provided important details. He collected tons of information on many different subjects. Taking an example from the section about his writings, it is obvious he did more with climate information than simply collect and list it. He made a table that averaged thousands of individual statistics. He also made charts with dates for planting vegetables. And he listed the most important 147 books on fine arts, politics, religion, law, history, philosophy, and natural history that a learned person should have in a library. More than that the list showed he was able to select the most important books after considering hundreds. He could pick out the most significant information in a sea of information. That is *specific-to-general thinking.*

Looking at a lot of specific details and then piecing them together is how people with Asperger's think. All my thinking goes from specific details to forming a general principle. I have learned from interviewing many people that most go from a general concept to specifics. Their thinking is "top down" and my thinking is "bottom up."

How does specific-to-general thinking work? Imagine that a 1,000-piece jigsaw puzzle is presented to you in a paper bag, and you have no idea what the picture on the puzzle is. As you start to put the puzzle together the picture will start to reveal itself. When less than twenty percent of the puzzle is completed you may be able to see what the picture will be. If there was a horse's ear in the upper right hand corner and a horse's back foot in the lower left-hand corner, you could be fairly certain a horse was the main picture of the puzzle. That is how I solve problems and do trouble-shooting in the livestock industry. I look for little clues and small details that can be put together to form a new theory.

When I was a child I used specific-to-general thinking to form concepts. I was able to figure out that dachshunds and cats were different animals even though they were the same size. I observed that all dogs, regardless of size, had the same type of nose. I found a common detail that was on all the dogs, and none of the cats had a dog nose.

In Jefferson's case, specifioto-general thinking is what made Monticello such a masterpiece of architecture. Ask anyone to draw a floor plan for a house, and that person will start with a square or rectangle. Not Jefferson. He thought first about natural light and windows, so his plan made use of other shapes such as half-octagons. He pieced them into a functional and aesthetic whole.

When planning the University of Virginia Jefferson went far beyond laying out a campus. He was concerned with who, specifically, would be teaching, what they would teach, exactly where in the university that would be done, how the students would be quartered, and even what their off-hour rules of conduct should be. The University of Virginia was another of Jefferson's expressions of specific-to-general thinking.

Genius Is an Abnormality

In my book *Thinking in Pictures* I stated that genius may be an abnormality. People who are very social and emotional are not going to be willing to spend all their time away from other people to invent new technologies or write complex documents fundamental to our democracy. Civilization would probably pay a terrible price if the genes that cause autism and Asperger's Syndrome were eradicated. The world might become a place full of highly social yakkity-yaks who would never do anything new or creative.

I hypothesize that it takes a lot of computing space in the brain to accommodate fancy circuits linking the emotion circuits with the frontal cortex and all the data files. The frontal cortex is where the executive function of the brain is located. In order to get speed to process complex rapid social information, the brain may have to sacrifice consideration of all the details. Brain scan studies show that in people with autism and Asperger's some of the circuits that would ordinarily link the frontal cortex to the amygdala, which is the brain's emotion center, are not hooked up.[1]

People on the autism-Asperger's continuum are forced to use problem-solving circuits in social situations. This makes them socially awkward, but perhaps it frees more brain circuits for pure reasoning and a greater attention to detail. To handle social situations I have to use pre-rehearsed and memorized responses.

Research is showing that the beautiful and precise drawings such as Jefferson's design layouts and the phenomenal memory of autistic savants come from deep memory circuits and brain areas which cannot be fully accessed by the normal social/emotional person. German researchers have found that nonautistics who are good at calculating can learn to access those lower circuits.[2] People with frontotemporal lobe dementia, an Alzheimer-like disease that destroys the language centers, will reveal art talent. As the dementia progresses, the art work of the patients grows more detailed and realistic.[3] A businessman with no prior art talent drew pictures of animals that won art awards.

There is a whole layer of highly abstract emotional consciousness that I simply do not have. I do not understand purely abstract thought. I only understand pictures, details, and facts. I can find common denominators and basic principles in great piles of information. What is subconscious in most people is the part of the brain I use to think with. Language is used to narrate and describe the pictures I see in my imagination, or it is used to download prerecorded mental audio tapes that have been well rehearsed.

Allan Snyder and John Mitchell at the Australian National University hypothesize that autistic savants who can perform great feats of memory like the savant in the movie *Rain Man*, or like Jefferson's single-handedly cataloguing 6,860 books for the University of Virginia library, have privileged access to lower brain centers.[4] They can access memories stored in the primary cortical areas that most people cannot access directly. Brain scan data show that people with autism rely more on the visual parts of their brains than normal people.[5] Normals use their frontal cortex when they do a task such as finding a hidden figure in a picture.

Being on the autism-Asperger's continuum provided Jefferson with the ability to have a tremendous breadth of knowledge on many subjects. Recently I attended a lecture on Asperger's by Simon Baron-

Cohen from the University of Cambridge in England. He has studied and interviewed many brilliant people with Asperger's. It is likely that many physicists and computer programmers with talents similar to Jefferson's are on the autism-Asperger s continuum.

A detail in the Ledgin manuscript that really caught my attention was that Jefferson preferred to sit at his desk and write quietly rather than debate in public. I, too, would rather sit quietly and write. Looking at much detailed information and making sense of it requires a great amount of time. While being on the autism-Asperger s continuum is a handicap in the social world, it is an advantage if you are doing work where details are important, for your social deficits free you to attend to time-consuming detailed examination. Furthermore, specific-to-general thinking is a great advantage when one is making a detailed objective analysis of the facts. In my field I have developed a reputation for being totally objective. I look at all the details, and I do not rely on emotion to make judgments.

A Developmental Disorder

Autism and Asperger's Syndrome are neurological disorders that a child is born with. Brain autopsy studies and imaging studies now show clearly that some parts of the brain are underdeveloped and immature and other parts are normal or possibly overdeveloped. The amygdala (emotion center) and the cerebellum—which is involved in movement and the timing of activities of different parts of the brain—are both underdeveloped.[6]

Autism and Asperger's Syndrome are on a continuum from normal to abnormal. Many people with Asperger's appear to others as totally normal. Moreover, there is no black-and-white dividing line between normal and abnormal. Many scientists agree that Asperger's Syndrome is just a milder variant on the autism spectrum. When I was three years old I had obviously abnormal behavior. I did not speak, and I threw constant tantrums. The Asperger's child may not have totally normal speech development, but it is normal enough that parents are not seeking out doctors and special educators when the child is only three. The typical Asperger's child is recognized in third or fourth grade because at that point he has no friends and he may be teased. When does mildly-eccentric turn into Asperger's Syndrome? It is a matter of degree. It's like asking, When does good math ability turn into genius level?

The severity of autism is highly variable. Autism ranges from high-functioning with an advanced college degree to completely nonverbal and handicapped. I just cannot emphasize enough that autism and Asperger's Syndrome are on a continuum from normal to abnormal.

Research has shown that there is a strong genetic basis to autism. I noticed Ledgin believes Jefferson's autism may have been passed down through his mother's family, the Randolphs. In such a hereditary process it is likely that several different genes are involved.[7] It is not inherited in a simple manner like blue eyes or blond hair.

I have had the opportunity to know hundreds of close relatives of autistic and Asperger's children and adults. When I talk to these family members it becomes obvious that the traits of autism and Asperger's Syndrome can be found among them as well in a milder form. It is common for the father to be a brilliant computer programmer or an aloof doctor with a poor bedside manner. One father I met had a small high-tech firm that developed specialized graphics programs. He was definitely Asperger's himself, and several of his employees were probably Asperger's. The children in these families will often have autism, Asperger's Syndrome, or some other learning difficulty. Intellectual giftedness is another trait which is often observed in these families. Some researchers have speculated that a little bit of the autism trait may provide an advantage, and too much will cause a severe handicap.

Depression is a disorder of too much emotion. Why would a disorder of too much emotion be in the family history of people who have an underdeveloped emotion center in the brain? Maybe the same genetic mechanisms affect the *degree* of emotion. Dr. John Ratey in his book *The Shadow Syndromes* (1998) provides many examples showing that depression and other disorders are on a continuum from normal to abnormal.

There are two kinds of autistic-Asperger's thought. Some who are affected are visual thinkers like me, and others are numbers and word thinkers. Both types concentrate on the details instead of the overall concept. Visual thinkers like me and visual thinkers like Jefferson are good at building things and good at mechanical design. The nonvisual detail thinkers are good at accounting and mathematics. Both types have enormous memory. People on the autism-Asperger's continuum have more memory for detail than most others.

People also think in many different ways. Once I was interviewed by a woman connected with a radio station who was totally a verbal thinker. Many verbal people are highly social and emotional. They excel in social situations. In fact there is a syndrome that is just the opposite of autism and Asperger's. It is called William's syndrome.[8] People who have William's are very verbal, emotional, and social but they have a small memory. Study of the brain indicates that their visual cortex is underdeveloped.[9]

People who are verbal thinkers have the advantage of being able to think and process information very rapidly. The disadvantage is that their analysis of the information may be superficial and shallow and based on emotion. The person on the autism-Asperger's continuum has the advantage of analyzing information in great detail, but the thinking process is very slow. I must bring each picture out of memory and put it on the "computer monitor" in my imagination to look at and compare and contrast with other information. This kind of thinking is an advantage for doing technical or design work, but it is a real handicap in a social situation. In a social situation one has to process information that changes rapidly.

My own family history is typical of the problem. On my mother's side of the family my grandfather was an engineer who was co-inventor of the automatic pilot that guides airplanes. I also have a second and third cousin who are a NASA space engineer and a mathematician. Other traits on my mother's side are visual thinking, anxiety disorder, and depression. It is common for anxiety and depression to be present in the family histories of autism and Asperger's.[10] On my father's side there is Asperger's with nonvisual thinking and ability with numbers. As one consequence our family was known for the "Grandin temper."

All my thoughts are in pictures. People who think in words find this difficult to understand. I reply that it is like seeing videotapes in my head. My mind works just like an Internet web browser. If I punch in, mentally, a key word such as "peaches," I start seeing very specific images of peaches. A picture of eating fresh peaches at my grandmother's house pops up. I then see a can of peaches I ate when I was little. The next image is eating peaches in a car on a trip and getting sick from eating too many of them.

Visual thinking is associative thinking. If I hold the picture of being at grandmother's house up on the "computer monitor in my brain," I then get other associations of being at grandmother's. I remember the day of the great apple fight on the back stairs and getting in trouble for exploring all the neat old stuff that was up in the attic. Each one of these events pops into my consciousness like a photo. If I hold the "photo" up and look, it will turn into a full-motion video.

Being able to see full-motion video in my head is a great asset for an equipment designer like me. I can test-run equipment in my head. I used to think that everybody could test-run equipment in their heads. I did not know it was a special skill until I interviewed many people about how they think, and I learned that most people only get vague still pictures in their heads.

I was also shocked to learn that there are some people who have no visual thinking at all. I spent the night with a nice lady who was a speech therapist. That night I learned that she lived in a world of completely verbal thought. I asked her if she could walk through her university office in her mind. Most people would see a picture of their offices in their imagination. She just verbally described where things were. In her own house she could not see her dining room in her head. She said only that it was to the left of the kitchen. Her husband remarked to her, "The camera is turned off in your head."

I can be very good at public speaking, although you may wonder how that can be. When I lecture I am actually downloading files I already have in my brain. The thinking which would ordinarily take much time has already been done. But debating on the floor of a legislature, on the other hand, would be difficult. That would require too much time for me to search memory files and analyze new data quickly. Obviously that is why John Adams observed that Thomas Jefferson was extraordinarily quiet during proceedings of the Continental Congress. Later, while isolating himself a few days, Jefferson completed his draft of the Declaration of Independence.

Today I am on the faculty in the Department of Animal Science at Colorado State University. I teach classes on cattle behavior and the design of handling facilities. My job at the university is part-time. The rest of my time I consult with the livestock industry on the design of cattle and pig-handling systems. About a quarter of my time is spent lecturing on my experiences with autism all over the United States and in other countries. I have written two books to describe my experiences, *Thinking in Pictures* and *Emergence: Labelled Autistic*.[11] Now, as a result of this discovery about Thomas Jefferson, I take satisfaction from realizing I have something in common with a Founding Father.

Notes:

1   Baron-Cohen, S., Ring, H.A., Wheelright, S., Bullmore, E.T., Brammer, M.J., Simmons, A. and Williams, S.C. 1999. Social intelligence in the normal and autistic brain: an MRI study, *European Journal of Neuroscience*, 11:1891-1898; Hazneder, M.M., Buchsbaum, M.S., Metzger, M., Solimando, A., Spiegal-Cohen, J. and Hollander, E. 1997. Anterior cingulate volume and glucose metabolism in autistic disorder, *American Journal of Psychiatry*, 154:1047-1050.

2   Birbaumer, N. 1999. Rainman's Revelations, *Nature*, 399:211-212.

3   Miller, R.L., Cummings, J., Mishkin, E, Boone, K., Prince, E, Ponton, M. and Cotman, C. 1998. Emergence of artistic talent in frontotemporal dementia, *Neurology*, 51:978-982.

4   Snyder, A.W and Mitchell, J.D. 1999. Is integer arithmetic fundamental to mental processing?: the mind's secret arithmetic. *Proceedings*, Royal Society of London.

5   Ring, H.A., Baron-Cohen, S., Wheelright, S., Williams, S.C, Brammer, M., Andrew, C. and Bullmore, E.T. 1999. Cerebral correlates of preserved cognitive skills in autism: a functional MRI study of embedded figures task performance, *Brain*, 122:1305-1315.

6   Bauman, M.L. 1991. Microscopic neuroanatomic abnormalities in autism, *Pediatrics*, 87:791-796; Kemper, T.L., and Bauman, M.L. 1998. Neuropathology of infantile autism, *Journal of Experimental Neurology*, 57:645-652.

7   Szatmari, P. 1999. Heterogeneity and the genetics of autism, *Journal of Psychiatry and Neuroscience*, 24:159-165.

8   Tager-Flusberg, H., Boshart, J. and Baron-Cohen, S. 1998. Reading the windows of the soul: evidence of domain specific sparing in William's syndrome, *Journal of Cognitive Neuroscience*, 10:631-639; Bellugi, U., Lichtenburger, L., Mills, D., Galaburda, A., and Korenberg, J.R. 1999. Bridging cognition, the brain and molecular genetics: evidence from William's syndrome, *Trends in Neuroscience*, 22:197-207.

9   Bellugi et al., *op. cit.*

10 Delong, G.R., and Dwyer, J.T. 1988. Correlation of family history with specific autism subgroups: Asperger's Syndrome and bipolar affective disorder, *Journal of Autism and Developmental Disorders*, 18:593-600; Piven, J., and Palmer, P. 1999. Psychiatric disorder and the broad autism phenotype: evidence from family study of multiple incidence autism families, *American Journal of Psychiatry*, 156:5 57-563.

11 Grandin, T. 1995. *Thinking in Pictures*, Doubleday, New York. Now published by Vintage Press, Random House, New York; Grandin, T., and Scariano, M. 1986. *Emergence: Labelled Autistic*, Warner Books, New York.

APPENDIX ONE

100 Topics

The following is a sampling of subjects in which Thomas Jefferson made notations or written comments of varying lengths, demonstrating either his practical interests or those of a literary, architectural, scientific, or political nature. In many of these instances he betrayed his fixations—attention to subjects in which he seemed overfocused to a degree strongly characteristic of an Asperger's condition. Such a practice was compounded by his occasionally presenting information in great detail that was of no apparent interest to anyone but himself.

This list is far short of completeness in representing all subjects of Jefferson's writings or chartings. Selected topics are offered here in capsule reference to show the breadth of interests to which he contributed observations, knowledge, logic, speculation, opinions, proposals, or sketches accompanied by detailed instructions.

Where the work appeared typical of the detail-oriented mind of a high-functioning autistic person, or as a fixation of Jefferson's—or where it seemed to have been elaborated by him more than was necessary and in a way characteristic of Asperger's behavior—I added this symbol after the bold-faced heading: [#]

Some may view the list also as a graphic clue that an important identification is often omitted from lists of Jefferson's talents—that of simply "writer" (not far from his epitaphic self-designation of "author"). Writing was an activity for which he maintained an obvious compulsion—to be productive in it at every opportunity, to be thorough, and to find relaxation. His written efforts at humor and homily, poetry and punditry were in a range comparable to that of present-day columnists and essayists, and the largest portion of his writing went into letters.

Agriculture [#].
Jefferson detailed procedures of crop rotation as a means of obtaining maximum yield from his lands. Jefferson to John Taylor, December 29,1794, *Thomas Jefferson: Writings*, Merrill D. Peterson, editor (New York: The Library of America, 1984), 1018-22.

American character.
He covered virtues and vices to be found from north to south. A traveler in America "may always know his latitude by the character of the people among whom he finds himself." Jefferson to the Marquis de Chastellux, September 2, 1785, *Writings*, 826-28.

I will give you my idea of the characters of the several states.

In the North they are:	In the South they are:
cool	fiery
sober	voluptuary
laborious	indolent
persevering	unsteady
independant	independant
jealous of their own liberties and just to those of others	zealous for their own liberties, but trampling on those of others
interested	generous
chicaning	candid
superstitious and hypocritical in their religion	without attachment or pretensions to any religion but that of the heart

American revolution.

Jefferson recounted the political events in which he was involved before and during the period of separation from Great Britain—in an autobiography he undertook at age seventy-seven and soon abandoned. *Autobiography, Writings*, 5-54. See also Jefferson's corrections of other accounts of the period in his letter to Samuel Adams Wells, May 12,1819, *Writings*, 1417-22.

Architecture [#].

A Roman relic in France, the Maison Carree, became for Jefferson (obsessively) the standard he proposed for the capital at Richmond. Jefferson to James Madison, September 20,1785; to William Buchanan and James Hay, January 26,1786; to Madame de Tesse, March 20, 1787, *Writings*, 828-30, 845-48, 891-93.

> Here I am, Madam (deTesse), gazing whole hours at the Maison quarree, like a lover at his mistress. The stocking weavers and silk spinners around it, consider me as a hypochondriac Englishman, about to write with a pistol, the last chapter of his history. This is the second time I have been in love since I left Paris. The first was with a Diana at the Chateau de Laye-Epinaye in Beaujolois, a delicious morsel of sculpture, by M.A. Slodtz. This, you will say, was a rule, to fall in love with a female beauty: but with a house!

Aristocracy, natural and artificial.

The natural aristocracy was said to be based in "virtue and talents," the artificial in "wealth and birth." Jefferson saw the former "as the most precious gift of nature for the instruction, the trusts, and government of society." The latter was a "mischievous ingredient in government." Jefferson to John Adams, October 28, 1813, *Writings*, 1304-10.

> I think the best remedy is exactly that provided by all our constitutions, to leave to the citizens the free election and separation of the aristoi from the pseudo-aristoi, of the wheat from the chaff. In general they will

elect the real good and wise. In some instances, wealth may corrupt, and birth blind them; but not in sufficient degree to endanger the society....

A constitution has been acquired which, tho neither of us think perfect, yet both consider as competent to render our fellow-citizens the happiest and the securest on whom the sun has ever shone. If we do not think exactly alike as to it's imperfections, it matters little to our country which, after devoting to it long lives of disinterested labor, we have delivered over to our successors in life, who will be able to take care of it, and of themselves.

Aviary
He described a large bird coop kept by a merchant in Amsterdam. *Writings*, 630-31.

Birds of Virginia [#].
His extensive list included their Linnaean designations. *Notes on the State of Virginia, Query VI, Writings*, 193-97.

Brickmaking.
Jefferson drew detailed specifications for bricks and mortar. They involved requirements for earth, lime, water, procedures for the molding of bricks and the firing, costs, weight of finished bricks, labor, and production outcomes. *The Garden and Farm Books of Thomas Jefferson*, Robert C. Baron, editor. (Golden, Colo.: Fulcrum, 1987), 352-53.

Burial place.
Jefferson's elaborate initial plans for the cemetery at Monticello showed a high regard for letting nature ease bereavement. His earliest recorded interest in English gardens appeared here (December, 1771), as well as epitaphic tributes he composed and borrowed. The subsequent layout of the family graveyard was a modification if not a substitution for his early plan. *Jefferson's Memorandum Books*, James A. Bear, Jr., and Lucia C. Stanton, editors—two volumes (Princeton, N.J.: Princeton University Press, 1997), 1:245-50.

Thin the trees. Cut out stumps and undergrowth. Remove old trees and other rubbish except where they may look well. Cover the whole with grass. Intersperse Jesamine, honeysuckle, sweetbriar, and even hardy flowers which may not require attention. Keep in it deer, rabbits, Peacocks, Guinea poultry, pidgeons &c. Let it be an asylum for hares, squirrels, pheasants, partridges and every other wild animal (except those of prey.) Court them to it by laying food for them....Inscriptions in various places on the bark of trees or metal plates, suited to the character or expression of the particular spot. Benches or seats of rock or turf passim.

Climate and nature [#].

Here he gave vital statistics of Virginia—temperatures, rainfall, wind directions, and the first appearance of blooms, insects, and birds, the data "reduced to a mean at this place" (Monticello). Jefferson to Jacob Bigelow, *Garden and Farm Books*, 206-7. He tracked wind directions two or three times a day, averaged rain accumulations, and offered low and high temperatures representing thousands of measurements over five years (1772-77) in order to design a month-to-month reference table. *Notes, VII, Writings*, 201.

Coinage, weights, and measures [#].

Jefferson as Secretary of State proposed uniformity of weights and measures to the U.S. House of Representatives and based the plan wholly in scientific and mathematical principles. *Writings*, 393-415. Reprised in Jefferson to Dr. Robert Patterson, November 10, 1811, *Writings*, 1250-58.

Condensation effects [#].

He compared factors of humidity in homes of brick or stone in detail with those of wood. *Notes, XV, Writings*, 279-80.

Constitution for the United States.

He praised and criticized efforts of the Constitutional Convention. The criticism was primarily for failure (so far) to provide for a bill of rights. Jefferson to James Madison, December 20, 1787. *Writings*, 914-18.

> I like much the general idea of framing a government which should go on of itself peaceably, without needing continual recurrence to the state legislatures. I like the organization of the government into Legislative, Judiciary & Executive....There are other good things of less moment. I will now add what I do not like. First the omission of a bill of rights providing clearly & without the aid of sophisms for freedom of religion, freedom of the press, protection against standing armies, restriction against monopolies, the eternal & unremitting force of the habeas corpus laws, and trials by jury....Let me add that a bill of rights is what the people are entitled to against every government on earth, general or particular, & what no just government should refuse, or rest on inferences.

Constitution for Virginia [#].

Jefferson drew a proposal for "new-modelling the form of Government" for the Virginia Legislature in 1776. *Writings*, 336-45. He wrote comments forty years later for reforming the state constitution through more direct democracy. ("I am not among those who fear the people.") Jefferson to Samuel Kercheval, July 12, 1816, *Writings*, 1395-1403.

Cotton.

Jefferson had questions about the efficiency, maintenance, output, and availability—even the cost-benefit—of a new invention, the cotton gin. Jefferson to Eli Whitney, November 16, 1793, *Garden and Farm Books*, 186-87.

Crime and punishment [#].

He drew a comprehensive proposal outlining a detailed criminal code for consideration by the Virginia Legislature. *Writings*, 349-64.

Currency [#].

He recorded changes in money values by month for Pennsylvania,

New Jersey, and Virginia for five years of financial uncertainty during the revolution, 1777-81. *Memorandum Books*, 1:514-16.

Distance measurements [#].

Jefferson recorded miles between stops (as measured by an odometer), the elapsed time, and other notations in a carriage ride from Philadelphia to Monticello September 3-12, 1791. *Memorandum Books*, 2:835.

> These measures were on the belief that the wheel of the Phaeton made exactly 360 revolutions in a mile, but on measuring it accurately at the end of the journey it's circumference was 14 feet, 10 1/2 inches and consequently made 354.95 revolutions in a mile. These numbers should be greater then in the proportion of 71:72 or a mile added to every 71.

Doubts on race.

Jefferson seemed hopeful that he might, on the basis of a second look and broader consideration beyond the "limited sphere" of Virginia, recant his early views about unequal intellectual potential between races. Jefferson to Henri Gregoire, February 25, 1809, *Writings*, 1202.

> Be assured that no person living wishes more sincerely than I do, to see a complete refutation of the doubts I have myself entertained and expressed on the grade of understanding allotted to them by nature, and to find that in this respect they (black persons) are on a par with ourselves.

Dung.

He described precise mixing of dung into the ground for best results, along with preferred positioning of livestock for natural fertilizing. He outlined standards for determining ground acid content. *Garden and Farm Books*, 332-33.

Elevators [#].

Jefferson made a detailed examination of principles of mechanical "elevators, conveyers, and hopper-boys" and questioned whether anything unique since ancient times was truly involved in newer modifications. Jefferson to Isaac McPherson, August 13, 1813, *Writings*, 1286-94.

English gardens and landscaping.
He described a detailed plan for the layout and contents of an English garden at Monticello. Jefferson to William Hamilton, July, 1806, *Writings*, 1166-69. For a more detailed examination of plans actually put in place, first on a small scale at his Paris dwelling and later at Monticello, see Jack McLaughlin, *Jefferson and Monticello: The Biography of a Builder* (New York: Henry Holt and Company, 1988) (pb), 339-48, 353-56.

English prosody [#].
He prepared an analysis of poetry for the Marquis de Chastellux, using precise factors of accent and rhythm and offering opinions about their effects. Jefferson relied on Greek models to make his point. *Writings*, 593-622. (See excerpt used in Chapter Six.)

Etiquette (with canons).
Jefferson proposed rules of conduct for officials, *Writings*, 705, and for everybody, Jefferson to Thomas Jefferson Smith, February 21, 1825, *Writings*, 1499-1500. A Decalogue of Canons for observation in practical life.
1. Never put off till to-morrow what you can do to-day.
2. Never trouble another for what you can do yourself.
3. Never spend your money before you have it.
4. Never buy what you do not want, because it is cheap; it will be dear to you.
5. Pride costs us more than hunger, thirst and cold.
6. We never repent of having eaten too little.
7. Nothing is troublesome that we do willingly.
8. How much pain have cost us the evils which have never happened.
9. Take things always by their smooth handle.
10. When angry, count ten, before you speak; if very angry, an hundred.

Female education.

Jefferson's response on this topic made him appear to be at sea, "a subject on which I have not thought much." Yet he made suggestions that seemed emancipating of women to a limited extent. They were in reality no more advanced in effect than would maintain "the order and economy of a house." That phrase defined a role that was acceptable to him (and his contemporaries) as a woman's "place." Jefferson to Nathaniel Burwell, March 14, 1818, *Writings*, 1411-13.

Fence [#].

He computed how much stone would be required to enclose 400 acres and how long it would take for "one hand" to lay it. *Garden and Farm Books*, 76.

Foreign commerce [#].

As Secretary of State Jefferson detailed exports and their principal European customers for the House of Representatives, with little or no benefit of consultants or staff. *Writings*, 435-48.

Free expression.

To combat Alien and Sedition Laws, Jefferson relied on interposition —a tenuous stand that places states' rights ahead of powers of the United States—in order to show in "Kentucky Resolutions" that restrictions on First Amendment rights and other freedoms were unconstitutional. *Writings*, 449-56. See also his position against book censorship in Jefferson to N.G. Dufief, April 19, 1814, *Writings*, 1333-35. (The book in question, "On the Creation of the World," a French work of a Monsieur de Becourt, disputed Newtonian philosophy with which Jefferson agreed and appeared also to have attacked religious dogma. Jefferson maintained that no person, cleric or layman, should intervene in its direct sale. Such intervention was evidently a local issue affecting the Philadelphia book dealer Dufief. "It is an insult to our citizens to question whether they are rational beings or not," Jefferson wrote, "and blasphemy against religion to suppose it cannot stand the test of truth and reason.")

Free press.
He emphasized the importance of newspapers' aiding in the formation of public opinion. Jefferson to Edward Carrington, January 16, 1787, *Writings*, 879-81.

> The basis of our governments being the opinion of the people, the very first object should be to keep that right; and were it left to me to decide whether we should have a government without newspapers or newspapers without a government, I should not hesitate a moment to prefer the latter.

See also Jefferson to Judge John Tyler, June 28, 1804, *Writings*, 1146-48.

French citizens' rights.
Jefferson "ventured" a draft of guarantees of French people's rights in a ten-point "charter" tailored to needs that he perceived from relevant contemporary circumstances. Jefferson to Rabout de St. Etienne, June 3, 1789, *Writings*, 954-56.

French revolution.
For a peak period of the political and revolutionary upheaval in France he chronicled (often as eyewitness) the acts of leaders and the masses. Autobiography, *Writings*, 78-79.

Fuel and light [#].
Jefferson described in brief detail the "Comparative expence of candles and lamps...which shews the advantage of oil," obviously on the basis of experimentation. *Garden and Farm Books*, 318.

Furniture design.
Blessed by the services of an in-house craftsman, John Hemings, and wishing to avoid the expense of stuffed furniture of the period,

Jefferson designed a number of tables, chests, chairs, and other items, many of them original for their functionalism. *McLaughlin*, 365-67

Governmental history [#].
He described charters dating to Queen Elizabeth I and efforts to establish constitutional government in Virginia. *Notes, XIII, Writings*, 235-55.

Grammar and etymology [#].
As a result of evidently detailed study, he offered recommendations for a practical evolution in language. "These are my visions on the improvement of the English language by a free use of its faculties." Jefferson to John Waldo, August 16, 1813, *Writings*, 1294-1300.

> ...retro-location
>
> re-location
>
> se-location
>
> sub-location
>
> super-location
>
> trans-location
>
> ultra-location
>
> Some of these compounds would be new; but all present distinct meanings, and the synonisms of the three languages (Greek, Latin, English) offer a choice of sounds to express the same meaning; add to this, that in some instances, usage has authorized the compounding an English root with a Latin preposition, as in de-place, dis-place, re-place. This example may suffice to show what the language would become, in strength, beauty, variety, and every circumstance which gives perfection to language, were it permitted freely to draw from all its legitimate sources.

See also Jefferson to the Hon. J. Evelyn Denison, Member of Parliament, November 9, 1825, *Writings*, 1502-5.

Historical bibliography [#].
Jefferson listed upwards of 200 documents by titles, descriptions, and dates of issue beginning in the year 1496 that would form the basis

for an accounting of the development of the Virginia colony and state. Notes, *XXIII, Writings*, 303-25.

Holistic medicine [#].

"I would wish the young practitioner...to be a watchful, but quiet spectator of the operations of nature," Jefferson wrote among his thoughts on illnesses, biochemistry, and a cautious application of healing arts. Jefferson to Dr. Caspar Wistar, June 21, 1807, *Writings*, 1181-85.

Hot-air balloons [#].

Jefferson gave an account (two months before he sailed for France) of principles of ballooning. He included a record of 1783 French ascents with descriptions, illustrations, lifting weights of the crafts, altitudes, and distances covered. Jefferson to Dr. Philip Turpin, April 28,1784, *Writings*, 794-97.

Indians (aborigines) [#].

He drew lists of native people's tribes, populations, sub-groups, and residence areas in Virginia and throughout the United States of his time. *Notes, XI, Writings*, 218-32.

Indian vocabularies
[# applicable to the research he described]

Jefferson had for years collected and compared key words of "about fifty" languages of native peoples. In shipment from Washington to Monticello the trunk containing the collection was stolen and later found to have been trashed and thrown into the James River. He maintained that significant words were common to "languages of the other quarters of the globe." Jefferson to Dr. Benjamin S. Barton, September 21,1809, *Writings*, 1212-13.

Injustices against (and eloquence of) Indians.

Jefferson traced circumstances leading to a 1774 retaliatory war by Mingo Chief Logan against whites, then quoted Logan's moving message to those assembled at the treatymaking for peace. *Memorandum Books*, 1:385-86.

International law [#].

At the request of President Washington, Secretary of State Jefferson analyzed treaties with 1793 France, without reliance on consultants, concluding they were "still binding, notwithstanding the change of government in France." *Writings*, 422-34.

Jesus [#].

The Jefferson Bible: The Life and Morals of Jesus of Nazareth (Boston: Beacon Press, 1989). Also Jefferson to Dr. Benjamin Rush, April 21, 1803, *Writings* 1122-26. See also Jefferson to John Adams, October 12, 1813, *Writings*, 1300-4, and Jefferson to William Short, August 4, 1820, *Writings*, 1435-40.

Justice system and criminal codes [#].

Jefferson evaluated the operation of Virginia's court system and the administration of laws for effects on the lives of citizens and slaves. He also presented here unfortunate opinions on race, which he wrote later he would be willing to recant. *Notes, XIV, Writings*, 256-75.

Kings.

Comparing "the regimen in raising kings" to the way people kept and bred animals, Jefferson concluded European regents had become "all body and no mind." He named twelve, of whom ten deserved to be called "fool," "idiot," "hog," or "really crazy." Only Catherine of Russia and her grandson, Alexander, escaped such judgment, but that line was "not yet worn out." Jefferson to Governor John Langdon, March 5, 1810, *Writings*, 1218-22.

Law practice.

Legal notations of Jefferson's law practice appeared throughout his earliest of *Memorandum Books*. They were listed in aggregates of cases or as scattered references. In many instances the entries included case details. *Memorandum Books*, Vol. 1.

Legal training [#].

He recommended a self-instructional regimen involving forty source books and time "for exercise and recreation, which are as necessary as reading: I will rather say more necessary, because health is worth more than learning." Jefferson to John Garland Jefferson, June 11, 1790, *Writings*, 966-68.

Lewis and Clark expedition [#].

Jefferson sent Meriwether Lewis instructions for his and William Clark's maintaining good relations with Indians, and for scientific observations he expected them to make while they sought a route to the Pacific. Jefferson to Meriwether Lewis, June 20, 1803, *Writings*, 1126-32.

> Your observations are to be taken with great pains & accuracy, to be entered distinctly, & intelligibly for others as well as yourself, to comprehend all the elements necessary, with the aid of the usual tables to fix the latitude & longitude of the places at which they were taken, & are to be rendered to the war office, for the purpose of having the calculations made concurrently by proper persons within the U.S. Several copies of these as well as of your other notes, should be made at leisure times & put into the care of the most trustworthy of your attendants, to guard by multiplying them against accidental losses to which they will be exposed. A further guard would be that one of these copies be written on the paper of the birch, as less liable to injury from damp than common paper.

Libraries [#].

He outlined the books every person should read and keep handy for well-rounded intellect: He drew a list of 147 works of fine arts, politics and trade, religion, law, ancient and modern history, philosophy, and natural history.   Jefferson to Robert Skipwith, August 3, 1771, *Writings,* 740-45. See also his approval of the notion of circulating libraries. Jefferson to John Wyche, May 19, 1809, *Writings,* 1207-8. And his proposal for replacing the Library of Congress, burned by the British, by the sale of his own collection. Jefferson to Samuel H. Smith, September 21, 1814, Writings, 1353-55. And his suggestions for cataloguing. Jefferson to George Watterston, May 7,1815, *Writings,* 1366-68.

Livestock [#].

He kept a census of stock, in certain cases by age and sex, and of slaughterings at Monticello-Tufton, Shadwell-Lego, and Poplar Forest, 1781-97. *Garden and Farm Books,* 252-54. Then at Monticello, Tufton, Lego, Poplar Forest, Bear Creek for the years 1809-20, 391-97. Other livestock data were scattered throughout the books.

Locusts [#].

By tracing recorded and remembered dates of locust appearances, Jefferson determined that Virginians were dealing with a recurring phenomenon of every seventeen years. *Memorandum Books,* 1:388.

Madison's books [#].

Ever the helpful mentor, Jefferson found in his European trip an opportunity to expand the library of the multi-lingual James Madison, whether or not by the latter s request. In a single shipment in two trunks, the works Jefferson listed numbered nearly fifty, some in multiple volumes. Jefferson to James Madison, September 1, 1785, *Writings,* 820-25.

Manufacturing

(as a means toward national economic self-reliance). Late in coming to this belief, Jefferson wrote, "We must now place the manufacturer by the side of the agriculturist...Experience has taught me that manufactures are now as necessary to our independence as to our comfort." Jefferson to Benjamin Austin, January 9, 1816, *Writings*, 1369-72.

Matches

From Paris he described "Phosphoretic matches" to James Madison. Jefferson to James Madison, November 11, 1784, *The Republic of Letters: The Correspondence Between Jefferson and Madison, 1776-1826*, James Morton Smith, editor—three volumes (New York: W.W. Norton & Company, 1995), 1:351.

> I will send them to you. These matches consist of a small wax taper, one end of which has been dipped in Phosphorus, and the whole is inclosed in a glass tube hermetically sealed. There is a little ring on the tube to shew where it is to be broken. First warm the phosphorized end (which is the furthest one from the ring) by holding it two or three seconds in your mouth, then snap it at or near the ring and draw the phosphorized end out of the tube. It blazes in the instant of it's extraction. It will be well always to decline the tube at an angle of about 45 degrees (the phosphorized end lowest) in order that it may kindle thoroughly. Otherwise though it blazes in the first instant it is apt to go out if held erect. These cost about 30 sous the dozen. By having them at your bedside with a candle, the latter may be lighted at any moment of the night without getting out of bed. By keeping them on your writing table, you may seal three or four letters with one of them, or light a candle if you want to seal more which in the summer is convenient. In the woods they supply the want of steel, flint and punk. Great care must be taken in extracting the taper that none of the phosphorus drops on your hand, because it is inextinguishable and will therefore burn to the bone if there be matter enough. It is said that urine will extinguish it.

Mechanical water flow [#].

Using Archimedean principles, Jefferson described and illustrated machinery he observed at Kew in England for automatic water recirculation. *Writings*, 627-28.

Militia [#].

By region and county he presented a table showing a count of manpower available to serve Virginia in 1780-81. Notes, IX, *Writings*, 215-16.

Music [#].

He made an offer to subsidize temporary resettlement here of Italians with dual talents—a practical skill or trade on the one hand and musicianship on the other, with a preference for players of wind instruments. Jefferson to Giovanni Fabbroni, June 8, 1778, *Writings*, 760 62.

Nailmaking [#].

Jefferson charted detailed weights and measures of nails for several American locations (because there was no agreed standard except British measures). He set out the weights and measures for his own nailery, as well as prices based partly on labor and materials, partly on market rates. *Garden and Farm Books*, 364-67.

Natural bridge

Jefferson's description of a rock phenomenon he visited for the first time August 23,1767—though reflecting some youthful awe—was detailed to evoke a visual image. By 1774 he was able to acquire the land in Rockbridge County on which the natural bridge rested. *Memorandum Books*, 1:38-39.

Natural history [#].

He prepared descriptions of North American animals for a French naturalist who doubted their relative importance. Jefferson to

Georges Buffon, October 1, 1787, *Writings*, 909-10. He also described items gathered by Lewis and Clark that he arranged to send to the Cabinet of Natural History, Paris. Jefferson to B.G.E. de la Ville Lacepede, July 14, 1808, *Writings*, 1189-92. And he commented, at times with the soul of a poet-philosopher, on classification. Jefferson to Dr. John Manners, February 22, 1814, *Writings*, 1329-33.

> Nature has, in truth, produced units only through all her works. Classes, orders, genera, species, are not of her work. Her creation is of individuals. No two animals are exactly alike; no two plants, nor even two leaves or blades of grass; no two crystallizations. And if we may venture from what is within the cognizance of such organs as ours, to conclude on that beyond their powers, we must believe that no two particles of matter are of exact resemblance. This infinitude of units or individuals being far beyond the capacity of our memory, we are obliged, in aid of that, to distribute them into masses, throwing into each of these all the individuals which have a certain degree of resemblance; to subdivide these again into smaller groups, according to certain points of dissimilitude observable in them, and so on until we have formed what we call a system of classes, orders, genera and species. In doing this, we fix arbitrarily on such characteristic resemblances and differences as seem to us most prominent and invariable in the several subjects, and most likely to take a strong hold in our memories.

Navigable rivers of Virginia and western areas [#].

He provided great detail about waterways that were then being relied on for local commerce, as well as rivers to the west that he believed would serve the expanding nation. *Notes, II, Writings*, 129-40.

Olive tree. He described the hardiness and nourishment value of the fruit of this "least known" tree in a letter to William Drayton from Paris, July 30, 1787, *Garden and Farm Books*, 181.

Organized religion.

Writing of Jesus as "the great reformer of the Jewish religion,"

Jefferson maintained "his principles were departed from by those who professed to be his special servants, and perverted into an engine for enslaving mankind, and aggrandising their oppressors in Church and State." Jefferson to Samuel Kercheval, January 19, 1810, *Writings*, 1213-15.

Paris weather [#].

Away from Virginia and prior to his trip abroad, Jefferson recorded high and low temperatures daily in Annapolis for several months. He resumed the practice in Paris and other European cities of his travels, June 9, 1785, through September 25, 1789. He added hygrometer (humidity) readings the final twelvemonths. *Memorandum Books*, 1:771-806.

Parliamentary practices [#].

Jefferson's Parliamentary Writings: "Parliamentary Pocket-Book" and A Manual of Parliamentary Practice. Wilbur Samuel Howell, editor. (Princeton, N.J.: Princeton University Press, 1988).

Personnel policies [#].

He detailed "articles for contracts" with plantation overseers as to pay, obligations, and even rules of conduct. He added rules governing laborers, together with some food allotment references. *Garden and Farm Books*, 326-27.

Piano tuning [#].

As with "everything mechanical that he owned," Jefferson mastered the workings of keyboard instruments and "tuned and repaired them." He corresponded with others about details of the mechanical maintenance of harpsichords. *McLaughlin*, 367-68.

Philadelphia temperatures [#].

Jefferson recorded precise times and temperatures, sometimes six measurements in a day, and weather comments for the Continental capital in the summer of 1776. He resumed the practice in the fall at Monticello and at Williamsburg. *Memorandum Books*, 1:432-35. Resumed in Philadelphia (and trips home to Monticello) with hygrometer readings January 1, 1791, and continued until March 11, 1794. *Memorandum Books*, 2:841-60.

Planting of grapevines [#].

Jefferson described precisely the elaborate planting procedure followed by Tuscan vineyardists who were directed by his friend Philip Mazzei at Monticello. *Garden and Farm Books*, 65.

Plows [#].

"The awkward figure of their mould-board," Jefferson wrote in observations of plows used near Nancy in France, "leads one to consider what should be its form." He then drew and described modifications. *Writings*, 650-51.

Population [#].

He traced the growth of Virginia over a period of 175 years. *Notes, VIII, Writings*, 209-14. He gave attention also to population theories of Thomas Malthus, which he called "sound logic." Jefferson to Dr. Joseph Priestley, January 29,1804, and to Jean Baptiste Say, February 1, 1804, *Writings*.

Potash [#].

He presented details for the making of potash, used in fertilizer and soapmaking. He directed the reader from the tree-cutting stage of the process to data about the worth of potash on the market. *Garden and Farm Books*, 371.

Public schools [#].

Jefferson sketched in legislative form a Virginia system for the establishment, geographical placement, administration, staffing, curricula, and operation of schools in "A Bill for the More General Diffusion of Knowledge." He was ambiguous about the system's funding, but he stipulated that children of poor families should be educated "at the common expence of all." *Writings*, 365-73.

> ...it becomes expedient for promoting the publick happiness that those persons, whom nature hath endowed with genius and virtue, should be rendered by liberal education worthy to receive, and able to guard the sacred deposit of the rights and liberties of their fellow citizens, and that they should be called to that charge without regard to wealth, birth or other accidental condition or circumstance; but the indigence of the greater number disabling them from so educating, at their own expence, those of their children whom nature hath fitly formed and disposed to become useful instruments for the public, it is better that such should be sought for and educated at the common expence of all, than that the happiness of all should be confided to the weak or wicked.

Quadrupeds of Europe and America [#].
He recorded the aboriginal species, many of them by weights, for both the North American and European continents. -*Notes, VI, Writings*, 165-82.

Reconciliation of friendship.
Jefferson saw the break with John Adams over political differences as "disgraceful" and "indicating minds not sufficiently elevated to prevent a public competition from affecting our personal friendship." Jefferson to Dr. Benjamin Rush, January 16, 1811, *Writings*, 1234-39. See also a reminder of their "laboring at the same oar" in Jefferson to John Adams, January 21, 1812, *Writings*, 1258-60.

Refrigeration [#].
Jefferson prepared precise instructions in 1802 for building and maintaining an ice house at Monticello. The facility was sixteen feet

into the ground, eight in diameter, and lined with a stone wall that extended four feet aboveground, with a side access door and a wooden top covered with earth-insulation. He also devised a tube-and-bucket apparatus to draw out the water of melted ice. *McLaughlin*, 296, 301.

Religious freedom [#].

Jefferson argued that the ten commandments and other religious tenets failed to qualify as common law. He used supporting excerpts from his common-place book in a detailed letter on religious freedom to Dr. Thomas Cooper, February 10, 1814, *Writings*, 1321-29. His bill to guarantee church-state separation in Virginia was a work of which he was very proud. *Writings*, 346-48.

Road building [#].

He kept a diary of road work at and near Monticello to show grades, dimensions, labor including average yards of earth moved per man, duration of project, and other details. *Garden and Farm Books*, 314-15.

School of botany [#].

About two months before he died Jefferson proposed establishment of, and resources for, botanical studies at the University of Virginia. Jefferson to Dr. John P. Emmet, April 27, 1826. *Garden and Farm Books*, 210-11.

Scientific phenomena [#].

His observations ranged from chemistry, both organic and inorganic, to the origin of rainbows. Jefferson to the Rev. James Madison (the teacher, not the statesman), July 19, 1788, *Writings*, 923-27.

Servants (slaves) [#].

Jefferson kept a roll by name and year of birth of house servants, tradesmen, and those serving separate farms. He mixed the lists with work schedules as well as with related and unrelated accounts and chartings. He updated the servant rolls periodically to show distributions of blankets, clothing, and other materials. *Garden and Farm Books*, 382-485. See also *Memorandum Books*.

Sheep breeding [#].
He described the propagation and yield of three varieties of sheep. Jefferson to William Caruthers, March 12, 1813. *Garden and Farm Books*, 201. And to bypass the greedy practices of sheep traders, Jefferson proposed distributing Merinos in every county of Virginia. Jefferson to James Madison, May 13, 1810, *Writings*, 1223-25.

Ships in dry dock [#].
Jefferson proposed the imitation of practices he observed in Europe for keeping naval vessels in dry dock. This was intended to protect the investment in ships as well as keep them in readiness. Jefferson to Benjamin H. Latrobe, November 2, 1802, *Writings*, 1108-9.

Slavery and emancipation.
The letter to Edward Coles must be read in its entirety for best understanding. He never surrendered his belief that a way could be found to end both the slave trade and the practice of slavery. Jefferson to Edward Coles, August 25, 1814, *Writings*, 1343-46. And for an end to slavery by deportation to a friendlier environment, Jefferson to Jared Sparks, February 4, 1824, *Writings*, 1484-87.

Spinning, weaving [#].
His proposal for home manufacture of woven materials included work schedules, raw materials, output by fabric type, costs, and other details. *Garden and Farm Books*, 370.

Supreme Court [#].
He challenged Chief Justice John Marshall's rationale for judicial

review. Jefferson to Judge Spencer Roane, September 6, 1819, *Writings*, 1425-28.

> The constitution, on this hypothesis, is a mere thing of wax in the hands of the judiciary, which they may twist and shape into any form they please. It should be remembered, as an axiom of eternal truth in politics, that whatever power in any government is independent, is absolute also; in theory only, at first, while the spirit of the people is up, but in practice, as fast as that relaxes. Independence can be trusted nowhere but with the people in mass.

And to Justice William Johnson, June 12, 1823, *Writings*, 1469-77.

Taxidermy [#].

Only a few days after his wife died, he described a procedure for gutting and then stuffing and preserving a bird. *Garden and Farm Books*, 81.

Terracing [#].

Jefferson described in detail an erosion-reducing method for leveling hillsides into horizontal steps. He credited the plan to his son-in-law, Thomas Mann Randolph. Jefferson to Tristran Dalton, May 2, 1817, *Garden and Farm Books*, 204-5. (Also in *Writings*, 1405-6.)

Tories.

Jefferson penned a cutting description of "anti-republicans" in response to a foreign professor's critical observations of American politics in 1795. *Writings*, 697-701. The Anti-republicans consist of

1. The old refugees and tories.
2. British merchants residing among us, & composing the main body of our merchants.
3. American merchants trading on British capital. Another great portion.
4. Speculators & Holders in the banks and public funds.
5. Officers of the federal government with some exceptions.
6. Office-hunters, willing to give up principles for places. A numerous & noisy tribe.

7. Nervous persons, whose languid fibres have more analogy with a passive than active state of things.

The Republican part of our Union comprehends

1. The entire body of landholders throughout the United States.
2. The body of labourers, not being landholders, whether in husbanding or the arts.

Trees, plants, and fruits of Virginia [#].

He offered a comprehensive list of the state's natural and best-cultivated flora and produce, including Linnaean designations. *Notes, VI, Writings*, 160-65.

Unitarianism.

Applauding the Unitarian creed, he feared its believers would be lured toward the kind of formalism that had affected other denominations. Jefferson to Dr. Benjamin Waterhouse, June 26, 1822, *Writings*, 1458-59.

University of Virginia [#].

He drew a plan for curricula, student entrance qualifications, student accommodations, the organization of administration and faculty, and the relationship between public education at lower levels and that at the college level. *Writings*, 457-73. A predecessor outline appeared in Jefferson to Peter Carr, September 7, 1814, *Writings*, 1346-52. And for a defense of the exclusion of religious instruction, Jefferson to Dr. Thomas Cooper, November 2, 1822, *Writings*, 1463-65.

Vegetable calendars [#].

Following his retirement from the Presidency, Jefferson prepared charts annually to mark places and dates of planting and transplanting dozens of types of garden vegetables and herbs, noting also when they came to table and offering other observations. *Garden and Farm Books*, 95-170.

Vocational training.

He proposed the use of government lands near the frontier settlement of Detroit to accommodate a school and farm where young native people could be trained in domestic and agricultural skills. Jefferson to James Madison, December 7, 1809, *Republic*, 3:1611-13.

Warships [#].

His 1807 message to Congress included naval design and deployment details. *Writings*, 539-42. Also, Jefferson to Robert Fulton, August 16,1807, *Writings*, 1185-86, and Jefferson to James Madison, May 21, 1813, *Republic*, 3:1719-21.

Washington [#].

Jefferson wrote a valuable account of the political relationship he had as Secretary of State with President George Washington in the 1818 work, "The Anas," (loosely meaning "revisit"), *Writings*, 661-90. For valuable comments upon Washington's character see Jefferson to Dr. Walter Jones, January 2, 1814, *Writings*, 1317-21.

> His mind was great and powerful, without being of the very first order; his penetration strong, though not so acute as that of a Newton, Bacon, or Locke; and as far as he saw, no judgment was ever sounder. It was slow in operation, being little aided by invention or imagination, but sure in conclusion... He was incapable of fear, meeting personal dangers with the calmest unconcern. Perhaps the strongest feature in his character was prudence, never acting until every circumstance, every consideration, was maturely weighed... His integrity was most pure, his justice the most inflexible I have ever known, no motives of interest or consanguinity, of friendship or hatred, being able to bias his decision. He was, indeed, in every sense of the words, a wise, a good, and a great man. His temper was naturally high toned; but reflection and resolution had obtained a firm and habitual ascendency over it. If ever, however, it broke its bonds, he was most tremendous in his wrath... His heart was not warm in its affections; but he exactly calculated every man's value, and gave him a solid esteem proportioned to it...his col-

loquial talents were not above mediocrity, possessing neither copiousness of ideas, nor fluency of words. In public, when called on for a sudden opinion, he was unready, short and embarrassed...On the whole, his character was, in its mass, perfect...and it may truly be said, that never did nature and fortune combine more perfectly to make a man great...

Western territorial government [#].

Jefferson drafted a plan for temporary governance in areas where the nation was beginning to expand (by 1784). The plan included such place names as Sylvania, Michigania, Cherronesus, Assenisipia, Metropotamia, Illinoia, Saratoga, Washington, Polypotamia, and Pelisipia. *Writings*, 376-78.

Whale oil [#].

He provided a vast amount of detail about the sources and the qualities of various forms of whale oil and trade factors affecting them. The product was used in his day in manufacturing and as a principal lighting fuel. *Writings*, 379-92.

Wheels.

Jefferson described the making of wooden-wheel circumferences from a single piece, a custom among New Jersey farmers that he traced directly to a procedure described by the Greek poet Homer. A young sapling was cut, bent "while green and juicy" to form a circle, and left until seasoned. The work was not copied from English farmers, Jefferson argued, because "ours are the only farmers who can read Homer." Jefferson to St. John de Crevecoeur, January 15, 1787, *Writings*, 877-78.

Wine [#].

He offered details about how French Moselle wines were made, bottled, and sold in *Writings*, 637-38; of vineyards and the wine industry near Cologne and "Mayence" (Mainz) in Germany, 641-44, and of French winemaking generally, 653-58. See also a nearly two-years' accounting of his wine stocks in Paris, frequently showing costs. *Memorandum Books*, 1:807. And records of wines used and their costs during his Presidency. *Memorandum Books*, 2:1115-17.

Appendix Two

Selected Internet Resources

Following are websites about Thomas Jefferson and about Asperger's Syndrome. All contain links to other sites. Some "sub-links" are included where a specific web page on a host site is of special interest or importance. Any popular search engine (Altavista, Yahoo, Hotbot, Excite, Infoseek, Lycos, etc.) can also be used to find other sites. Occasionally web addresses (URLs) change or become obsolete.

Commercial or service references will appear on a few sites, but the listing of their host sites here is no endorsement.

This list of sites is by no means complete, for increased interest since the Sally Hemings confirmation has led to a burgeoning of material on the Internet in a number of topic areas relating to Jefferson.

Thomas Jefferson on the Web

General biographical/historical
http://www.monticello.org
Now includes a Hemings-Jefferson resource page.

http://www.monticello.org/foundation.html
Monticello, Jefferson's home, is owned and operated by the

Thomas Jefferson Memorial Foundation, a private, nonprofit organization whose twofold mission is preservation and education.

http://www.history.org/almanack.htm
Colonial Williamsburg Foundations Historical Almanack. The "Meet the People" link will take you to Thomas Jefferson, his family, and others.

http://www.liberty1.org
Historical information from the Institute for American Liberty, a nonprofit corporation established for educational and literary purposes.

http://etext.lib.virginia.edu/jefferson/icjs/
International Center for Jefferson Studies.

http://www.pbs.org/jefferson/
http://www.pbs.org/wgbh/pages/frontline/shows/jefferson
About the PBS-TV presentations, *Thomas Jefferson and Jefferson's Blood.*

http://www.nps.gov/thje/index2.htm
The Thomas Jefferson Memorial in Washington, D.C.

Jefferson's Architecture and Inventions
http://www.bc.edu/bc_org/avp/cas/fnart/fa267/jeffersn.html
Description of the architectural expression and style of Thomas Jefferson.
http://jefferson.village.virginia.edu/wilson/catalogs/catalog.html
Catalog of Jefferson's drawings.

http://www.poplarforest.org/history.html
Story of the octagonal-shaped retreat that Jefferson designed, which is located near Lynchburg, Va.

Jefferson's Writings

http://memory.loc.gov.ammem/mtjhtml/mtjhome.html
The complete Jefferson papers from the Library of Congress Manuscript Division. Approximately 27,000 documents including correspondence, commonplace books, financial account books, and manuscript volumes.

http://lcweb.loc.gov/exhibits/treasures/trt001.html
Evolution of the Declaration of Independence from its original draft by Jefferson to the text adopted by the Continental Congress.

http://www.h-net.msu.edu/reviews/showrev.cgi?
path=20551896221096
Online scholarly review of Jefferson's *Memorandum Books*— accounts, legal records, and miscellany—edited by James A. Bear, Jr., and Lucia C. Stanton. The two-volume work published in 1997 covers the period 1767 to 1826.

Relationship with Sally Hemings

http://www.discoverrichmond.com/pages/bhistory/1999/
hemings.shtml
A Black History newspaper profile of Sally Hemings.

http://www.villagevoice.com/features/9905/jones.shtml
Newspaper interview with Barbara Chase-Riboud, author of the novel, *Sally Hemings* (1979).

http://www.upress.virginia.edu/books/onuf_lewis.html
Information about the book, *Sally Hemings and Thomas
Jefferson: History, Memory, and Civic Culture*, edited by Peter S.
Onuf and Jan E. Lewis and published in the wake of the DNA
verification.

Asperger's Syndrome on the Web

http://www.asperger.org
Asperger Syndrome Education Network of America, Inc. (AS-
PEN), a national nonprofit organization providing compre-
hensive, up-to-date information.

http://www.aspennj.org/index.html
New Jersey regional chapters of ASPEN provide education,
emotional support, advocacy, public awareness for families affected by developmental disorders.

http://grandin.com
Home page of Temple Grandin, autistic author, lecturer, and
livestock-facilities designer. An excerpt from Dr. Grandin's
book, *Thinking in Pictures—and Other Reports from My Life with
Autism*, is available at http://grandin.com/inc/
visual.thinking.html

http://amug.org/~a203
On-The-Same-Page: definitive Asperger's Syndrome and autism
resource authored by three people who are autistic or have
Asperger's Syndrome. Provides valuable U.S. and foreign links.

http://www.udel.edu/bkirby/asperger/
Online Asperger Syndrome Information and Support (OASIS),
maintained by a parent of an Asperger's child, with local,

national, and international links.

http://www.aspergers.com
Scientific links by a medical professional.

http://www.FHautism.com
Resources of the largest publisher of books on autism in the
world, Future Horizons, including conferences featuring world-
renown authorities.

http://www.autism-society.org
Autism Society of America, support organization for autistics
and their families as well as a leader in advocacy, public awareness, education, and research.

http://www.autism.org
Center for the Study of Autism, an information resource that
researches therapeutic interventions, much of it in collabora-
tion with the Autism Research Institute, San Diego.

http://www.autism-spectrum.com
Spectrum, an online community of parents, caregivers, and people with autism in their lives.

http://www.faaas.org
Families of Adults Afflicted with Asperger's Syndrome, a nonprofit organization promoting educational awareness and providing emotional support.

http://ww2.netnitco.net/users/chart/index.html
Newsletter for the organization, More Advanced Individuals
with Autism, Asperger's Syndrome, and Pervasive
Developmental Disorder (MAAP).

http://www.autism-resources.com
The parent of an autistic youngster furnishes links to many online resources.

Acknowledgments

I received special help in this work from Temple Grandin, of Fort Collins, Colo., the autistic animal scientist, lecturer, and author, who pored over three drafts before agreeing I had made my point credibly. Her patience with me was unlimited, and there was a driving force to her enthusiasm. She is truly an inspiring person. My older daughter, Stephanie P. Ledgin-Toskos, Piscataway, N.J., a music journalist and Director of the New Jersey Folk Festival at Rutgers University, urged me to try to overcome readers' negative perceptions about autism. Her research, her preparation of Internet website references, and her encouragement were crucial. My cousin, Gladys Hosch, Boynton Beach, Fla., pulled me "out of the closet," so to speak. Unless I admitted being the parent of an Asperger's child, which I had avoided doing in the early drafts, my qualification for making this study would be in question. My very supportive wife and longtime work partner, Marsha, smoothed the path to that admission by talking it over with our son, Fred, for whose patience and help through all this I am also grateful.

Jean-Paul Bovee, Kansas City, Mo., has Asperger's Syndrome and works in the area of developmental disabilities. On the basis of my preliminary findings he said I had made a valid connection with Thomas Jefferson's behavior. So did Brenda Smith Myles, of Overland Park, KS, an author and lecturer in the Asperger's field who made a helpful formatting suggestion. She anticipates young people will derive support from identifying themselves with Jefferson. An old friend and graduate-school classmate, Stanford Gerber, Kansas City, Mo., applied his long experience in the social sciences to a critical review of my findings, agreeing they were sound and making suggestions for my manner of presentation.

As a lawyer my oldest son, David H. Ledgin, who lives in Merrick, N.Y., added a dimension of worth to my effort when I was forced to deal with such things as publication contracts. My editor, Hillel Black, of New York City, used his pen like a sword, slashing at inappropriate colloquialisms and redirecting my passive voice into a presentation that should now make more sense to everyone. Without his faith in the soundness of my theory I might be using the manuscript pages for kindling.

I owe thanks for support also to Tony Attwood, of Queensland, Australia, who expressed great interest in what my study might mean to young people. And I thank Polly McGlew, Jennifer Gilpin, and R. Wayne Gilpin, of Future Horizons, Inc., all "present at the creation" with Tony, Fred, and me in a discussion that moved this work into print. Wayne's strong commitment has been especially inspiring, and I will always be grateful for the confidence he placed in me.

There are people in the background—those who introduced me to Asperger's when they diagnosed Fred or aimed me toward greater knowledge in that field, and those who first inspired my interest in Thomas Jefferson. I am thankful to Dr. Rochelle Harris of Children's Mercy Hospital, Kansas City, Mo., and her medical chief, Dr. Michele G. Kilo, developmental pediatrician, for arriving at a diagnosis that gave Marsha and me, after years of anguish, our first grasp of what was truly going on. Robin Wells, of Overland Park, Kans., put us on a track of learning about Asperger's that we will never leave. Going back half a century to my time at Rutgers University, I must credit my professor in undergraduate American history, Richard P. McCormick, and my political science mentor in graduate school, the late Edward McNall Burns, for awakening me to giants like Jefferson. Harriet L. Moeller, Ithaca, N.Y., who values public education as highly as Jefferson did, taught me later that— once stirred and ignited toward doing a little good in this world—I would probably never be able to get Jefferson out of my mind.

For kindnesses or suggestions I thank Susan R. Stein, curator at Monticello, and Bryson Clevenger, reference aide in the Alderman Library, University of Virginia, Charlottesville, Va.; Ellen Welch and Sharon Khoury, Johnson County, Kans., Public Library; Barb Hoist, Colorado State University, Fort Collins; Stacey Jones Bock, Autism/Asperger Syndrome Resource Center, University of Kansas Medical Center, Kansas City, Kans.; Patricia Breinin, Scarsdale, N.Y.; Jo Anne Shaw, Pompton Lakes, N.J.; Sherry Lomax, of the Westport Post Office, Kansas City, Mo.; Charles A. Hammer, Shawnee, Kans.; Matt Grogger, Overland Park, Kans.; Hal and Dee Pottle, Oxford Township, Kans.; my sister-in-law, Pamela Johnston, Olathe, Kans., and my son-in-law, Ted Toskos, Piscataway, N.J.

For cheerful encouragement I thank Roy Schatt and Elaine Vorgetts-Schatt, New York City; Rita Compter, Toms River, N.J.; Linda McShann-Gerber, Kansas City, Mo.; Alex Everitt, Jr., Lafayette, N.J.; Jodi Dinkins, Olathe, Kans.; Wanda Brussell, Overland Park, Kans.; my younger daughter, Allison Jucha, Santa Cruz, Calif., and her children, Calla and Zachary (Zach's observation—"Grandpas writing a book about Thomas Jefferson!"—helped keep me going), and my youngest son and head cheerleader, Nick.

Eternal gratitude to Sheba, my late Chow-mix companion, for her loving sacrifice.

Abbreviations of Sources

Adams-Jefferson

The Adams-Jefferson Letters, Lester J. Cappon, editor (Chapel Hill, N.C.: The University of North Carolina Press, 1959)

Adams/Monticello

William Howard Adams, *Jefferson's Monticello* (New York: Abbeville Press, 1983)

Adams/Paris

William Howard Adams, *The Paris Years of Thomas Jefferson* (New Haven: Yale University Press, 1997)

Attwood

Tony Attwood, A*sperger's Syndrome: A Guide for Parents and Professionals* (London: Jessica Kingsley Publishers, 1998)

Brodie

Fawn M. Brodie, *Thomas Jefferson: An Intimate History* (New York: W.W. Norton & Co., Inc., 1974)

Burstein

Andrew Burstein, *The Inner Jefferson: Portrait of a Grieving Optimist* (Charlottesville, Va.: University Press of Virginia, 1995)

DSM-W

American Psychiatric Association, Diagnostic and Statistical Manual of Mental Disorders, Fourth Edition. Washington, D.C., American Psychiatric Association, 1994

Ellis

Joseph J. Ellis, *American Sphinx: The Character of Thomas Jefferson* (New York: Alfred A. Knopf, 1997)

Family Letters

The Family Letters of Thomas Jefferson, Edwin Morris Betts and James Adam Bear, Jr., editors (Charlottesville, Va.: The University Press of Virginia, 1966)

Foster, et al

Eugene A. Foster, M.A. Jobling, P.G. Taylor, P. Donnelly, P. deKnijff, Rene Mieremet, T. Zerjal, C. Tyler Smith, "Jefferson fathered slave's last child," *Nature*, Vol. 396,

November

5, 1998, 27-28.

Frith

Autism and Asperger's Syndrome, Uta Frith, editor (Cambridge, England: Cambridge University Press, 1991). Article references that are repeated will appear by author and editor, as *Asperger/Frith, Gillberg/Frith, Happe/Frith, Tantam/Frith.*

Gordon-Reed

Annette Gordon-Reed, *Thomas Jefferson and Sally Flemings: An American Controversy* (Charlottesville, Va.: University Press of Virginia, 1997)

Grandin

Temple Grandin, *Thinking in Pictures—and Other Reports from My Life with Autism* (New York: Doubleday, 1995)

Guidebook

Monticello: A Guidebook (Charlottesville, Va.: Thomas Jefferson Memorial Foundation, 1997)

Happe	Francesca Happe, *Autism: An Introduction to Psychological Theory* (Cambridge, Mass.: Harvard University Press, 1995)
Jordan	Winthrop D. Jordan, *White Over Black: American Attitudes Toward the Negro*, 1550-1812 (Chapel Hill, N.C.: University of North Carolina Press, 1968)
Malone	Dumas Malone, *Jefferson and His Time*—six volumes (Boston: Little, Brown and Company, 1948-81)
Mapp	Alf J. Mapp, Jr., *Thomas Jefferson: Passionate Pilgrim* (Lanham, Md.: Madison Books, 1991)
Martin	Edwin T. Martin, *Thomas Jefferson: Scientist* (New York: Henry Schuman, 1952)
McLaughlin	Jack McLaughlin, *Jefferson and Monticello: The Biography of a Builder* (New York: Henry Holt and Company, 1988)
Miller	John Chester Miller, *The Wolf by the Ears: Thomas Jefferson and Slavery* (Charlottesville, Va.: The University Press of Virginia, 1991)
Memorandum Books	Jefferson's *Memorandum Books: Accounts, with Legal Records and Miscellany*, 1767-1826, James A. Bear, Jr., and Lucia C. Stanton, editors—two volumes (Princeton, N.J.: Princeton University Press, 1997)

Monticello: Recollections	*Jefferson at Monticello: Recollections of a Monticello Slave and of a Monticello Overseer,* James A. Bear, Jr., editor (Charlottesville, Va.: University Press of Virginia, 1967)
Myles/Simpson	Brenda Smith Myles and Richard L. Simpson, *Asperger Syndrome: A Guide for Educators and Parents* (Austin, Tex.: Pro-Ed, Inc., 1998)
Peterson	Merrill D. Peterson, *Thomas Jefferson and the New Nation* (New York: Oxford University Press, 1970)
Randall	Willard Sterne Randall, *Thomas Jefferson: A Life* (New York: HarperPerennial, 1993)
Republic	*The Republic of Letters: The Correspondence Between Jefferson and Madison, 1776-1826,* James Morton Smith, editor - three volumes (New York: W.W. Norton & Company, 1995)
Wills	Garry Wills, *Inventing America: Jefferson's Declaration of Independence* (New York: Vintage Books, 1978)
Writings	*Thomas Jefferson: Writings,* Merrill D. Peterson, editor (New York: The Library of America, 1984)

Index of Proper Names

M

Machiavelli, Niccolo, 168

Maclay, William, 122-23, 126, 130, 151,154

Macpherson, James, 71

Madison, Dolley, 168

Madison, James, 34, 41-43, 147, 167

Malone, Dumas, 19-20, 26-27, 30-31,37,39,52-53,63,79-80, 103, 106, 115, 118, 121-24, 126-27, 129, 136-37, 139, 151-52, 154, 162, 165, 168

Mapp, Alf J., Jr., 39, 123, 126, 138, 155

Marshall, John, 26, 169

Martin, Edward T., 90, 96

Maury, James, 27, 176

Maury, James, Jr., 27

McLaughlin, Jack, 51, 79, 89, 93-95, 107

Mendel, Gregor, 18, 99

Merry, Anthony, 156, 167

Merry, (Mrs.), 168

Miller, John Chester, 39, 65

Mitchill, Samuel L., 123-24

Monroe, James, 42

Moore, Dennis, 184, 190

Myles, Brenda Smith, 13, 21-22, 118, 120

N

Nagy.J., 164

P

Page, John, 165-66

Palladio, Andreas, 89, 91

Parton, James, 195

Peak, Rembrandt, 119

Peterson, Merrill D., 20, 39, 50, 63, 71,76,82,91-92, 100, 106, 126, 139, 144, 162, 164, 167

T

Tantam, Digby, 147

U

Ursula, 48
Utley, Vine, 163

V

Van Buren, Martin, 42

W

Walker, Betsey, 2, 170, 180
Walker, John, 30
Washington, George, 26, 34-35, 41-42, 84, 88, 119, 146, 151, 168-70
Wayles, John, 2, 30, 49, 53
Webster, Daniel, 154
Wills, Garry, 30, 39, 78, 82, 84, 126, 154
Winfrey, Oprah, 188
Wing, Lorna, 111-12, 168
Wiltshire, Stephen, 99
Witelson, Sandra, 5
Wright, Pamela Darr, 190
Wright, Peter W.D., 190
Wythe, George, 28-29

Z

Zinn, Howard, 84

In this exceptionally humanizing portrait, the author assembles clues to Thomas Jefferson's deepest nature—reports and testimony from Jefferson's contemporaries as offered in a number of biographies, most notably the monumental six-volume work by Dumas Malone.

Historians confess confusion over seeming contradictions in Jefferson—behavior out of step with his writings, apparent flaws in his character. The author of *Diagnosing Jefferson* puts to rest the inconsistency and character issues, explaining features of a condition Jefferson probably inherited through his mother.

The neurological disorder Asperger's Syndrome, or high-functioning autism, relies on observation for diagnosis, not on purely medical procedures. While no two Asperger's-diagnosed people are exactly alike, they may have traits in common. Norm Ledgin's family experience made him watchful for signs of the condition. Ledgin offers a comprehensive table of Asperger's traits, any combinations of which may be found in people with the condition. He relates Jefferson's behavior to two-thirds of them. He also associates five criteria in the *Diagnostic and Statistical Manual* of the American Psychiatric Association with Jefferson. The minimum for the diagnosis is four.

Jefferson fought stress through writing that gave free rein to fixations, by tinkering and undertaking exacting construction projects, by means of music (he hummed or sang under his breath constantly), and by following pointless routines all his life. He reasoned on an either-or basis, infuriating political contemporaries. Unable to deal with middle-ground contingencies, he kept strictly and literally to the promises he made. Two of them eased the way for his long-term relationship with Sally Hemings.

In the context of educational issues that affected young Jefferson, a closing chapter lashes at modern public-school treatment of students with disabilities.

Appendices include a first-ever list of "100 topics" of Jefferson's writings, most illustrating fixations. Another is a list of internet web sites about the Sage of Monticello and about the brain condition that governed him—in much the same way scientists are beginning to believe it affected Albert Einstein.

NORM LEDGIN earned degrees at Rutgers and has been a country weekly editor in Illinois and Kansas and traffic safety specialist in Louisiana and Missouri. He now writes and lectures in history. Here with son Fred, Ledgin lives in Oxford Twp., Kans., near Kansas City.

Printed in the USA
CPSIA information can be obtained
at www.ICGtesting.com
JSHW082155140824
68134JS00014B/245